DR ROBERTA SYKES was born in the 1940s in
Townsville, North Queensland, and is one of
Australia's best known activists for Black rights. In
the 1980s she received both her Master and
Doctorate of Education from Harvard University. She
has been a consultant to a wide range of govern-
ment departments, including the Royal Commission
into Aboriginal Deaths in Custody and the NSW
Department of Corrective Services, and was Chairperson of the Promotion Appeals Tribunal at the
Australian Broadcasting Corporation. A guest lecturer
at universities and tertiary institutions throughout
Australia, and in demand as an international speaker,
she is also the author of seven books, including
Eclipse (1996) and *Murawina: Australian Women of High
Achievement* (1994), as well as having written, contributed to or co-authored numerous publications,
journal articles and conference papers. In 1994 she
was awarded Australia's highest humanitarian award,
the Australian Human Rights Medal. She lives in
Redfern, Sydney.

Snake Circle

Roberta Sykes

ALLEN & UNWIN

First published in 2000 by
Allen & Unwin Pty Ltd
9 Atchison Street, St Leonards, NSW 2065 Australia
Phone: (61 2) 8425 0100
Fax: (61 2) 9906 2218
E-mail: frontdesk@allen-unwin.com.au
Web: http://www.allen-unwin.com.au

National Library of Australia
Cataloguing-in-Publication entry:

Sykes, Roberta B.
   Snake circle.

   ISBN 1 86508 335 6.

   1. Sykes, Roberta B. 2. Authors, Australian—Biography.
   3. Aborigines, Australian—Civil rights. 4. Aborigines,
   Australian—Land tenure. 5. Afro-Americans—Australia—
   Biography. 6. Afro-American women—Australia—Biography.
   I. Title. (Series: Sykes, Roberta B. Snake dreaming; v. 3).

920.00926073

Set in 12/15 pt Novarese by Bookhouse Digital, Sydney
Printed by Griffin Press, Adelaide

10 9 8 7 6 5 4 3 2 1

'I *wish* you wouldn't keep calling yourself BLACK. You're not BLACK.'

I'm surprised that this white woman would think I should take her wish-list on board, as if I have no wishes of my own.

'So—am I white?' My question is rhetorical, my dark skin and hair a brazen confrontation.

'Well, no. You're not black and you're not white. You're perhaps sort of somewhere in between.'

Yes, perhaps sort of somewhere in between.

1

'How can this be happening to me? Not *to me!*' This question is a burning sensation coursing through my whole body, every nerve ending affected. I feel limp with anguish and expectation, knees so weak that I'm glad I'm sitting and will not be expected to stand for quite some time.

Exhausted, I visualise the journey that I have made, how I have laboured long and hard, over torturous terrain, for too many years to recall, starving and sweating, to reach this mountain peak where the air is so thin I can barely draw breath. Now I am confronted with a precipice, a drop so sheer I can see nothing at the bottom, no outcrop along the way to grasp if I should fall.

This is a personal plateau, and I'm so afraid. But I can't let anyone see just how afraid I really am. My hands are wet, so wet, though I've waved them around a bit and run them discreetly along my slacks to dry them many times. I hang on tightly to the armrests to stop my hands from shaking, keep them steady.

I sneak a quick glance at my daughter, Naomi,

sitting beside me. She has caught my anxiety. Her face looks strained and pinched, and she is dabbing at the tears in her eyes with a tissue. Though just twelve years old, she senses, rather than understands, the gravity and enormity of my situation, but her innocence also allows her to translate this into the beginning of a huge adventure. She is sitting beside her mum, and no harm has ever come to her there. Mum, she thinks, will look out for the both of us—which serves to make my own burden heavier.

Muted voices and the rustle of movement break into my consciousness. The soft tinkle of muzak adds to the incongruity. A quick scan around confirms my suspicion that my daughter and I are the only two Black people here.

I turn my face towards the window, so that those seated near me can see only the back of my head, and lean my forehead against the pane, pretending I'm peering outside. I feel the fear overwhelm me. My eyes begin to sting and tears well to overflowing, making their way slowly down my cheeks.

I have succumbed to the tension of the past few days, weeks, months, perhaps years. Embarrassingly, a shudder, a deep sob, tugs at my shoulders for a moment before I regain my self-control. I worm around in my seat, my face still averted, hoping anyone looking won't see my distress.

The question forms in my mind once more: How can this be happening *to me*?

Static interrupts the muzak.

'Please, ladies and gentlemen, fasten your seat belts for take-off.' The deep male voice crackles over the speakers. As he speaks, the jet engines begin to rev and throb. We are preparing to leave, to leave

Australia, the home I hold so dear, and heaven alone knows what lies in store for me. I feel that I am stepping onto that big global stage now, and should I stumble or fall, heaven alone knows how many people may be watching me.

My primary job, as Education/Liaison Officer with the New South Wales Health Commission, keeps my waking hours very busy, and it's a real effort to find time to fit in the other part-time work I do around it. Still, I have two children to support and they want to eat every day, and there is no one to help me. It helps to stay focused on my work, the needs of the children, our extremely derelict house, and the enormous tangled growth we jocularly refer to as the 'back garden'.

For a large part of my job, I crisscross New South Wales almost constantly, mostly alone in my unmarked Health Commission car. My mission is to visit Aboriginal communities, listen to people, and search for solutions to the overwhelming host of problems which become obvious to me. It's dangerous to be out on these backroads, a woman alone. I put in a request to the Department for a rifle for my protection and, although everyone agrees I need one, it never appears.

These journeys are, in themselves, exciting. Travelling along country roads in the early mornings and at dusk, I often see kangaroos and wallabies, occasionally in mobs but mostly just one or a pair. Driving on dusty, unsealed and corrugated roads, often little more than glorified tracks, with occasional signs to reassure travellers that they are still heading in the right direction, I spot these majestic creatures grazing in the distance, a joey or two around. They turn their heads sombrely to watch the car as it rattles by, sometimes abruptly bounding away at the sound. On bitumen roads, it's quite a different story. They seem lured to the macadam by the dew which collects there, and are reluctant to leave until the car is almost upon them. At night, I catch the flash of their eyes in the head-lights and hit the brakes, long before I can make out the shape of their erect, watching bodies.

From time to time, the flash of eyes turns out to be that of wandering stock. I loudly smack the side of the car with my hand in an effort to get these beasts to disperse as I inch a path through them. Kangaroos invariably leap off at the sound but cattle turn and give me a withering look. Once, very late on a pitch black night, on a particularly narrow backroad enclosed on each side by fields of thick tall millet, I was forced to creep along at cows' pace for almost an hour. The half dozen or so large beasts before me merely ambled along, at times unable and obviously unwilling, to leave the road, pausing to throw disdainful glances in my direction. From experience I knew better than to try blowing the horn, because the sudden noise can star-tle them, and then there's no knowing what they might do. A tonne or more of wild beast lumbering at speed towards a vehicle can do almost as much damage as if I had hit it, rather than that it had hit me.

Smaller native creatures, plump wombats, possums and even koalas, can be seen along the roads at almost any hour, but especially at night. I seem to have my own internal radar, my foot automatically lifts from the accelerator long before these animals come into view. I pride myself on never having run into or over a crea-ture of the bush. Even snakes have continued their graceful and leisurely slither across my path without harm. A quick red-eye flash and a disappearing tail is usually all the notice I get of having passed a dingo in the night. Goannas and other reptiles watch me as I carefully watch them.

I am constantly horrified and distressed by the conditions at most of the Aboriginal reserves and missions. People are living with so little in the way of material possessions in often appallingly unsanitary environments. It is 1977, ten years since the Referendum which acknowledged Aboriginal citizenship, but what's changed? Not much. People remain in pockets of misery, ten or fifteen miles along a dirt track, away from the main roads, outside the town levees, separated by distance and poverty from the nearest store, hospital and phone. The few possessions they own, mostly second-hand clothes and some pots and pans, blackened from cooking over their open fires, are washed away with each flood. In the city between visits I routinely beg replacements and try to carry boxes of things people might need when I travel.

Women tell me of the valuables they have lost in these floods—a photograph, a treasured memory, of the child who died of gastro two years earlier; a copy of an old magazine, *New Dawn*, which published pictures of people in the old days, showing a grandfather, a great aunt, even a lost sister, brother or child. Their eyes brim with tears at these recitals, and I am helpless. These are not things I can beg in the city and replace.

I am happy to walk around the reserves, to have the women point things out to me. What looks from the distance like a surly group of dark tattered figures sitting in the dirt behind the rudimentary sheet-iron ablutions block is actually a lively card game. When we approach, the game slows. The players do not like anyone standing behind them, perhaps we can see what's in their hands. 'Sit down and join in—or move on.'

Sometimes I carry *Ebony* magazines I have brought from home. The colourful pictures of American Blacks—entertainers, models and sportsfolk—decked in finery and standing beside sleek modern cars or in front of solid mansions, with their slick well-dressed children and salon-groomed pets, are a million miles away from the lives of the similarly dark-skinned people who steal the magazines from my car if I don't offer them. Not just the young girls, either. One time I gave a lift to three old ladies, and when the two women sitting in the back seat got out, so did the magazines. They weren't carrying bags so I could only imagine that they'd stuck them down their dresses. Strange though this may seem, I was quite pleased by this because our transaction, such as it was, had been carried out without the need for words. I would like to have offered the women the magazines to keep, but was too shy and thought they may have been offended to accept, to be seen to condone the flamboyant clothes and glossy makeup of the women in the photos. The old women, of course, were also far too shy to ask, but the need for something, anything, to confirm their prayer that there were Black people like themselves somewhere in the world whose lives were not squalid was overwhelming. I was just a messenger carrying a small symbol of hope. The women looked back and smiled as they walked away. In my mind's eye I could see them later, devouring each page, sharing them with their friends and relations, making sure all the young people realised the possibility of a life beyond poverty, a life they could reach for, perhaps study towards.

I gave presentations at conferences, sometimes in Sydney, at other times in country regions. For some of the Aboriginal Health Workers, this was their first job, and for others, the first position they had held which wasn't domestic or menial. Quite a lot of the Health Workers spoke of their fear of the paperwork and record-keeping involved, even though the work had been tailored to minimise these requirements and to maximise the skills they brought with them, their cultural knowledge, the status they carried in their own communities. They were able to bring health education and assistance into homes where the most experienced white professionals would never have been allowed inside the door—even if they had been prepared to go, which many were not.

Their greatest bugbear, I learned early on, was not the crucial work they had been entrusted to perform, or even the fairly minor paperwork requirements of the Department, such as petrol and vehicle records, but the terror many had of the Taxation Department. Although I didn't think any one of these people actually *knew* someone who had been imprisoned for not filing income tax returns, a rumour had spread like bushfire that this could happen. The Health Workers, mainly women, the majority being senior women, that is, mothers and grandmothers, were law-abiding and highly respected in their own communities. In some cases, their Health Worker positions gave them an additional status. However, they shared with their communities not only the traumatic events of the past, but also the legacy of past policies of exclusion which had left them with insufficient education to perform basic literacy and numeracy tasks. Their accommodations, too, were often of the same standard as their clients', that is, run-down, overcrowded and, at times, without electricity or hot running water and subject to floods. The idea that they could keep a full year's worth of receipts for work-related expenses, sorted and held in one safe place, was ludicrous. They feared imprisonment by the Taxation Department as a consequence of holding down a job—even a job which saved lives and was so important and highly skilled that no one else could do it.

I don't think there was a single Aboriginal Health Worker's family untouched by the prison system, so the Health Workers' fear of imprisonment was awesome. They recognised the benefits that flow, over time, from having a regular income that was higher than the dole or the deserted wife's or widow's pension, such as being able to buy a generator, fridge or television on hire purchase. Also, they were enormously pleased to learn new information which they could share with their communities. However, they were also very concerned that their efforts to do good might instead end up with them behind bars. Even though their wages were taxed at source, they feared the Income Tax Department and its annual requirement. Although I was loath to report it to the Commission at the time, I learned of a few new employees who abandoned their positions for this reason.

I made up my own travelling rules, such as never to drink the water in country towns unless it had been boiled. I broke this rule accidentally just once, in Wilcannia. I was reporting my whereabouts to Head Office on an Aboriginal organisation's telephone and absent-mindedly accepted a cup of lukewarm tea from a young girl who worked there. I reflected on the source when, a few hours later, I was doubled up with stomach pains. I'd been allocated a room at the nurses' quarters of the hospital, and spent the next day either in bed or losing bodily fluids at both ends in one of the toilets. There was no doctor at the hospital and no local chemist, the nearest medico coming in just once or twice a week from Broken Hill, many miles away, and I felt too weak to drive there. I wondered how local Aboriginal families coped, drinking polluted water all the time, and without cars to drive to Broken Hill if anyone became ill.

Two white nurses, twin sisters, worked at the hospital. When I had sufficiently recovered from my gastro bout to sit around in the lounge, one of the twins joined me and wanted to talk. She told me that she and her sister went to Fiji each year for their holidays because men in Fiji like big women, and both she and her sister were indeed big women. I thought her indiscreet for sharing this aspect of her life with me and wondered if she realised the sharp contrast between her attitude to these annual pleasure jaunts and the condescending manner she maintained towards the local Black population. Still, I held my tongue.

In the countryside, I often learned terrible truths through dramatic experiences. Once more in Wilcannia, I was walking to the petrol station in the main street for a cool drink, when I was joined by a group of five or six young Aboriginal girls from the nearby camp. They walked along with me and chatted. As the camp had no electricity and therefore no refrigeration, camp residents ambled towards the petrol station or the sprinkling of shops several times a day for basic provisions and cool drinks. The temperature was often almost 40° Celsius, and the air still, dry and dust-filled from clouds of parched soil stirred by the cars and semitrailers that passed through on this main highway to and from the west.

A police wagon slowly came around the corner and one of the girls suddenly ran onto the road and began hurling abuse at its lone male occupant. As the wagon slowed, I saw the policeman smirk at her, then raise his eyes and catch sight of me standing with her group of friends. He drove off.

'He been rape me,' she said angrily, by way of explanation for her actions. 'In the cells, he been rape me.' I was shocked by her candour.

'Yeah, he rooted all of us,' one of her friends piped up. Horrified, I looked around at their pinched little faces, dark eyes swimming with anger and frustrated indignation, not one of them yet sixteen years old, and I felt sick to my stomach.

'When?'

They were all answering at once. 'Anytime he can take us off to the station.'

'You gotta watch out for him all the time.'

'My boyfriend said next time he do it to me, he'll kill him.'

'Yeah. One time I even told him I had the rags on, and he jus' said, "Well, jus' open your mouth".'

'He call us names all the time, too. Like "Poxy bitch" and "Black cunt".'

I stood around with the girls for a while and tried to get enough information to make a case. Although they had each been subjected to various gross indecencies and in many ways corroborated each other's stories, the policeman had always taken the precaution of never taking two girls at the same time, never providing them with a witness. So it would always be one girl's word against his own.

I heard similar stories in several country towns, and was always sickened. Yet I was never able to get evidence, apart from hearing over and over about such incidents from different girls at different times, which I doubted would stand up in a court. I was told that young Aboriginal men who threatened the police offenders who had molested their girlfriends always found themselves in jail. Some even became what was later called a 'death in custody'.

I wondered a lot about these towns, their isolation from centres that would investigate these incidents, their social structure which ensured that what was common knowledge in the Black community never leaked over into the white community—did not penetrate the consciousness of, for instance, the wives of the offending officers.

I realise the paradox in saying how much I enjoyed this work, because I was so often confronted with misery and situations that made me feel impotent. Yet the small things that I could do to alleviate suffering were often so pleasing, so satisfying, that my life still felt, in a strange way, perhaps a busy way, fulfilled.

The thing I liked best about all the travelling was being alone in the car and being in the bush. Often I would see a good place to stop, sometimes beside a creek or under a shady tree, and just pull up and kill the engine. The sounds of the bush took over, because there seems to be no real silence, that is, the total absence of sound, in the bush. Birds caw in the distance, flies buzz constantly, and the smell of water in perspiration, I swear, attracts every little flying and stumbling creature within coo-ee. For a brief moment after the motor dies, there is the illusion of quiet, but it's a quiet only in contrast to the mechanical sound.

In those periods of tranquillity I had time to think, to focus on the things I had seen and try to place them in the context of what I knew, in the search for solutions. I still read avidly and was constantly learning—about the law, the environment, economic development—and I always came to the same conclusion. There had to be radical change and economic independence before the situation of Aboriginal people could be rectified. We had been on the right track in 1972, in Canberra, when the Aboriginal Embassy had put forward its demands. Land rights and land rights compensation were the only just way out of the quagmire. This would enable the Black community to develop sufficient economic, social and political power to force change on this society. But eighteen million white people were yet to be convinced.

In Sydney I was busy supporting a range of Black community and women's endeavours, in the hope that the prototypes we were developing would ultimately spill over into the country areas and bring a measure of relief. Rape crisis centres, rape counselling, refuges for victims of domestic violence—all were on my agenda. I was later to become disillusioned by the fact that racism by white crisis and refuge workers as well as from their white clients continued, in many cases, to make these services unavailable to Black women.

I kept myself so busy that I rarely had time to consider my own situation or pause to address the psychological problems which I knew to be driving me furiously on. In the country, unless I had been able to get a message through to one of the many Aboriginal

safe-houses at which I was assured of a warm welcome, I routinely drove through the night towards my
destination until tiredness overtook me. I then slept
curled up on the bench seat of the Health Department
car, rather than confront the racism that would almost
inevitably arise if I tried to book into many of the way-
side motels. At home in Sydney, I worked until,
exhausted, I would often fall asleep with my head down
on my desk or on top of my typewriter, only to wake
in a few hours, freezing cold, and crawl, fully dressed,
under the covers of my bed.

Despite these efforts to keep myself bombed out
with work, on occasions I was still troubled with the
nightmares.

I am hovering in a corner above and, looking down
in the darkness, I see a small crowd of men. They are
passing around brown beer bottles, taking swigs,
laughing, jostling each other and talking amongst
themselves. On the ground lies a small naked form, a
girl, very thin, her ribs clearly etched beneath her
brown skin. She is motionless. Her eyes, full of fear,
are wide open, yet there is no recognition, no indication that she is seeing anything at all.

A square of moonlight, streaming through a hole
where a window and glass panes may once have been,
provides the only light, brightening portions of the dirt
floor and walls where it falls. A man unzips his trousers
and stumbles to his knees upon the girl, fumbling for
purchase. A tremor of laughter rises from the assembled men inside the room. Outside the hut, others
stand in earnest mumbled conversation, waiting their
turn. Several cars are parked haphazard, doors left
open and interior lights softly glowing, illuminating the

faces of more men, smoking cigarettes, a hand drumming on a dashboard in impatience.

As I lift my eyes I suddenly see the girl rise up from the earth, her movements effortless and fluid. With an amazing bound, she is out the windowframe. Her feet barely touching the ground, moonlight clearly outlining her thin limbs, her frail shoulder bones, her small childish buttocks and giving her an almost silver glow as she runs. I watch her disappear, slip silently amongst a sparse clump of trees. There is freedom in her graceful form. I stare after her until she has completely vanished.

But when I look back to the dirt, in reality the girl is still there, still lying motionless, and I realise that the escape happened only in my mind.

The man who had laid upon her has been hoisted to his feet by his friends. He stands unsteadily, groping at his clothes. The others turn to watch the second-comer, who smiles lasciviously, drops to his haunches and pulls the young girl's legs so that they are straight. 'Looks good enough to eat,' he announces to his audience, receiving 'Ugh' and 'Uh-uh' responses from his friends. He leans forward and I see his teeth flashing for a moment before they sink into the girl's lower abdomen. Even his friends are startled. He looks up at them, his teeth stained with blood, and smirks his approval. The small gasp and sob that rose up from the girl's mouth does not appear to have been heard by any of the men, but it echoes around the shack, piercing my ears and numbing my senses. I feel that I am about to burst.

My eyes open and, in half my mind, I realise I am lying safely at home in my own bed. But somehow, in another part of my mind, I am now also inside the body of the young girl. Rough skin, gravelly with stubble, rasps brutally against my shoulder, hurried breathing and grunts insult my ear, and I am overcome with the reek of beer fumes. A hard hand grasps my left hip as a flabby body over heavy bones assaults me, pounds upon me, smack, smack, smack. I struggle to become fully awake, to leave this nightmare, to find sanity in the security of my own familiar bedroom in my locked house. My pillow is soaked with my tears. How often, I frequently rage to myself, must I wake from death?

Tea. I get up and make myself a cup of tea. I'll sit here, willing myself to stop shaking, try to calm myself, sitting at the kitchen table until dawn, if necessary, in order to give myself time to recover.

I prowl the house, check on my sleeping children, sit quietly for a while on the corners of their beds, watch their innocent faces and imagine them growing as they rest, their breathing even, their faces beautiful in repose as they are in activity. These children are my anchors, forcing me to stay with them, though I so often yearn to escape. I find so few brief moments of peace in the struggle of my days, the agony of my nights, that I long for oblivion. Death looks so sweet.

In my occasional rare daytime examinations of my nightmares, I always realise there is something wrong with me and with the dream. Until I work out exactly what that is, I will always be plagued. But I can't speak to anyone about this. I feel there is no one whom I trust enough to share my secret and shameful inner life. At the same time, I worry about my sanity. The psychology books I am reading keep informing me of a host of possible consequences of carrying around a concealed trauma.

ROBERTA SYKES

It is easier for me, then, to concentrate on what I have done with my trauma, rather than on the trauma itself. I create fantasies. I imagine these awful events of the past as the small stone in an oyster, my mind being that oyster. I can't dislodge the stone, so instead I put down layer after layer of nacre, which are my layers of pretence, everything's all right Jack, until, over time, there will be no jagged stone, just a lovely smooth and quietly luminescent pearl.

Inside myself, I can do with the happy ending, so the fantasy always has to stop right there. I consciously reject the thought that threatens to follow: pearls before swine.

2

Since the early days of my arrival from the north and my leap into so-called radical Black politics, I have learned many lessons. Some later stood me in good stead, others make me laugh now when I recall them. If I'd known any seriously rich people in Townsville, I had been unaware of it. As a public educator about Aboriginal problems and a key community organisation fund-raiser, though, I had found myself rubbing shoulders with the rich, famous, and sometimes notorious.

Initially I had been intimidated by rich people, by their wealth actually, not by their minds or personalities. At the same time, the women's movement was pushing equality and I had taken it to heart. Rich people would invite me to lunch to talk about possible sponsorship of projects and community services for which I was trying to drum up support. When it came time to pay the bill, as an advocate for women's equality, I always fought them to pay my share.

After one such performance, the memory of which causes me enormous embarrassment, a woman who had also been at the lunch took me aside and talked to me about my reasons and the outcome.

'Do you think rich people go away thinking, "My, isn't she equal"?' she asked.

I was amazed because I had never stopped to wonder what they thought at all. I realised I had only been concerned about proving to myself that I was equal.

'You didn't choose this fancy place to eat, one of these guys did. And when you go home and count the pennies you have left to feed your children, you're going to miss the dollars you insisted you contribute as your share. Do you think paying the bill is going to make any difference to the lifestyle of any of those blokes? No. But it'll probably make a big difference to yours. So just let it rest, okay.'

I later learned that this adviser had married a man with money, but had not forgotten her childhood and her own mother's struggle to put food on the table. Though grateful for her advice, I continued to fret about accepting generosity when it was offered, and struggled with the notion that my equality did not depend on whether I could beat the host to the bill to pay my share. The reality of my situation caused me to closely examine much of the rhetoric of the women's movement and its manifestations in my daily life.

I often felt I was in no man's land, caught up in rapidly changing times vis-a-vis the advancement in the status of women. This alone would have been heady and confusing, but I also had to deal with being a spearhead in the Black community's charge on white society in an effort to gain equal rights, and the changes in perception which this forced upon all of us. There was also angst in the Black community which I felt was caused, curiously enough, by both the slowness and the rapidity with which social changes were taking place. Over time I began to appreciate that it was the unevenness with which these social changes were distributed throughout the community that was weakening our community structure, leaving it frail and vulnerable.

Fortunately MumShirl was my chief mentor. While she was never a social analyst, she had devised her own set of behavioural rules which, for a long time, had stood her in good stead. MumShirl ignored anything she didn't understand and concentrated her energies on those things she did. She had an innate understanding of the full range of human emotions and could spot their manifestations almost immediately. I recall a meeting she and I attended, a lunch with a man who had contacted me to offer help with some community project we were working on. I found the man's conversation quite confusing, he had arrived with a briefcase of notes, newspaper clippings and quotes from, well, he called them philosophers but neither MumShirl nor I had ever heard of any of them. And he never did reach whatever point he'd come to make.

I walked away from that meeting a bit discouraged, I felt as though nothing had been resolved. Meetings with potential sponsors usually had a pattern about them. We rarely contacted potential sponsors ourselves for fear of rebuff, so, with just a few exceptions, they usually made the first move. They would tell us of their area of interest, whether it was to aid medical or legal services, or if they had been touched by the plight of needy children, for instance. We would then give them a range of options until we had a match between their interests and current needs in the Black community, and we would proceed from there. At this particular meeting, we hadn't even reached the first step. By the time we took our leave, the man had still not divulged his area of interest, though he bought us a delicious lunch. He was waiting for a receipt when MumShirl and I made our way back out onto the street.

'Well, what did you make of that, Mum?' I asked, still trying to get something out of the quotes he had read to us from his scraps of paper.

'Greedy,' Mum replied, which elicited from me my standard reply when I couldn't see how she had put fragments together to come up with a total. 'Huh?'

'What does he do? D'ya get his card?'

'No, I'll run back and ask him for one now.'

'Don't bother,' Mum said, looking about for a taxi. 'I'll bet you anything he sells insurance. He's read in the papers the government's going to spend money on the Black community, and he wants some of it. Probably a big slab of it. You'll see.'

With a rush, everything the man had said over lunch fell into place. He had never mentioned 'insurance' as such, but he had spoken about vagaries such as 'gains in the area', 'protection against the future', and 'the balance on the slates'. I had sort of forgiven him as he talked, considering his terminology 'businessmen's jargon' and thinking he was slowly working his way around to telling us what he had in mind, how he thought he could help.

Mum said she'd pinned down his personality by just watching him, she hadn't understood a word of what he'd said. A week or so later he rang again and asked if Mum and I had thought about his 'offer', would we like to have lunch again?

I was tempted to accept, to rat out this guy, make him put his cards on the table. Then I would give him

a big rouse for wasting our time and for trying to get
something out of the poorest people in the land. Mum
said if I went, it wouldn't be the man wasting my time,
I'd be wasting my own time.

Was it because I was so deeply involved with understanding the connections between the causes of
poverty and despair in the Black community, that it
hadn't occurred to me that a white, apparently wealthy
and successful business person would see us as grist
for his money-making mill?

Over time, however, as governments increased their
allocations and trumpeted what sounded like fantastic sums of money to be spent in Aboriginal Affairs,
all manner of greedy opportunists tried to climb
aboard. And we began to watch out for them. We knew
that they were unaware, as we were, that the bulk of
government funding went to white agencies and admin-
istrators, contractors and career Black-helpers, while
very little trickled down to the Black people in need.

On the other hand, I was also fortunate to meet
people with what MumShirl and I called 'heart'. Some
of them were rich, though many were only pensioners
and battlers. They were people who were saddened by
the poverty of others, by the death of a child, or by
the plight of the homeless and despairing, no matter
what colour, and they made an effort, however small,
to do something about it. I still like to think they out-
number what MumShirl called the 'greedy', but I
learned that they don't cancel out the greedy. The
greedy walk amongst the poor every day and connive
to take the shirt from their backs, even knowing that
he or she only had one shirt. The problem, as I see it,
is that often the poor are unaware of this, and because
kindness is almost a currency between themselves and

other poor people, they even offer their shirt, while the greedy merely add it to their extensive wardrobe.

But these are by no means the only white people I met on the streets, hanging around in the Black community. There is a rawness, an earthiness, about poverty, material or spiritual, that, in some instances, seems to transcend differences.

Driving MumShirl, who had no car or licence, whose size and health prevented her from travelling on public transport, I was exposed to an array of people in such diverse circumstances.

In her efforts to keep the Black community together, keep families together, and locate and shepherd people back into the flock, I trailed after her, often in the midnight hours, through churches, graveyards, prisons and brothels. We slept in convents and were feted by nuns. We took shelter in the houses of strangers and were sometimes met with hospitality but occasionally suspicion. I have lost count of the number of times I caught a few hours sleep in the car by the side of the road with my head resting on Mum's handbag or leg while she kept guard against marauders. We chatted on our long drives through the countryside about almost every subject under the sun. Even Mum's frequent snores were punctuated with, 'Uhuh, yes, keep talking. I'm not really asleep.'

Love blossomed between us. We happily sang out of tune as I drove, and told jokes and laughed a lot. We were able to cry in each other's company without embarrassment as we struggled to make sense of some of the terrible things we saw and heard together. Although I never shared with her the traumas of my past life, she watched as I strove to keep a roof over my children's heads, food on the table and clothes on their backs. And she appreciated the many personal sacrifices I had to make in order to do so. In many ways we shared a world view and a rare intimacy born of mutual respect. Initially she had introduced me to people as her daughter, but over time our relationship changed. I became something more than an acolyte amongst many who rendered her services in exchange for her company and for the satisfaction of helping her to accomplish her missions. I was one of a very few people who would and could chide her when necessary and have her turn towards me to listen. She sought my opinion and often called upon me to accompany her to any place where she was likely to be asked 'high-falutin' questions'.

Mum had easily over a hundred children placed in her care by courts and parents and institutions. I never saw her raise her hand to any of them, but she sometimes verbally lashed out at them in ways that I found quite unacceptable, and frequently told her so.

During many of our trips, Mum had the older children looking after smaller ones in her absence. When we arrived back we would be met with bedlam. The house in total chaos, the reek of urine-soaked mattresses would overwhelm us at the door, and radio and television blaring. She would be greeted with a long list of complaints, requests for money and sometimes food, and the sight of often half-naked kids galloping noisily around at whatever hour of the night. We may have just spent hours comforting a rape victim, a threatening suicide, or a victim of domestic violence, rounded off with a five-hour drive back to Sydney, and Mum's temper would be hair-trigger.

Stepping past the children who raced each other to get to the door first, and over whatever piles of clothes or sheets were stacked up in her way, Mum would bellow down the hallway, 'What *** pigs have been living in my house while I've been away. Start cleaning up this *** bloody mess straight away. You littlies with your shitty pants, get out of my bloody sight. And you big ***, when I get hold of you I'm going to kick all your arses up to breakfast time.'

If I had time, I would take her by the elbow and draw her back outside, into the car, where we would sit and talk for a while. From inside the house, sounds of furious activity assured me that everyone there knew that Mum was back and that she was on the warpath.

'When you rouse at the kids like that, Mum, you make them feel bad about themselves.'

'Well, they're cleaning up the place now, aren't they?'

'Sounds like it, but I'm talking about long-term damage to their self-esteem.'

I took particular exception to any name-calling that had a sexual or criminal reference, and often told Mum that if she talked to the kids like that, she shouldn't be surprised if they began to act like that. She was always sorry, pleading tiredness, and I'd urge her to ignore the mess, close her bedroom door and get some rest before trying to deal with anything.

'How can I rest when there's three kids have to sleep in my bed with me. And two of them bed-wetters?'

Mum sometimes rang me to come and get her, spirit her away to my house, where, despite the enormous discomforts endured by myself and my kids, such as no hot water for a shower, she could steal a few hours or days of peace.

'If anyone rings, looking for me,' she'd say, 'tell 'em I'm not here.'

At other times Mum's demands could be quite exasperating, although I found out over time that there was always a point to them, even if that point wasn't immediately obvious.

Once MumShirl asked me to pick her up at four in the afternoon and take her to Newcastle. I said it wasn't a convenient time for me to leave as I'd made no arrangements for my children. I would pick her up at three, get across the Sydney Harbour Bridge before peak hour traffic, supervise the children when they came home from school, cook dinner and arrange for a neighbour to keep on eye on them overnight. She agreed.

Liz Milne, an emergency surgery nursing sister at Royal North Shore Hospital, lived across the street from us. Often she allowed herself to be roped into over-night duties at my house if she wasn't rostered on night duty in her regular job. Liz also had a lemon tree growing in the side of her yard.

MumShirl shared the little food we had for our evening meal, waited while I got the children settled, and, as I was about to pull out from the kerb, said, 'Get me some lemons from that tree.' More precious time wasted, I thought, as I shinned around, scooping up a bag of lemons for her. 'I want some salt to eat with them.' Mum eating lemons and salt, or sometimes raw onions and salt, set my teeth on edge, so I made her get out of the front seat and sit in the back. Then she decided she needed to go to the toilet again before we hit the road. It was quite dark by the time we set out, and I'd begun to wonder why she was employing such obvious delaying tactics. I thought that her mission was urgent and I knew that nuns at a convent in Newcastle were awaiting our arrival. I wondered if she had decided she didn't want to go, that we'd stay at my house and leave early in the morning, but when I asked her, she said no.

We were almost at Hornsby when Mum suddenly said, 'Turn right here at this next corner—I know a short-cut'.

MumShirl seemed to know Sydney like the back of her hand, and was always directing me to drive through alleys so hidden and narrow that I felt only she and immediate residents knew they were there, so I turned as I'd been told. We were in an ordinary poorly-lit sub-urban street on which even the darkened houses petered out after a while, and our passing was noticed only by a few surly dogs which rose like ghosts in the headlights. The street grew narrow, became a road, became a country lane of only one car's width, and still we travelled along it. I peeped in the rear vision mirror to make sure Mum was still awake, still moni-toring our progress, and that we were still headed in the right direction. She was happily munching away on a lemon, peel and all, and when she spotted me watch-ing her, she just nodded me on.

A few miles further along, I felt her lean on the back of my seat and peer out into the darkness. There was no moon, no lights, only the car headlights cutting a swath through the jet black night that surrounded us, occasionally casting a glow on a the slender trunk of a tree as we sped by.

'Okay, slow down a bit now,' she said. We were nowhere. 'Watch for the next break in this fence on the right.' Turning the car a little so that the headlights veered off towards the side of the road, I could faintly make out a fence.

'Okay, here. Turn here.'

I trundled off the road and heard the crunch of

gravel beneath the tyres. Now this, I thought to myself, is not the way to Newcastle.

We travelled some distance along this gravel road, surrounded by complete silence. My curiosity was piqued, but I thought it prudent just to wait and see, rather than try to prise information out of Mum. There was something eerie, too, about the night quiet outside the car, which seemed to demand a reciprocal silence inside.

The car shuddered as we drove over a bridge of pines, a barrier to prevent stock from straying. We seemed to be in a very large field.

'Brakes,' Mum whispered. I stopped but kept the engine idling. Two men came up from behind the car, I could barely make them out in the darkness. Mum wound her window down and spoke to them in tones so low that I couldn't hear what was being said. A short conversation ensued.

'Okay, drive on.' I was bewildered. A few hundred yards further and I was instructed to turn left. As I did so, the headlights lit up a field of cars and trucks. It was all very mysterious.

MumShirl directed me here and there, along this row, then another, before motioning towards a space where I was to park. She opened her door in a flash and as she clambered out, she just said, 'Wait here.' I killed the engine and watched her walk off, zig-zagging through vehicles until she was out of my sight.

'Well, damn, what are we doing here?' I spoke to myself in the darkness. Long minutes ticked by. For a while I just sat at attention behind the steering wheel, waiting for Mum's return. As my eyes relaxed from the tension of driving, I realised I could see the twinkling of a spread of stars in the night sky. I turned the radio on, looked at the dashboard clock, and relaxed to hear a human voice and music coming over the air.

Twenty minutes passed and I began to grow resentful, sitting out there in the dark, waiting for God only knew what. I would give her ten more minutes and then, well, I'd leave her there. She could find her own way home or to Newcastle—there were plenty of cars about. I'd go to my own house and my own increasingly attractive bed. I was tired.

In ten minutes, the news came on, so I extended her deadline. I'll make up my mind what to do after I've heard what's been happening in the world, I thought.

Still no sign of Mum, so, thinking there might be dogs about, I scrambled up onto the car roof for a look around. I didn't see any dogs, but in the distance I could faintly see what looked like a very large shed, similar to a tractor shed, but much much longer. I stared at it for a while, and twice I briefly saw slivers of light from doors at one end. Gathering up my courage, I slipped off the roof onto the ground and made my way soundlessly towards them.

I could hear nothing as I approached, no dogs, no cars arriving or leaving the field, and there appeared to be no lights on in the shed. When I reached the building, I stood still for a moment, taking stock. As I did so, I was able to make out three or four men standing at a distance, smoking, watching me. I was about to bolt back to the safety of the car when a door opened slightly and two more men came out, lighting cigarettes, speaking to each other in low tones, obviously waiting for their eyes to adjust to the dark.

Through the crack in the door, I saw two other men, standing with what looked like a sheet strung up to a line behind them. I sniffed the air, sensed no hostility, and walked over to the door. The two men inside looked at me.

'I'm with MumShirl,' I said with as much nonchalance as I could muster, and walked the two steps towards the sheet shielding the room from my view. One of the men pulled a corner of the sheet aside to allow me to enter.

Inside, there were bright lights, dozens of people milling around, and lots of noise and activity. For a moment I wondered why I hadn't been able to hear anything from outside. I was standing there with a startled look on my face, about as comfortable as a fish out of water, when a man came up and asked me what I wanted. I was concerned he might tell me to leave and I had just begun to mumble something when a cheer broke out and the people who'd been standing shoulder to shoulder, their backs toward me, broke rank.

I found myself looking at a big square of canvas on the floor, with a crowd of people standing and squatting around it.

Heavens above, I suddenly thought, this is an illegal two-up school!

The man wandered away and I was left to my own devices. As I glanced around I saw a lot of strangers— but also a few familiar faces. They weren't people I knew personally, but they were faces I'd seen in newspapers and magazines, on television, in corridors or at demonstrations. There were police, though not in uniform, detectives, possibly others higher up in the chain of justice and law enforcement, all looking very relaxed and happy. There were men in suits, others in a casual form of uniform, badges and ties removed, and just a few women. Money was changing hands. I noticed looks of recognition flicker over some of the faces in the crowd as they saw me, but no one spoke or made any movement in my direction.

I looked across the canvas and there was MumShirl, standing with some people, and they were all bent forwards staring at something on the floor. As she rose, she cast her eyes about and saw me. A guilty, 'caught-out' look fluttered across her face, and without another word to her companions she came across, grabbed me by the arm and tried to hustle me back outside. A lot of people there obviously knew her, and she them, but still no one spoke.

Out at the car, Mum could sense that I was fuming. I wished I had just driven away and left her there. I had more to do with my time than sit around waiting for her at a two-up game. I had children at home, work to do, things to attend to. The silence as we drove away was broken only by Mum's words of leave with the two men guarding the field.

The nuns were tired and anxious when we arrived in Newcastle at an ungodly hour. But they served us a cup of tea and a few biscuits before showing us to a narrow cell with two single beds. Barely a word had been spoken on the journey. I lay awake in the darkness for a short while, exhausted by the long day and the thought of the work we would have to do in just a few hours, and tried to reconcile what had transpired. What did it all mean? Being one of those people who draw comfort from the companionable snores of others, when MumShirl's regular deep and noisy breathing filled the air, I settled down.

Over time I realised that attending these sorts of illegal places was part of MumShirl's modus operandi, which is not to say that she didn't also enjoy participating. She had very little cash to gamble with, but I think she would have been delighted to win a bundle and have lots of money to give away. I became convinced, however, that her main reason for going along was to people-watch, to see who was doing what and where. Sometimes when we were on a mission which involved calling at a brothel to rescue some poor soul who had fallen into 'the life', we often sat out-side either before or after our visit, MumShirl watching who was going in and out. She gathered up this useful information and used it to enormous advantage by never overtly using it against anyone. I could always tell when she was dealing with a police officer, magistrate or politician with whom she had rubbed shoulders in some unsavoury environment, somewhere she or he would rather not have been seen.

Her reasons for not telling me where we were going on that night were complex. She would have been con-cerned about my disapproval, not being a gambler, and that I may have refused to drive her there, because I was such a worrier about leaving my children for any-thing other than urgent missions and emergencies. She may have felt unable to explain her attendance as part of her MO, because I hadn't yet seen all of it pieced together. Also, it became obvious later, from events that occurred when I was working on her autobiogra-phy, that she was worried about my safety if I knew too much. By the same token, there weren't a lot of people she could comfortably impose upon to take her to these places. She had a number of drivers, from time to time, drawn from religious orders and very strait-laced, who would have been mortified at the things Mum got up to in order to generate the power she had. Mum walked with both saints and sinners, but found it hard to find a companion and helpmate who could straddle these two groups with ease and without too much conflict. I think, for her, I had become one such person.

3

I often found it hard to maintain a sense of balance, much less humour, about my life. Working virtually non-stop, and unable to arrange someone to cover for me, I couldn't take holidays. Routinely, notices arrived on my desk at the Health Commission telling me that I had fifty days leave outstanding and unless I took some, I'd lose them.

The Commission had moved from Young Street at Circular Quay to the McKell Building, Rawson Place, near Central Station, a much busier area with very little parking. Because I used the Department's faster vehicle to respond to midnight emergency calls, I was obliged to keep it at my house, even though I had my own trusty little Morris Nomad for personal use. It was often more convenient to drive through the city and into Redfern, park and catch a train back to the office when I had desk work or meetings to attend. I learned that some of my neighbours resented the fact that there were often these two cars parked outside my house, regarding this as a sure sign that the government was wasting tax-payers' money on Aboriginal problems, but I was kept too busy dealing with the problems to do anything about it.

Life at home brought its own strain, too. A seemingly endless legal dispute involving the owners of the house we were living in prevented them from finalising its sale to us. Their mother's will and their inheritance of the property was being challenged by someone on the South Coast who, quite coincidentally, shared the same surname. As a result they were reluctant to undertake any repairs and the house was falling down around our ears.

At the first drop of rain, Russel, Naomi and I rushed around with buckets and rubbish bins, placing them strategically under the leaks, and we were up and down all night emptying them. Yet water still frequently soaked the children's beds. On one occasion, water on the electric wiring in the ceiling started a fire, and it was only the asbestos panelling that saved us. I fretted about the children's safety every time I was away from the house, but there was little I could do. As I was not the owner, I wasn't entitled to undertake major repairs.

Over the Christmas school holidays my mother agreed to take care of the children at her place at Tweed Heads. This meant that I could respond to the increase in threatening suicides that came in over that period, but it was always difficult for me to save the money for the children's plane fares. Mum, accompanied by her rogue boyfriend, Arthur, also lobbed on my doorstep several times a year. As well, she thought nothing of bringing Aunty Glad or some other of her friends with her, despite there being no space in the house. Gratitude was expected if she timed these holidays to coincide with the children's mid-term vacations, because she saved me the fares, although I usually ended up cooking and cleaning up after everybody. Now in her seventies, Mum tried hard to help me, but her eyesight was failing and clothes or dishes that she washed had to be washed again once she'd gone to bed.

She made every effort to find me a husband, flirting madly on my behalf on the phone with any male voice on the other end. I often snapped at her about how she was compromising me with men with and for whom I worked, but it made no difference. Mum, with backup from Aunty Glad, chided me about working too long and too hard, about not going out socially. They both said I was suffering from 'nerves', and that living alone with just the children for company was 'most unnatural'. When they realised I wasn't about to heed their well-intentioned advice, they began turning up with 'remedies' in the form of beer, whisky, Guinness, tonics, vitamin supplements and even sleeping tablets. It seemed that they wanted to get me drunk, drugged or both—supposedly for my own good.

At work, I began to notice signs posted around the Commission informing employees that they had to attend seminars on superannuation. I asked what this was about, and was told that because I wasn't a permanent employee, I wasn't entitled to attend. None of the Aboriginal staff was entitled to attend. Like the other Black staff, I was so grateful just to have a job, a regular paypacket coming in, and so busy doing the job, that I had completely overlooked the significance of our lack of status and job security.

Over the next couple of years, however, I gradually became aware that, while I'd often been at meetings all around the city, fighting for acknowledgement, funding and improvement in services to a range of disadvantaged people, it had never occurred to me, or apparently to any of the Black staff with whom I worked closely, to explore our own situation. We were all too outward looking.

Once I realised this, during the short periods of time I spent in the office I began to keep my ears open to see what I could find out. The Aboriginal Health Section had been established because the mainstream services were inaccessible and culturally inappropriate to meet the needs of the Black community. But the Black community represented the largest pool of ill-health, morbidity and mortality in the country.

Although we were therefore delivering specialist services that no one else was either able or prepared to deliver, the skills we brought to the Health Commission were not valued. A special range of employment categories had been designed for Black workers—we were not employed on a permanent basis, and the categories of our employment attracted lower remuneration than white workers doing comparable work. Indeed, in our office even much less skilled white employees were earning more than the most highly skilled Black workers.

This situation bothered me but I was at a loss to know what to do about it, apart from writing and talking about it. And frankly, I didn't have a lot of time. The unfairness of it all, though, simmered in my gut, adding to the burden of other problems I encountered every day, such as racism and sexism. However, it was impossible to remain focused on something so abstract when I frequently had to rush to young Black women who were putting their heads into gas ovens or trying to throw themselves under the wheels of a bus. There was still a great deal of overt racism around too, in those days before the anti-discrimination laws. People called me racist names, 'Abo', 'Boong', 'Nigger', and told me to 'go back to the jungle'. As well, I worried that if I began to make waves before I had formulated a plan and enlisted the support of all the senior Black staff, I would be sacked.

From time to time over the years, following spates of positive publicity given to activities within the Black community, including my own, people from my past began to contact me. No doubt this was because they then knew how to find me.

Adrian Keefe, for instance, a friend who had worked at the Sound Lounge in William Street, Kings Cross, during the period when I had been dancing with snakes, contacted me quite out of the blue. I remembered him from that time as having been deep into drugs, mainly speed. I had often voiced my disapproval then, and I was curious to know how he had turned out and what he could possibly want from me now.

Adrian had cleaned up his act, married, had a son, and his ex-wife had taken the child to live in South Africa. He said he thought that the child might become racist in that environment, an idea which worried him deeply, as did the notion that his child would associate with other members of his family. Adrian confided in me that he was trying to devise ways to rescue his son. I must say that at the time the intrigue surrounding his plans seemed fanciful, making me unwilling to assist him, not that I would have been able to do much anyway.

Adrian had a sister, Gaye, a former nun, also living

in South Africa, who married Clive Derby-Lewis. Over a decade later, his sister and brother-in-law were charged and tried, along with another white right-wing extremist, Janusz Jacub Walus, with murder, conspiracy to commit murder and illegal possession of arms and ammunition. This was following the assassination of Chris Hani, General Secretary of the Communist Party, an African National Congress leader and popular South African community organiser. I realised only then that Adrian's fears about his son's associations with other members of his family had not been groundless at all.

Another 'blast from the past' came walking right into the Health Commission to find me.

I looked up from my work one day to see a dishevelled, but vaguely familiar, figure making his way towards our space. An employee from another section was with him, pointing towards my desk. Pushing the employee away, the man ambled over noisily. When he was still a few feet from my desk, a question flashed through my mind. I thought I somehow ought to know who this man was, but I didn't.

He leaned across the desk and breathed enough beery fumes into the air to alert the entire office staff.

'Hullo, sis!'

Good grief, the ragged shape before me was Reg Mills, ex-husband of Desma. She had grown up in my mother's house and for many years I had regarded her as a sister. After suffering years of terrible physical abuse at Reg's hands, she had moved out with her six children and picked up with another man, Pete. Then she and Pete together had stolen from me everything I owned at the time. I'd vowed never to speak to her again, a promise I'd kept. Reg had tried to sexually molest me when I was a very young teenager, so the sight of him reeling over my desk and loudly claiming some relationship with me was quite appalling.

'Well, aren't you going to get me a chair?'

'No. What do you want, Reg?'

'This is urgent, and it's Health Commission business, sis. I'm sick.'

'You're sick alright. So what are you doing here?'

Some of the other staff, alerted by Reg's loud voice, were hovering in case I needed help. Reg looked around, saw them and whimpered. He looked more pathetic than dangerous.

'I want to talk, sis. I want to tell you my troubles.'

O, dear Heaven, I thought, how can I get out of this?

I rose and went to speak with my colleague Bob Jones. 'Bob, this guy used to be married to someone I once knew. He's drunk. I'm going to take him downstairs to the cafeteria and I'd like you to come down in about fifteen minutes and interrupt. Okay?'

Bob Jones, a six foot two inch ex-football player, was as peaceful as a lamb, but he looked quite formidable.

As we sipped coffee, Reg laid out his long tale of misfortune. It was an alcoholic's story, variations of which I was already awfully familiar with. He said he was living in a room in a nearby flea-bitten hotel, and that he had 'a new lady' whom he wanted me to meet. I shuddered. He admitted that they were both alcoholics, but that they were trying to get their lives together. He had been in and out of Callan Park Psychiatric Hospital, and knew that if he kept on with the drink he was dead meat.

When Bob appeared, I excused myself and directed Reg back out onto the street.

I spent so little time at my desk that I felt sure I would not run into him again. But no, hey presto, Reg began turning up and turning up. I had no idea whether this was merely his good fortune and my bad luck, or if he came by so often that he was bound to run into me. Maybe he even loitered outside, watching for my arrival. On one of these occasions he brought with him a very frumpy woman, quite short and dumpy, whose most remarkable feature was that she had no front teeth. This was Margaret.

One day Margaret came into the office alone and in a great state. Reg was crook in bed, she couldn't get him to wake up. I was glad that the Head of the Section, Tom Gavranic, was in the office that day. Tom was a physician, and he accompanied Margaret and me to the hotel. It seemed to be more a door on the street with a few rooms above it than what I would have thought of as a 'hotel'. We had to step gingerly up the rotting staircase and wait outside while Margaret went in to make sure Reg was 'decent'. Tom and I both thought it likely that he might be dead.

He wasn't dead, just very close to it. Tom was able to rouse him, and Reg pleaded with us not to send for an ambulance or take him to a hospital. No doubt from experience he knew this to be an indirect path back to Callan Park. The smell in the room was over-powering and, having made the introductions and stood by for a few minutes, I took my leave. Tom stayed and later told me he would continue to monitor Reg's condition, and that I didn't need to worry—which I had no intention of doing anyway.

Not long after, Margaret came into the office again. This time she wanted to know if the Health Commission would allow me to drive her to Callan Park. She had to visit Reg. I felt sorry for this foolish woman who was wasting her life. She looked so pitiful and needy that I took her to the psychiatric hospital against my better judgment. Reg, on the other hand, looked the best I had seen him—clean, sober and reasonably well. He also looked very sheepish when he saw me walk in. I left them alone to talk and was approached by a nurse.

I don't believe Reg knew I was coming, but he had been talking to all the nurses about his 'famous' sister-in-law. I quickly apprised this nurse of the truth, and told her that I had merely brought Margaret to visit. She was not about to let me go that easily. She thought she had located someone who could be made responsible for Reg so the staff could get him off their hands. Margaret, it appeared, had moved out of the hotel and was either camping with a friend or living rough. She had no address to give the hospital. No, I would not give the nurse my address, and no, Reg could not look forward to living at my house!

Some time later a nurse phoned looking for me at the Health Commission. I was working from home that day, but had left instructions that reasonable and vetted calls could be re-directed. It seemed that a call from the psychiatric hospital was considered reasonable, as it was forwarded on to me. A nurse informed me that Reg was due to be released that afternoon, would I please come and get him? I said no.

I prefer not to think that the nurse gave Margaret my personal and unlisted phone number, but from then on, Margaret began to ring me at home. She was always sober when she rang, but she had such a long list of woes that she kept my phone line tied up for hours when I was working. When I told her so, she started ringing at night.

Reg had been taken away, put in Chelmsford Hospital, and Margaret was worried about him. She told me horror stories about what a zombie he was becoming. The exposé of Chelmsford was still years in the future, so I had no way of knowing whether she was telling me the truth. What could I have done anyway, and would I have wanted to do anything?

Then she rang and told me that Reg had disappeared and urged me to do something about it. I worked at the Health Commission, it was my job to do something, she demanded. She accused the hospital of killing him and spiriting his body off somewhere. It all sounded far-fetched and I was short with her on the phone. Above all, I was in no position at the Health Commission where I could start an inquiry into a hospital. I could barely get a civil response from some of the hospitals I had to contact about any matter that had to do with an Aboriginal patient, for whom I did have some responsibility.

I was in a deep sleep when Margaret rang again, days later, at some time after one o'clock in the morning. She couldn't find Reg, and she had spent all her time looking and trying to force Chelmsford to give her information. If she didn't find him, and if I wasn't prepared to help, she was going to commit suicide. She said she couldn't live without him.

I was so exhausted that I laid the receiver down and let her talk while I went back to sleep. When I woke up next morning, the phone sounded as though it had been cut off. I hit the bar, got a dial tone, and decided Margaret had got the message and hung up. I never heard from her again.

This was one of those life episodes for which there is no closure. I never knew Margaret's surname, or where she made those calls from. I resented the way she always badgered me on the phone. I resented whoever had given her my phone number. Still, if I had not been so utterly worn out by the work I undertook each day and by looking after two children, I might have got in the car and gone to wherever she was, if only to assure myself that her threats were bluff. But were they bluff? I will ever know for sure.

Thoughts about this woman sometimes come uninvited into my head, as well as the many other white women I have met who remind me of her. Most are alcoholics, though some are not, but they have in common a heavy sorrow about themselves. In the main, the ones I have met seem to reach out to Blacks, and from time to time I have found myself counselling them. They share unhappy and often abused—sexual, physical and emotional—childhoods, followed by a string of relationships which mirror their early life. Perhaps in their acute pain they seek solace amongst people who they know can understand pain.

Christine Kankindji also miraculously reappeared. Christine had been my friend before my marriage to William. She had helped me prepare for our wedding and it was only with her expert culinary skills that I'd managed to feed the wedding guests. Christine, with her daughter Justine, had gone to live in Belgium, where she had married an African. Now she had a couple of small children, though her husband seemed to have abandoned her.

Christine had a small flat in a somewhat derelict-looking building in Brougham Street, Kings Cross. She received a deserted wife's pension and, although forced to live very frugally, she remained a generous person, readily sharing the little she had. She was something of a bower-bird, throwing away nothing and always picking things up in the street, pieces of discarded furniture, clothes, and sorting through anything anyone else had thrown away in case they had turfed out something of value. She also picked up people, particularly people in need.

One night Christine phoned me in distress—she had noticed a young girl crying in a Kings Cross coffee shop and approached her to see if she could help. The girl, who was Lebanese, had a room in a hotel of notorious repute, which, unknown to the management it seemed, she shared with her two even younger brothers. Christine wanted me to come at once—there was something wrong with the girl, she had been in an accident of some description and needed my attention.

The girl gave me a story, which I disbelieved, about how she had been alone in her room, washing her face in a washbowl, when she looked around and saw a man who had thrown some sort of acid at her. I went with her and saw the room, the washbasin in the corner, her few clothes strewn about over the floor and draped on the furniture. It was obvious that she worked as a prostitute, though I didn't feel it my business to ask. There was no evidence of acid anywhere, but the girl had a very serious injury of quite mysterious origin on her little finger. The digit was completely black and numb. I made arrangements to have her seen by a friend of mine, Dr Mick Asher, who had been my physician for years.

Mick confirmed what I already suspected, the finger was gangrenous and would have to be amputated. Left alone, it would inevitably have just fallen off, he said, but the gangrene might have spread further. He made arrangements immediately for her to go to a private hospital to have a cosmetic amputation, to minimise the visual impact later on. I thought I ought to meet her two brothers, since I had deprived them of their support by removing their sister temporarily from the streets.

The older of the two was already street-hardened and sly, and I felt sure he would continue to survive somehow on his wits. The younger brother was a different matter, baby-faced, still naive and somehow, with his large and anxious eyes, quite pitiful. He had not yet reached compulsory school leaving age. So, concerned about what might happen to him if the police stopped him on the street, I offered him a bed at my house for a few weeks until his birthday.

I didn't have a spare bed, of course, but we found an old mattress and he happily slept on the floor of Russel's room. The first night he stayed with us, he and Russel sat out in the kitchen in front of the little fireplace, putting logs on the fire and talking far into the night, while I worked on my papers in the little 'parlour' which served as my office. On my trips into the kitchen for coffee or to go to the bathroom, I could hear their voices, and I worried that this lad might make street-life and the glitter of Kings Cross sound attractive to my teenage son.

At almost midnight, way after Russel's usual bedtime, he came in and said, 'Mum, that boy's an idiot', his favourite expression for anyone he thought wasn't using their brains. I breathed a deep sigh of relief.

From the girl I had learned the tragedy of their family, how they had been preparing to flee war-torn Lebanon to start a new life in Australia when their mother died. The father, she said, had valiantly decided to bring his four children to Australia anyway, and things had gone downhill from there. The father was technically skilled and, despite his poor English, had got a job with a public utilities company, but the culture shock was enormous. As well, three of his children were growing rapidly and ate everything he could earn. Tied by the children to the little flat he rented, he had been unable to socialise and make friends outside his work. I phoned him and made an appointment to meet him in a coffee lounge in the city during his lunch hour to see if any of the family's relationships were salvageable.

He had one younger son, whom he showed me in a snapshot, a very chubby boy. The other siblings had told me that he was treated like a baby and was favoured by the father. Yes, he admitted, he had put locks on the fridge and on the food cupboard, but that was because the older children used to get out of bed at night to eat all the food that was supposed to be the family's meals for the next few days. Yes, he had hit his daughter on the face and head, but that was because he found she was wearing lipstick. She sneaked out one night and he caught her coming back in at midnight. Although she said she had been out with school friends, her father accused her of being a slut and had thrown her out of the house. Within a short time, both of the older brothers had left him to go and live with their sister, but he was determined to keep the youngest child from the same fate.

Interspersed with the information he gave me about himself and his family, he tried to prise personal details out of me. How come a young woman like me was working at the Health Commission? Didn't I have a husband who would keep me? Did I have children? And finally, would I be interested in marrying him?

I had not broached the most poignant and critical of the allegations that his children had made against him—that he had tried to force himself upon his daughter when she came home and he had called her a slut. But his ready and very unapologetic admissions had already caused me to despair about the likely success of putting the family back together through any of the helping agencies I knew to exist. The father appeared not only reconciled to the fact that his three oldest children had left him, but happy to be rid of the responsibility of them and get on with his own life.

I made time to go to the hospital to visit his daughter. I had told him that she had had surgery and was in hospital, but he had not even asked which hospital she was in. I was informed by the nurses that the girl had so many drugs in her system that the medications they gave her to lessen her pain weren't working. I peeped around the door and she appeared to be sleeping, so I didn't disturb her, leaving the few gifts I had brought with the duty nurse. When I next rang, I learned she had signed herself out and staff had no idea where she was.

Meanwhile, her brother stayed quietly over at my house, spending his days mainly doing odd-jobs in the yard and, I hoped, reflecting on his life. He took a bus into the city once or twice, but was always back by nightfall. On his birthday, I made a cake and we celebrated the event. Afterwards, when we were alone, I told him that he was now at liberty to leave and unless he got up to mischief, the police were unlikely to be able to detain him. He was now old enough to get himself on the unemployment register and look for work, even apply for the dole.

While I was telling him his rights, he began to plead with me to allow him to stay. He would even go back to school, if he could go to the same school as Russel.

I was surprised because, after that first night, Russel had been dismissive towards him and they hadn't spent much time together. I looked about me, our house so small, dark and tiny, the boy had slept on the floor, and I recognised that, despite my wish to help him, I couldn't. My life was hard enough—I could not acquiesce to his pleas.

I took him into town the next day, and found his brother. Then I sat them both down and gave them a good talking to about being at the crossroads and offered what small back-up assistance I could, and did not see either of them from that day.

Christine mentioned that she had seen one of the brothers again. But after that they had disappeared out of our lives, as people often do. In banter, I asked Christine not to talk to girls in coffee shops, even if they were sobbing buckets. And if she did, she was not to call me.

Another wonderful soul who rose up out of my past was Phillip Pearce, whom I had met while working at Lowths Hotel in Townsville. Phillip had been a casual waiter at functions, his full-time job was working in a hair-dressing salon in Flinders Street, then the centre of town. He had given Naomi her first haircut. Before he began to trim her fair locks he had carefully snipped off a curl, tied it together with a thin ribbon and given it to me as a memento.

In Townsville, he had been a pleasant and thoughtful young man, quite shy and withdrawn. When I met him again, though, he had become a very confident man, co-owner and operator of an upmarket hair salon in trendy Oxford Street, Paddington. He had not known he was gay in the old days in Townsville, he confided, and realising and acknowledging his orientation had

allowed him to be his full self. He was in a monoga-
mous and loving relationship with his partner who
worked with him at the salon.

Over the years since I had met Phillip, I allowed my
hair to sprout and only cut it down once a year, at the
beginning of summer, to save money. Sometimes it
grew to extravagant lengths, although the texture of
my hair is so light that I used to joke that other people
grew their hair long and I grew my hair 'tall'. Indeed,
my wild hair was virtually a trademark, though few
knew how much care and effort it took to keep it looking so fine. Phillip was an expert at cutting 'Black hair',
and I later discovered that my friend, Faith Bandler,
was one of his regular customers, too. Phillip also
began to help me in my work.

I took many poor people to him for discount, sometimes free, haircuts, but one client stands out
particularly in my mind. She had been in an abusive
relationship in a small country town. Aware of her circumstances, I had urged her to make the break and
get away, an extremely difficult thing to do with many
of her husband's relatives living in the same town.

Once, after receiving a beating by her husband that
left her hospitalised with her injuries, a local doctor
and some nurses conspired to help her leave. She had
small children with her when she arrived in Sydney,
and I found her a safe house out on the northern
beaches.

My other commitments meant that I could not
spend any great length of time with her, and she soon
grew lonely and nostalgic for the friends and relatives
she had also had to abandon. When she learned that
an uncle had died in a town near her home, she felt
obliged to attend his funeral. She was determined just

to slip in and out for the service, and planned to leave the children with people she knew in Sydney.

A few days later I received a hysterical phone call asking me to pick her up in Redfern. While waiting for her train at Central Station to carry her to the funeral, she had been abducted, taken to an unknown destination and kept in an underground cellar. There she had been repeatedly raped and beaten before making an escape. A stranger to Sydney, she had found a railway station and noted its name. Although she had no money, she was desperate to keep moving because she thought the man who had grabbed her once would try to grab her again when he discovered she had gone. She boarded the first train and alighted at Redfern, where she had previously been with me. She made her way to Redfern Police Station where she tried to report what had occurred.

The police, however, were disbelieving and rude. An Aboriginal woman, she was somewhat overweight; perhaps they thought she did not look sufficiently attractive to be a rape victim. They suggested to her that she had just dumped her kids and gone away for a few days with a bloke who took her fancy, and, fearing she might be found out, she had made up a story to cover her tracks. They refused to take her account seriously or write a report, and sent her away.

She went next door to the Aboriginal Medical Service. Staff there gave her a more polite reception, but again she was met with disbelief, which I found really disappointing.

I picked her up and took her home to my place. She was in shock, traumatised with grief and as nervous as a skittish kitten. She told me brief details of her abduction, but by this time she had become even more disturbed by the fact that she had not been believed. She spoke disparagingly of herself and her worth, as a person and as a mother. I didn't push her for conversation, but sat with her in case she wanted to say something, just let her know I was there to listen. I realised I had a threatening suicide situation on my hands.

She kept lapsing into a silent wide-eyed state, a condition I diagnosed as sleep-deprivation. When I asked her if she wanted to lie down and rest, though, she was unable to do so. That afternoon, when my children came home from school, I left her with Naomi, who was only about eight years old, and went out to buy food for our evening meal. I felt she'd be safe with Naomi for a few minutes because Naomi was such a gasbag. I knew she wouldn't stop talking until I returned, and her remarks were always very positive. Even as I was preparing to leave, I could hear Naomi talking: 'Can I have a look at your earrings? Oh, aren't they beautiful! And your hair is so shiny. And, oh look, your skin is so smooth and soft.' That's just the sort of child Naomi was—when she wanted to be.

My guest's inability to settle down became a serious problem, and I knew sleeplessness would heighten her suicidal thoughts. I, myself, was exhausted, but couldn't go to bed and leave her alone. As well as my genuine and deep concern for her, I also had to consider the welfare of my own two youngsters. I had to think about the impact it would have had on them if they went into the bathroom and found her with her wrists cut. On the other hand, it would be of no benefit to anyone if I stayed awake all night to keep her company and was unable to function the next day. So I persuaded her to take a sleeping tablet, which I kept on hand for such occasions. Then I put her to sleep beside me in my double bed so that if she stirred in the night, I, being a light sleeper, would know.

Next morning I had a plan of action, with the welfare of my client foremost in my mind. The woman was adamant that she would not subject herself to further hostility from the police or any other agency. The Aboriginal Medical Service had said they were unable to find any bruising on her body, which might have confirmed for them her version of events. By the next morning, however, they had surfaced. She had obviously suffered very deep bruising and, being overweight, these had taken time to rise to the skin. She looked like she'd been used as a punching bag. Seeing the marks set her off on a crying spell, which I regarded as healthy. Tears can sometimes heal.

What she had told me of her abduction was fresh in my mind. She had arrived early at Central Station and, while waiting for her train, had walked out to the concourse in front of the station. A man in a car parked near the kerb had slid across the seat and called out to ask her the time. As she approached the car, looking down at her watch, she found herself being forced into the passenger seat, head first, and pushed under the dashboard. The man then put his foot on her head and drove away.

She had freed herself from under his foot for just a few moments before he secured her again, and she had described for me a sign she had seen in that brief glimpse. It consisted of just three letters and they appeared to be on the top of a tall building. The woman didn't know Sydney, but I did, and I had a good idea which building and sign she had seen.

After getting the children off to school that morning

we got into the car, and I told her that I had a call to make. I approached the building from the direction I felt her abductor was likely to have taken, and although she had been sitting quietly beside me during the ride, when it came into view and she spotted the sign on top, she held her hands to her breast and started to scream. I pulled over and we talked.

I thought back to my own experience when I had wandered around in a bizarre dream world, doubting my own sanity, until I was eventually believed and later confronted with tangible evidence. I wanted her to be able to confirm for herself the reality of the abduction and attack. Seeing the building and the sign enabled her to do so. She kept repeating between her sobs, 'I knew I wasn't making it up, I knew I wasn't mad.'

Her relief at seeing the evidence and realising that I believed her story was enormous, and she clung to me as though I was her only friend. While she talked, my mind raced ahead to the rest of my plan, which was to try to help her restore some sense of self-esteem. I knew this would be a long task, eventually completed alone, but there were steps I could take to help her.

First I brought her to Phillip Pearce's hair-dressing salon. Phillip could always sense when I had something critical going down, and needed no brief. While I flicked through magazines and rang the office on his phone, Phillip transformed her. He gently shampooed and massaged her head then cut off her long and badly neglected hair and created for her a style which curled cheekily around her face, flattering her features. When she caught a glance of herself in the mirror, the first flicker of a smile appeared. 'I didn't recognise myself,' she told me softly—which had been my intention.

Phillip waved us goodbye without charge. On the way to the car, the woman asked, 'Who's going to pay for that?' She'd noticed the schedule of fees on the wall, she told me, and had been worried about it the entire time. She had no money and she knew from the state of my house that I had very little.

'Phillip's a friend. You'll have to consider your new looks a gift from the gods,' I told her. 'You deserve it.' She was really pleased with her new image and kept patting her hair, smiling.

From there we went to North Sydney to the business of another friend, Maureen Pettit. I had met Maureen and her outrageously extroverted husband, Arthur, when they ran a hifi and record shop in Crow's Nest. Len Wallis, who went on to own a hi-fidelity audio company, worked with them. They had become committed to the cause of assisting me in whatever way they were able, on the strength of the few bits and pieces I had shared with them about my life and work. Maureen ran a clothing store, Blush, and a nod was all that was required for her to slide my client into a dressing room and hand in a wonderful assortment of clothes to try on. 'Just pick out a couple of pieces you really like,' she told her, 'and we'll worry about the bill later.' Of course there was no bill, and Maureen even treated us to lunch at a nearby coffee lounge.

By now my client was beginning to feel quite special. When we returned to the house, with just a little urging, she modelled her elegant new clothes. I was pleased with the enormous improvement—from the desperate soul of yesterday who had been racked with self-hatred and worry, to the woman who now stood before me, looking at herself in the mirror in wonderment.

I made arrangements for her and her children to be

re-united at the safe house the next day. Then I took her out with me to a discotheque in the hope that she would find music and dancing as relaxing as I did. Being mid-week, there were not a lot of people there, but enough for her to draw a few admiring glances and to be asked up to dance. I really wanted her to feel that she was still attractive, that the horrendous events she had been subjected to had not marked her permanently on the outside, and that, with fortitude, she could carry on with her life much as before, even as she hid her pain behind a facade of cheeriness.

Within a few days, however, I received a call from someone at the safe house—a man had come to the door asking for her, and she had gone out with him for a few hours. Later the person phoned me again to say the woman was now packing to leave.

I spoke with her on the phone. She had, she said, had time to think about everything that had happened. She was thankful that she had had a friend like me to turn to, but she had to think about her whole life. She'd phoned a relative of her husband's and asked her to tell him where she was. He had come straight down to Sydney on the train, and was taking her home that very night.

'Are you sure you know what you're doing?' I asked, and her answer chilled me to the bone.

'No woman's safe. I'm not safe in Sydney and I'm not safe at home. I know that now. So if someone's going to kill me, I'd rather it be someone that I know.'

4

My work brought me into contact with people who had flamboyant and unconventional lifestyles. John Newfong, whom I had met at a One People of Australia League (OPAL) conference in Brisbane in the 1960s, was one such person.

While always effusive and jovial to my face, during the 1970s John wrote a hostile article about me in the government-subsidised Black community magazine, *Identity*, when he was editor. Amongst other things, he wrote that I was a 'Johnny-come-lately', and implied a sexual relationship between Germaine Greer and myself when we travelled to Alice Springs in 1972. Not a word of this was true.

The more I learned about John, the more obvious it became that he often projected his own short-comings onto other people, myself included. After taking legal advice about the article, I contacted him. 'I would suggest that your best line of defence would be to write an article for my magazine...', he replied from his Canberra base. There were few writers in the Black community and *Identity* was always soliciting people to contribute material. However, the idea that I would submit an article to his editorial pen—instead of suing him—was ludicrous.

Brian Syron, Aboriginal Theatre director, who had recently returned from studying acting and directing overseas, was a close friend of mine. Jailed in his youth, Brian then left Australia and had, he said, been able to prosper abroad because he was fair-skinned and didn't identify himself as Aboriginal, a situation he makes quite clear in his autobiography, *Kicking Down The Doors*.

Both MumShirl and Brian regaled me with tales of the escapades of John Newfong, who, since our initial meeting, had 'come out of the closet', identifying himself publicly as homosexual. They were both people to whom John turned when he had 'problems'.

MumShirl's favourite anecdote, which always set her laughing until tears ran down her face, was about a time when love-lorn John had approached her to help him 'rescue' his love object, a slim, fair, long-haired white lad, from the clutches of a sect to which he had apparently fallen victim. John was a bear of a man, dark, tall, rotund, and gregarious, and he often seemed to attract his exact opposites.

John had learned the daily schedule of the recent recruits to this sect. So, with MumShirl and at least one other, a driver no doubt, to assist, he waited in a car in a street outside the sect's headquarters at night for the youth to have a break and emerge briefly for fresh air in the garden. After waiting unsuccessfully the first night, they returned 24 hours later to make a second attempt. On this occasion, they pounced on a long-haired blond lad and bundled him headfirst into the back seat, and John squeezed himself in too.

They had gone some distance in silence, Mum said, before John's voice broke the dramatic mood. 'God, I hope we've got the right one!' It was this comment that always cracked MumShirl right up.

A politically savvy conversationalist, through his work as a journalist, John had made contacts all over the world. But he was enormously self-indulgent and lost jobs because he thought nine in the morning was an entirely unreasonable hour of the day to be expected to arrive at work.

On one occasion when John was out of work, Brian had to travel out of Sydney for a week, so he agreed that John could use his house in his absence. He returned mid-morning to find John in the loungeroom, the cupboards and refrigerator bare and not even the makings of a cup of tea left in his house. Brian gave John money to go and buy tea and milk, as Brian couldn't live without his cup of tea.

While John was out at the corner store, Brian discovered that even the little money-boxes in which he saved coins for his nieces and nephews had been raided. He became livid and confronted John on his return. In response John pouted and said, 'I was hungry. What did you expect me to do?'

Brian said he realised John had not looked for work at all in his absence, and had spent his day lying around, watching television and listening to the stereo. Spending the coins from the money-boxes was the last straw. Brian ordered John to leave and retired to his bedroom to give him time to pack his few things and organise his departure. He heard John making some phone calls and rattling around.

At last Brian heard a car pull up, and went to the window to peep out, expecting to see a taxi. Instead he saw John, suitcase in hand, stride down the path and climb majestically into the back of a big white, privately owned limousine!

'Can you believe that?' asked Brian to the group of us with whom he was sharing this story. 'The man had friends all over the place so wealthy and keen to see him that they'd send limos to pick him up, and instead he pilfers money out of kids' money-boxes?' We all cracked. Strange as this may seem, tales of John's knavish behaviour often endeared him to people and many of his antics became embedded in urban Black folklore. In some quarters his appetites were legendary and his larrikinism lionised, much like Ned Kelly, I suppose.

Over time I tackled John about his feelings of hostility towards me, as shown in his *Identity* article and in the patently untrue things he had said to mutual friends. I had learned, from fragments of conversation he had dropped in my hearing, that my sister, Della, had married a boarding-school friend of John's with whom he had been enamoured. I asked him outright if my sister's marriage was the reason for his bitterness towards me. Della, by this time, had long ago divorced her first husband and had been living in New Zealand for almost a decade.

Eventually, after John had reflected on my words, he conceded his hostility and acknowledged the truth of my suspicions regarding my sister's marriage. He asked if we could put the past behind us and if I would be his friend. We were both doing work which often brought us to the Aboriginal Medical Service, and he said it would be to the advantage of the Black community if we were to 'bury the hatchet'.

Although I continued to run into John from time to

time over the years when he would try to inform me about his latest conquests or dramas, I was unable to feel confidences shared with him were safe and consequently we never became 'friends'. I thought too that, despite his general lack of sensitivity about such matters, he became aware that I disapproved of his frequent sexual coarseness, which he seemed to regard as titillating, and of the promiscuity about which he often boasted without any concern for the presence of children.

Brian Syron, on the other hand, had become a friend, after some initial misunderstandings between us. At first I had thought Brian dealt with problems lightly. He had an actor's manner of calling up quips and punch-lines from old movies in often quite inappropriate circumstances, and on one occasion I told him so. I think he thought me far too serious for my own good, and consequently not entertaining company. However, he took it upon himself to bring some cheer into my life, ringing to invite me to opening nights and performances. Over time we became very close, sharing a deep friendship and loyalty, while remaining trusted critics and supporters of each other's work and efforts.

My mother continued to visit me several times a year, as well as sharing fragments of her news with me by post. She was really beginning to show her age by this time, not only through her increasing forgetfulness, but also her inability to stay up with the times. If, while she was staying at our house, I had to fly to a meeting outside of Sydney, she would make a big fuss about coming to the airport to wave me goodbye.

'Mum, I fly out at 6.30 in the morning—and I'll be

back this very afternoon. Taking a plane now is like taking a bus.'

She seemed unable to comprehend the speed at which the world was changing. On one occasion, she sent Russel a few dollars cash in an envelope, telling him to take me out to dinner with it for my birthday. The small sum she sent wouldn't have come anywhere near paying the bill at even the cheapest restaurant. Instead, Russel used the money to buy mince to cook me a meal at home. She seemed to have completely lost track of so many things, though I was assured by my friends who had elderly parents that Mum was normal for her age.

In one of her letters Mum wrote that a nephew of hers had turned up at her home in Tweed Heads. Perhaps he had contacted Aunty Glad, who would have given him her address. With the exception of Aunty Glad, Mum had been wiped off for more than three decades by her large family for having the temerity to give birth to three illegitimate children of colour. Mum seemed delighted, therefore, that at long last she had been forgiven and she was now being, perhaps, welcomed back into the fold.

This nephew, she informed me, was in his fifties, lived in Sydney with his wife and family, and was a senior police officer. She just knew he would love to meet me.

I had to laugh at her naivety. If the theory I'd put together from the tiny clues that had littered her life was correct, that her family had been passing as white, then the chances of this man putting his hand up to be recognised as one of my relations was extremely remote. I was the family's 'black sheep', being so politically active. I also had the capacity to cause people to ask if Mum and her relations were really white? Or were they Black, too?

When she was next in Sydney, Mum spoke of her nephew in really glowing terms. He was such a 'lovely young man'. He had come by her house and they had spent such a nice afternoon together. Through him, she had caught up with all her family news—who had died, who was still living and in which town. From her handbag, which always held everything but the kitchen sink, she took out a scrap of paper and carefully copied from it his name and the police station at which he was the senior officer. Would I contact him?

After a few days of nagging, I phoned the police station, which was on the northern beaches. Mum was at my elbow, encouraging me. I thought that if I got him on the line I'd pass the phone to her. But he was on holidays, I learned from the officer who answered, and they weren't expecting him back; he was about to be transferred to another northern suburbs station. Mum seemed quite sad.

However, when she returned to Tweed Heads, she continued to hassle me to contact him, and in each letter she put another slip of paper with his name on it. Eventually, sitting at my desk with my little manual typewriter in front of me, Mum's square slip staring me relentlessly in the eye, I tapped out a letter to him at his new posting and, next day, mailed it.

Need I say more? The letter was never answered, nor was it returned. The phone never rang. Mum's nephew disappeared back into the thin air from whence he had come. I waited until she visited again before I told her, so that I could console her if necessary.

'Mum, he just didn't answer. I gave him my phone number and address. I'm so well known that I have no doubt he knows who I am. He just doesn't want me as a cousin.'

Mum's face grew rigid and she rose up from the kitchen table where we were sitting and went off to the lounge room where she was sleeping during this visit.

I would liked to have confronted her again about my suspicion that she and her entire family were living a lie, but I restrained myself. To be honest, by that time I think I no longer cared. I was living my own lie, keeping the dark secret of my son's conception and birth, and carrying the burden of pain and secrecy in my heart.

How then to raise questions of my mother's pain and secrecy? I felt also that I had to set some sort of example to my child, to accept what my mother wanted to tell me so that he would accept what his mother had to tell him. Mum had her reasons, and I had mine.

Over the years, I had been placed under a lot of pressure from some Black community members to explore my family roots. At first, when my son, the product of rape, was young, I had done so, often quite enthusiastically. But as time passed and my own experiences widened and deepened, it had become unimportant to me. I had questioned Mum, often brazenly and rudely, about my father, and when that had not been successful, I had used cajolery. As a maturing adult, though, with periods of my mother's absence from my life, combined with the struggle of raising my own children, I had had cause to reflect on just what constitutes fatherhood.

As my children had no father present in their lives, I realised I had had no one either. No one willing to put his hand up, to take responsibility for the life he had helped to create, whoever he was. He had not been there to help my mother put food in front of me, to hold me high in the air so that I could get a lofty vision of the world. There had been no one nearby to be my protector, to defend me against the horrors of the world. Instead, like so many others in my position, I had become a victim.

I had reflected, too, on the experiences of some of the Blacks, and a few whites, whom I had counselled, who had confided in me stories of their own searches. Many had gone out looking for fathers, sometimes mothers, and occasionally siblings, only to have their hearts broken by rejection. I was saddened by their stories, some of which no doubt influenced the way I thought about the notion of searching for a father who had abandoned me.

Eventually, I had come to a conclusion: why would I want to know a man who didn't want to know me? It boiled down to being that simple. I was glad for those people whose search stories seemed to have had a 'happy ending'. But their stories were the exceptions rather than the rule. I had enough unhappiness to deal with. I wasn't interested in going out of my way to find any more.

My mother, pretence or not, had stood by me. As an adult, I realised I cared enough and was grateful enough for her love and loyalty, to overlook whatever may have been her shortcomings. They were not mine to judge. When I was pressured by other Blacks, and sometimes whites, about my bloodlines, I silently accepted the burden of their pressure. I just hoped that over time, they too would mature enough to realise that no one can judge another person on anything other than what they themselves had done, and that they had no right to try to judge me.

I took heart from all the things that had been given to me in this life, and decided to waste no more energy and tears on those things that were beyond my reach. As time passed I was able to acknowledge that there are some things unknowable, unattainable, and I became happier in myself when I achieved this insight. People would undoubtedly keep nudging and hassling me, because it seems to be in the nature of some people to always cry for the moon.

My two children were a source of tremendous joy to me; they were, quite simply, the reason why I drew breath every day. I didn't want my son to know anything about who his father could be. And my daughter's father, William, refused to support her. I considered his threat to tell Russel of the criminal circumstances of his conception too high a price to pay, so his support too had become unattainable.

I had a warm coterie of friends, friends for every reason and friends for every season. Without some, like Mrs Owens, who had started as a reluctant occasional child-minder but had grown into an adopted 'grandparent', and Liz Milne, who cared about my children, my life would have been much harder. As we all do, I had friends for when I was up, and for when I was down. They all had their own lives, of course, but I was grateful for that bit of their lives which they spent on me.

I had a headful of warm memories, of beaches and blue sea and sky. My snakes had always been wonderful friends to me, and a great happiness and feeling of satisfaction flows over me whenever I think of them coiled or stretched on sunny hills, somewhere just beyond my immediate vision.

My identity was grounded in being who I was, in the work I was doing, and the mother I was being. I

ROBERTA SYKES

was who I found looking back at me from my mirror each morning: a Black woman of modest good looks, striving to live the only life we are given, as decently and honestly as I could.

5

When in 1997 I received, first, an invitation to fill out an application and then later an acceptance into the Master's program at the Harvard Graduate School of Education, I was filled with confusion. On the one hand, this felt like the opportunity of a lifetime (Pinch me quick, see if I'm dreaming?), and on the other, an awesome burden which I felt, at that point in my life, I could not assume. My work at the Health Commission was almost totally consuming, but it was so poorly paid that I was compelled to keep doing extra work outside whenever it was available. I wrote book reviews for newspapers, magazines and radio programs, and continued to freelance as a journalist, writing articles wherever I could place them.

I have collected quite a store of humorous stories about some of my written work, most of which was, by then, commissioned. One week I had just finished writing a piece for a Christian newspaper when I received a surprise phone call from Mark Day, then the managing editor of *Australian Penthouse* magazine.

Geraldine Willesee had introduced me to Mark years before when he was working at the *Mirror*.

We met again now in his office and he asked if I would be interested in writing a piece for his publication. *Penthouse* wasn't a magazine I read, and I had always thought of it as being tits, bums and porn, so I was shocked. Mark assured me, though, that they ran serious articles. I thought about his offer for a while because, although I didn't read it, I knew that it had a high profile and likely reached an audience possibly hitherto untouched by Black politics. Surely, I thought, readers of Christian newspapers do not also read *Penthouse*.

Health Commission policy, which I had often had to ignore, was that employees were not to make public statements without prior approval. However, if the public had to become informed before governments addressed the appalling state of Aboriginal health, then I felt I had a greater responsibility to do what I could. I would not allow myself to be stopped by red tape. My articles had appeared in a wide variety of newspapers and magazines, and I had never been reprimanded. Still, an article in *Penthouse*, I thought, might just draw flak.

After considering all the factors, Mark and I struck a deal. My article would run on two pages, and not be interspersed with pictures of partly undressed or naked women. I hurried home and wrote 'Killing Me Softly', a piece about the removal of Black men, through death, incarceration and other means, from the Black community, and the social consequences which eventuated and the genocidal conclusions which had to be drawn from this. When it went to press, I sat back and waited.

Surely, I thought, no one at the Health Commission reads *Penthouse*?

Within two days of the magazine's release, I received a phone call from Gary Foley. He had read it and warmly congratulated me. I said, 'Only for the articles, eh, Gary?'

'Yeah, sis. Just for the articles.'

I had perhaps envisaged rich old white men in raincoats as being *Penthouse* readers. It had never occurred to me that members of the Black militant sector might also lean in that direction, so Gary's phone call had me spluttering with surprise and laughter for years.

As promised, my article had been printed discreetly, on two facing pages and appropriately separated from nudity or anything that might have detracted from its political and informative value. Over the next week, photocopies of it were circulating through the entire Health Commission. So many people, including senior staff, spoke appreciatively to me about it, all careful to mention that they had read only the photocopy, that their implicit denials became something of a joke to me. *Someone* had read it in the original, but no one ever owned up.

My mother also phoned me, as she had previously when an article about me and my work had appeared in *Australasian Post*.

'Do you always have to write for rude magazines, Roberta? And why is it that everyone else has to tell me these things! Your Aunty Glad rings to say you've been on television, people pull me up in the street to say they've seen your picture or writing in magazines. How come I'm always the last to know, eh?'

Mum chose not to understand that these things were just part of my job as a public educator. She considered this to be 'fame', and was peeved that I didn't report directly to her.

I continued, in a voluntary capacity, to write, research and edit the Black community newspaper, *AIM*. It was being published by the Aboriginal Dance Company, where I also taught, through an arrangement with Aboriginal and Torres Strait Islander Skills Development. I was kept very busy and locked into work which I regarded as valuable. I remained in no position just to walk out and go off to Harvard, even if I could afford to, which I could not.

As well, my son Russel was doing his Higher School Certificate, to become one of the few Black students to successfully reach this level at that time. I could no more abandon him at this crucial period than I could fly. I wrote back to Harvard, spelling out the reasons why I was unable to take up their offer.

Professor Chester Pierce, who had initiated the invitation to Harvard, wrote to me supportively on a regular basis. His airmail letters in his familiar almost illegible scrawl mounted up, and I was always pleased to read his repeated reassurances that the work involved in gaining a Master's degree was well within my ability. Still, I harboured my doubts. If, I wondered, I was considered smart enough to get a degree from Harvard, why had Australian universities not picked up on this? Although I routinely gave guest lecture presentations in university courses in fields such as medicine, politics and English literature, I had been regularly told that in order to enter the university I would have to study for and pass a Matriculation exam. Being the sole bread-winner, I couldn't have afforded the time off to do so, and therefore the idea had never been on my agenda. Apparently it was alright for me to teach in universities which I couldn't get into, even as an undergraduate student.

Now I was being assured that, despite not having either secondary or undergraduate experience, I could succeed in postgraduate work. It was all very confusing.

My son passed his HSC at Crows Nest Boys High School in 1978 and entered the University of New South Wales in 1979. He was seventeen and I was terribly proud of him. Although he had shown aptitude for maths and his teachers had encouraged him to think about accountancy as a career, he had taken an elective in Psychology at high school and become fascinated with human behaviours. He said he hated the idea of being stuck at a desk with just lists of numbers for company. The training for psychology has a significant component of maths, percentages and graphs, so he felt well equipped to link up his two areas of interest. Prior to starting his university studies, we had a talk.

'You know it's very hard for me to be the sole breadwinner here, Russel, so if you start at the university, you have to finish.'

'You want me to go to work?' I knew that he had a lot of concerns about going to work without qualifications. Some of his school friends had found the going hard, unless their families had a business—and, of course, we did not.

'No, that's not what I'm saying. I want you to go to university and get a degree, but if there's any likelihood that you'll just go for a year or two and drop out, then I'm not prepared to help you. Do you understand me? We're not a rich family that can afford a playboy son.'

'Okay. I understand. You help me, Mum, and I'll stay the distance.'

His earnest young face was reassuring. Apart from

ROBERTA SYKES

the secret surrounding his birth, which I had constantly evaluated and decided he had not yet had sufficient life experience to deal with, our relationship had always been based on directness and truth. I knew when he gave his word, he would keep it.

For his seventeenth birthday, my mother bought Russel a very old, very tiny car. She told me that if he broke no road rules and carried no more than one passenger at a time for one year, she intended to buy him a new car when he turned eighteen. She was very worried that the profile of males killed on the road was that they were young and inexperienced, driving powerful cars, and often being egged on by a carload of their mates.

During his term vacation, he went up to Tweed Heads at her bidding, and together they went to a new car dealer. They wandered around the display area alone, this tall young dark man with this poorly dressed little old lady. The salesmen didn't bother giving any attention to this unlikely pair. However, they stayed so long, with Russel opening and closing doors and so on, that eventually one salesman sauntered out of the office towards them.

'Uh, can I help you at all, mate?'

'Do you have this Gemini panel van in that green?' Russel asked, choosing the car of his birth sign, and indicating the bright grasshopper colour on another vehicle.

'We don't have it, but we could get it,' the salesman replied, his voice loaded with scepticism.

'Is that the one you want, Russel?' my mother piped up. 'If the man can get it in green?'

When Russel nodded, Mum spoke to the salesman. 'We'll take it. How long before you can get it delivered?'

'How would you like to pay for it?' the dubious salesman responded.

'Oh, cash. How much will it be, with registration and delivery and everything?'

Mum had worked, scrimped and saved for years towards this big moment, when she would buy the apple of her eye a new car. That day she had gone to the bank and withdrawn her savings which she was carrying now in her old purse.

She told me the salesman was absolutely flabbergasted when, at last, he invited them into the office, and she pulled out this roll of cash and started counting out her bills on his desk!

When Russel's car arrived, we nicknamed it 'the grasshopper', and, like most young men, I suppose, he lavished his every attention upon it. No one was allowed to eat in the car, no one was permitted to drive it but him, and he made up so many other rules that I declined even to get in it. When it was brand new, he even carried a dust rag to wipe over the seats when anyone got out.

Next time Mum was in Sydney, though, she and I had a row. Not only had my mother never bought me a car, but although she saw me working so hard, apart from looking after the children during school holidays, she had never offered me any help. The house we lived in was so derelict as to be disgusting, and I had not been able to afford to buy myself anything new, not so much as a lipstick, for many years.

Mum, no doubt subscribing to the theory that the best means of defence is attack, was in the habit of using every opportunity to berate me about the poverty she seemed to think I brought upon myself. She erroneously equated fame with riches, and since I was often quoted in the press and appeared on television, she seemed to believe I deliberately eschewed payment for this work. She was unable to reconcile that those who spoke out about the Black community's struggle for justice were penalised, not paid, for doing so. And, as though I needed her reminder, she frequently held up to me that Naomi's father, William, contributed nothing to her upkeep. William, with his new wife, was in the habit of visiting Mum occasionally, and she knew it was well within his means to support his child.

'My girl,' Mum said flippantly in her own defence, 'if you don't like the way you are living, find a husband and get married. I don't want my grandson walking around in this area where he could be a target for white boys.'

There had been a spate of incidents, bashings and vandalism, in the northern suburbs committed by wealthy young men which could only have been recreational violence. I shared her concern. However, it did not seem to dawn on her that not only was the protection of a car something that she had never offered me, and my life had been almost destroyed by that, but she also had no intention of buying a car for any other of the grandchildren, even the girls who should have been considered to be of equal, if not greater, risk. My words fell on deaf ears.

'When Naomi's old enough, she's good-looking, boys will give her a lift home. She won't have to walk home after social events.'

I despaired, as I had often had cause to, at this sort of reverse sexism which seemed deeply ingrained in so many of her generation.

Mum stood up, indicating any discussion on the subject was reaching its end.

'All my other grandchildren have fathers, and their fathers can buy them cars if they want. Russel is the only child with no father. He only has me. And if you want a car, or someone to help you fix the house, my girl, you should get married and let someone buy these things for you.'

How absolutely unreasonable, I fumed as Mum stalked off. What sort of short memory did she have! My father had not even owned up to me, much less bought me a car. Her current boyfriend never bought anything for her, in fact the reverse was true. She was constantly dipping into her purse to keep him out of jail and buy and repair cars for him.

I tried hard to be happy at Russel's good fortune, because, in my mind, getting a car from your grandma was almost like winning the lottery. Often, though, I found myself swimming in tears at my own lack of comfort. This feeling was exacerbated at times by the presence of the car and the fact that Russel did not yet have the maturity to recognise the situation for what it was and appreciate how much I was hurt by my mother's good intentions directed only ever towards him.

The first year at university was a severe blow to, and a learning experience for, Russel. He had assumed universities were places that encouraged thought and welcomed new ideas, new ways of looking at things. But when he discovered that he was merely expected to parrot back in class and repeat again in essays whatever his lecturers had said, he was dismayed. He found this out the hard way, by having his work marked down and he was failed in one course.

One of the courses he took was Aboriginal Studies. After receiving his marks for this subject he came home and sat at the kitchen table with his head in his hands.

'Mum, it's just not possible for these white boys to have studied books for ten weeks and know more than I know about being Black. MumShirl almost lives here, Elders from everywhere come here. I've been reading—and you've been writing—on the subject for years. Even most of the Koori writers have been sitting here in our house, talking about their lives and what they think and write. For the course we were set a handful of readings by whites, and we had to take notes on what the white lecturer told us. Now the results are in, I find most of the white students in the class got higher marks than me. No one wants to know what it is to *be* Black, we've just got to learn what whites think *about* Blacks.'

Russel had learned a tough lesson: Just listen to what the teachers have to say and spout it back to them, even when you know it's wrong. Years later I would hear the same complaint from Geraldine Willesee when she went to university after being a political journalist for decades. Books on the Middle East conflict and troubles in some African countries, used in subjects she was taking, had been written by academics who had never been in the countries concerned. Geraldine, who had covered those conflicts on the ground for newspapers as a reporter at the time at which they occurred, despaired when she was expected to express no opinion other than what was in those books.

Russel, by this time, had grown into a tall, handsome young man, keen on sport and physical exercise. Also, perhaps because he had spent his life mainly in the company of women—his mother, sister and grandmother—he was wary of the responsibilities he saw flowing from relationships with the opposite sex. Consequently, although he was courteous and respectful to women, he had not yet ventured into dating. He found some of the white women at university, expressing their newfound sexual freedoms perhaps, extremely aggressive and often very racist in their approaches to him. So, at just eighteen, he was doing all in his power to avoid them.

I quite simply adored him. Years before, a friend had said to me, 'What women ought to do if they don't have a good man in the family—is grow their own.' Without consciously thinking about this advice, I realised I had done just that. Russel was a good cook, did his own washing, ironing, even neatly patching his own jeans and replacing buttons, kept the lawn mowed, helped take care of his sister, who was eleven, and train her in the right direction, and he would turn his hand to anything on request. A non-smoker and keen sports enthusiast, he enjoyed body building and running in the City to Surf and other marathon races.

Naomi was by far the more gregarious of the two, always had been. She was also what I regarded as a classic Taurus and, once she planted her feet on an idea, couldn't be pushed or pulled in any direction. In another word, obstinate. As our family unit could only function with a great deal of inter-dependence and flexibility, to allow me to earn a living for us all and not fold up under the burden, I sometimes felt the only reason I hadn't ended up strangling her was because she was 'my child'. I often had to remind myself that I was 'her mother/adult' in the relationship. It was a blessing that Russel had incredible patience with her, though she was able to reduce him to her level with her teasing when the mood took her.

At times, I would hear them arguing in the kitchen.

'Naomi, you chucked out the last of the bread, and now we have no bread for sandwiches for your lunch in the morning.'

'I'm allowed to.'

'You're not "allowed to". Why did you do it?'

'It smelled funny.'

'It was fresh bread, Mum only bought it yesterday. It didn't smell funny.'

'Yes, it did.'

'No, it didn't.'

'Did so, did so'.

'Did not, did not'.

I put my hands over my ears when their conversation descended to this childish banter. Naomi was always trying to 'get over' on Russel, and Russel, being the eldest, often got the blame. Rushing down the hall to stop the rising crescendo of 'dids' and 'did nots' in the kitchen before the neighbours called the police, I would hoe into Russel and try to make him see that he was responsible and that the din was interrupting my work. Meanwhile, Naomi would scuttle around to stand behind me smirking, pleased that her brother seemed to be the one in a spot of bother—for something she had initiated. When I caught sight of her from the corner of my eye, she'd be doing something juvenile, such as pulling faces at him, and the temptation to give her a good wallop would rise in my breast. Naomi, always canny and able to sense my pulse rate accelerate from across the room, would disappear in a flash, through the house and out into the street. By the time I reached the front door she'd be doing cartwheels in the park opposite in the company of Liz Milne's young son, Matthew, who, at about four years old, doted on her—a setting so playful and serene that I'd be smitten with guilt about the damage I had been about to inflict on her.

There were other times when Russel's maturity of approach towards Naomi's development was enormously insightful and protective. I came home from work one day and he sat with me at the kitchen table and dropped a bombshell. Knowing how I regarded the link that often existed between young kids hanging around certain milkbars and the increased likelihood of them falling into mischief (on the basis that 'the devil finds work for idle hands'), he had taken Naomi right around the area in which we lived to show her every corner shop and milkbar that had a pin-ball machine.

'Now why in heaven's name would you do a thing like that?' I asked, appalled.

'She's reaching the age where she's going to start finding them herself anyway. I wanted her to know I'll always know where she is, and I'll always come and haul her out!'

From quite early on, Naomi loitered on her way home from school. She was the sort of little child who couldn't resist stopping to look at everything wonderful in the world—puppies, chrysalises, two goats that ate the grass down on craggy land at the nearby tennis courts—anything, and she was always caught up in the moment and arriving home late. We'd laugh about it— 'born ten days late and she's been late ever since'—though not when I was out chasing over hill and dale anxiously looking for her. I did not want to give her my negative view about the depravity I knew to exist, but when I found her, dawdling along and chatting at a street corner with two men who were repairing the traffic lights, I came down on her hard.

'It's alright, Mum,' she replied breezily, 'I knew they weren't the "bad strangers". They were wearing uniforms.'

How do you convince a child that 'bad strangers' can wear uniforms too?

Still, her first major upset came not from strangers but from much closer to home, right next door to be exact. On one side, in a well-kept little weatherboard house, lived an older couple. Initally they had regarded a Black family moving into the street with a good deal of suspicion, but they had grown accustomed to us and were very helpful to us in many ways. While I think they continued to consider me a bit eccentric, they took particular pleasure in letting me know every time they saw me on a television program. On the other side, in a much fancier brick house with an in-ground swimming pool in the backyard, was a young couple who, as I recall at the time, had only one child, a little girl. I always had far too much to do to spend any great length of time socialising with the neighbours, but I spoke to anyone if I was digging or watering in the frontyard when they passed by.

I came home from work one day to find Naomi trembling and crying.

'Mum, she told me not to tell you, but I've got to. I don't know what else to do.'

'Who? What's the matter, child.' She was still young enough for me to take her on my lap, but she was too distraught to be comforted in this way, and instead stood, shuffling her feet and moving her slender weight from one thin bird's leg to the other.

'The lady next door—she said I've stolen her gold, and if I don't give it back she's going to call the police and they'll take me away.'

I had tried to discourage Naomi from going inside the houses of people in the street generally, except for Liz Milne's house where we were always welcome. But the woman next door had often called Naomi in to play with her small daughter who may have been lonely. I particularly didn't like Naomi going anywhere that I felt I couldn't follow, and I'd never been inside their house, had never been invited.

So I was cross with Naomi for having, once again, been into their house against my frequently expressed orders, and now I would have to deal with some problem which had arisen which sounded particularly nasty.

What 'gold' was my daughter being accused of stealing? Naomi was still at the age where a yellow plastic ring from Woolworths was 'gold' and the coloured piece at the top was 'a diamond'. The little girl next door, I was soon to learn, had been given genuine gold bracelets and chains as gifts, and allowed to keep them in her own bedroom. Naomi had been playing with the little girl in the room, the gold chains were missing, ergo Naomi had stolen them.

I stormed over to their house and, barely able to contain my anger, demanded to know what was missing. The woman was stern-faced while she recited a list of her daughter's missing valuables. When I asked why she, a mother herself, had told Naomi not to tell her own mother about what was going on and instead scared her witless by threatening to call the police, she said, a bit embarrassed, that she thought this would frighten Naomi into bringing them back. Then that would be the end of the matter and there'd be no need for me to know.

I was outraged. Naomi, quite simply, did not have the missing items. Our family were not thieves. To make the matter worse, Naomi was to leave the next day to spend the school holidays in Tweed Heads with my mother, and I could see that she was anxious because the whole thing was unresolved.

A day or so later I was walking towards my car parked in front of the house, when I was approached by the father of the little girl. He apologised for his wife's behaviour—and, yes, they had since found the missing gold. The little girl had put them in her own slippers in her wardrobe, or perhaps, he said, they had just fallen into them while she was playing, and she had forgotten what she had done with them.

I continued to choke over this classically racist episode. If anything goes missing, and a Black family lives in the street, blame them. Instead of going to work, I walked across the street to Liz who made me a cup of coffee to help settle me down. She was used to dealing with traumatised people, and we chatted idly for a while until I relaxed before we examined the whole issue. Liz, who had grown up in New Zealand, was acutely aware of the manifestations of racism, and this was not the first time, nor would it be the last, that I was able to confide in her. This gave me the support and energy I needed to just keep going. I was very glad to have such a friend.

About a year after I had received the letter from Harvard advising me that my admission had been deferred, I received a follow-up letter inquiring if I was coming for this academic year. Late at night, when my literary juices were flowing, I replied to the school. I wrote a long letter explaining my circumstances and why it was not possible for me to do so. I had no idea who would eventually read this screed apart from the signatory at the bottom of their letter, no clue that a whole admissions committee existed to whom all the correspondence was circulated, so my letter was very chatty, as if I were writing to a friend. In it, I weighed up the pros and cons, and shared the fact that I was full of wonder at their offer, but didn't know where their university was or what I could expect if I was ever in a position to take it up.

The idea had rested, for the year, very lightly on my mind. In fact, I rather thought it likely that in a big institution like a university, an offer of a placement made to a small person like me, so far away on the other side of the world, would have fallen through the cracks by this time. So I had been enormously surprised when their second missive arrived.

I mentioned this to MumShirl, and explained how it had come about and how long I'd been sitting on their original invitation. She did not appear overly impressed, probably because, like me, she had no idea where the university was or where this could lead.

Life went on.

I received a phone call one day from a man who asked me to give a presentation at the police academy which, at the time, was in Redfern. He was a psychologist whom the Police Service had hired to help with training recruits. His plan was to bring in people from the groups which had been negatively categorised and targeted by police, as reflected in their arrest rates. Homosexuals, long-haired demonstrators, those who carried placards to stop development and save the environment, and, of course, Blacks—we were all to be given an opportunity to present ourselves as people, to humanise ourselves in the eyes of the recruits, with a view to changing their perception of us.

By this time, I was a veteran at giving presentations—a regular lecturer at community nursing training programs, as well as the various casual posts I held in tertiary institutions. Nevertheless, I was concerned about addressing this particular audience. I figured the class would be all male, reflecting the composition of the Police Force at that time, and, as recruits, have a mean age of about eighteen with a maturity level to match, and with limited life experience.

I was worried about what to wear. I thought my blue jeans were too stereotypical, and I only owned two dresses, both of them more than ten years old. Eventually I settled on wearing one of the dresses, although I was concerned that the sight of my skinny legs on view to these young guys might distract from the substance of my talk—and at the outset, I wasn't wrong.

About thirty pairs of eyes zeroed in on my knee-length skirt as I came through the door in the company of the psychologist, and I felt flushed with embarrassment. I realised I could not afford any informality here, as I sometimes could in other settings, and I set up hopefully to alter forever their views on the Black community.

I gave them the usual—mortality and morbidity statistics, history of educational, employment, social and political deprivation stemming from the non-citizen status of Aborigines which had been relaxed less than ten years earlier, as well as a great deal of anecdotal evidence from the observations I had made through my role at the Health Commission. I did not share with them my own experiences with the hostility of police, how frequently I was pursued by their sirens as I drove through country towns in the Health Commission vehicles, stopped and questioned in front of crowds who then automatically assumed I had done something wrong. Instead, I held my tongue, and presented only information about which I could provide references.

Towards the end, I called for questions to give the recruits an opportunity to raise their own concerns. The first few queries demonstrated that the inquirer felt that Aborigines could change their own situations, if only they would make an effort. I talked then about reserves and missions that were without water, electricity, transport, a public phone, where the man of the house, where there was one, could find work only as a seasonal fruit-picker or cotton-chipper. Then I asked how they thought a family in these circumstances could even begin to change their situation.

A young man rose to his feet and said that he had been given a placement in Bourke, as part of his training. He had had the opportunity to see country conditions first hand, the reserve outside the levees, the poverty of the people, and he sounded quite upset. The officer in charge at Bourke had driven him past the reserve and told him that the government had given the families there houses in town, but they had all moved back to live in the shanties 'because they got free meals'. He wanted to know why they did that.

I had been to Bourke many times, and I realised we could both visualise conditions there, so instead of answering to the class, I spoke directly to the man.

'You saw the tiny shacks sprinkled around there, on the reserve?'

'Yes, I did.'

'And you saw the little demountable Health Commission clinic sitting up there on its own levee?'

'Yes, I did.'

'Did you see a big hall?'

'No. There's no big hall.'

'That's right. There's no big hall. I wonder where the people go to eat their "free meals" then?'

'Well, I don't know.'

'Hmm. Do the white people in town cook these free meals and take them out to the reserve, do you think?'

'I don't know. I don't think so.' He sounded doubtful, and the other cadets were now giving him their full attention.

'Well, do the Aboriginal people cook these "free meals" for themselves, perhaps?'

It was slowly dawning on all in the class, including the young man, that there were no 'free meals'.

He shook his head and banged his hand on his desk. 'Well, why did the sergeant tell me that?'

'I've no idea—but when anybody tells you anything, you've got to make sure it's feasible before you believe it. You're all going to be policemen in the very near future, and you've got a responsibility to only deal in facts.'

The next week I received another phone call from the psychologist. He had been sacked and was very distraught. He said he'd been told that he had overstepped the line by bringing me in. We both agreed that I hadn't said anything particularly controversial, and I felt badly for him.

A few weeks later the Aboriginal Section of the Health Commission received a request from his replacement for an employee to go to the police academy to give a talk. Joe Mallie and I concluded that the police were unaware I was a senior employee at the Health Commission, but decided that it might be too provocative and consequently counter-productive for me to go again. We decided that a group should attend instead.

Betty Little, daughter of the well-known singer, Jimmy Little, was a member of that group and she spoke to me about it afterwards.

'I had to laugh,' she said, with more than a trace of pride in her voice, 'because at the end, one of the recruits said to me, "You're as bad as Bobbi Sykes".'

Unlike me, Betty was quite a laid back person, more musician than politician, so it was amusing that we'd be bundled together like that. Our subliminal message, however—that Blacks were being treated unjustly—was the same whichever way one looked at it. Perhaps it was on this basis that we both caused ire.

Harold Hunt, alcohol counsellor for the Health Commission and another member of the group, also spoke to me about his concerns. He was alarmed that, with the attitudes he had heard expressed at the meeting, these young recruits were going to be put out on the streets in uniforms, armed and dangerous.

On another occasion, I was asked to give a joint presentation at the University of New South Wales Medical School. The doctor with whom I was to share the podium on the day came up with an idea. He would speak for about five minutes before passing the floor over to me. We were to rotate our presentations, if everything went well.

He began: 'The subject we are talking about today is Aboriginal health. It is no wonder Aboriginals have poor health. We stole the land, we poisoned the water-holes and distributed poison flour, we took the

children away from their mothers. We brought diseases, and then we withheld from them the cures and
treatments for the diseases we had brought.'

A hush fell over the audience of final year medical
students, and the air was charged with *mea culpa*. They
sat alert, waiting to hear what they were expected to do
about it. The doctor continued with a few current health
statistics before inviting me to take the microphone.

Reading from the page he had given me, I said: 'The
subject we are talking about today is Aboriginal health.
It is no wonder Aboriginals have poor health. You stole
the land, poisoned the waterholes and distributed
poison flour. You took the children away from their
mothers—'

That's about as far as I got before pandemonium
broke out. There was no *mea culpa* this time. Few students, if any, realised that I was merely repeating, in
the accusative, the words with which they had earlier
agreed. The doctor leapt up to defend me and pointed
out to them the experiment which had just occurred.
When several of them refused to settle down, he just
talked over them using the microphone, then dimmed
the lights in the hall and began to show a series of
very graphic slides until silence was restored.

We later talked about the difference in the reactions
we had received. The doctor was very concerned that
I might have been upset by the furore.

'No,' I assured him, 'hopefully some learning went
on in there today. Sometimes people don't know their
own attitudes until they're confronted by them.'

The Aboriginal Medical Service had been nominated
for an award, and MumShirl and I, and two others,
were to attend the dinner presentation. The other two,

Aboriginal men, failed to turn up, later explaining they did not have the money to hire suits to wear.

MumShirl and I sat side by side at a table with perhaps six others, all white men, members of the civic club that was making the awards. The AMS did not win but received an honourable mention. After the dinner, MumShirl sat talking with the man on her right, while I chatted with the fellow on my left. At events of this nature, MumShirl was sometimes a bit of a braggart, and I became aware of her voice rising.

After some conversation I heard her say, 'and my daughter', nudging me savagely with her elbow to get my attention, 'has been invited to' and turning to me, she continued, 'what's that place you've been invited to?'

I shook my head, unwilling to buy into this and feeling quite embarrassed at having been made the centre of her conversation with this man.

'No, go on, tell him,' she ordered. I actually couldn't see around her so I leaned forward to speak to a large man with a florid complexion. He was looking at me quizzically, so I said, 'Harvard.'

'No.' He banged his closed fist on the table, rudely and emphatically, and I could tell my answer displeased him. 'You mean Howard.'

I had, I am sorry to say now, never heard of Howard University, a Black tertiary institution with a long history and solid academic reputation. At that time, though, until I had received their letters and handbook, I hadn't really known much about Harvard University either. Still, I was not so illiterate as to have confused the name on the materials they had sent me. I felt very insulted and turned my back on him.

MumShirl, on the other hand, took it to heart. On

leaving soon after, she said to me, 'This university must be really important if that man doesn't want you to be going there. So—when are you going to go?'

From that point on, MumShirl was on my back almost every time we spoke, and seemed determined to drive me to go. Once, during dinner at my house, she threatened me. 'When we go out to the schools and you talk to those Aboriginal kids, you're always telling them what a big chance they're getting. "Now you've got an opportunity", you tell them, *go for it!*"' She was repeating my own words back at me and using my own inflection to boot.

'Well, the next time we go out and I hear you saying that, I'm going to yell out "Hypocrite". Do you understand me? You've got the chance to do something over at that university over there, get an education, and instead you're always making excuses why you can't go.'

I knew she'd do it, too. When I thought about it I realised that, while I did still have some outstanding things I wanted to do, I probably could organise to be away for the nine months I had been assured that it would take to complete my Master's degree. Some of the real reasons for my procrastination were fear, funds, and more fear. I had put my son's need to have a stable home during his HSC before my own educational opportunity, but now he was attending university and, well on his way towards independence, was supplementing his meagre study allowance by lining himself up work for when he wasn't studying.

I had trained members of the Aboriginal Skills Development Scheme to publish the Black community newspaper, which I had been concerned about leaving previously. At the Health Commission I had brought in as many innovations as I'd been capable of up to

that point. Although I knew I could keep doing valuable work there, it would, to a large extent, just be the
same work in which I had already demonstrated my
capability. I'd be giving much the same lectures to different faces every year, the thought of which was not
particularly attractive and would not have been mentally challenging. I had always been scornful of people
who claim to have twenty years experience in a job,
but in reality only have the one year multiplied by
twenty, that is, the same year over and over. So, I felt
I had gone as far in the Health Commission as I could
go without the input of fresh ideas.

I discussed the possibility of going to Harvard with
my children. Russel would have to stay, continue his
studies and take responsibility for the house. Naomi
would need to come with me. She would turn twelve
by the time we were likely to depart and was still in
a critical stage of her development. Russel was
sombre—no doubt perplexed that, at an age where he
might consider flying the coop, his mother instead was
considering the very same thing—but agreeable. To
Naomi, the idea seemed both romantic and remote,
and her main concerns were whether she would be
able to go to Disneyland and who would look after her
beloved pet, Catso, if we went.

Work had kept me so busy, I soon realised as I
began to mentally prepare myself to go, that there'd
been no time at all to reflect, to step back and look
at the big picture.

At the time I was also emotionally involved with an
Aboriginal man whom MumShirl had introduced me
to. However, she and I had discovered, too late, that
he was a chronic liar and a cheat. This was part of his
manifestation of the emotional deprivation he had

suffered as a baby when he had been removed from his mother and fostered out to a white family. I think MumShirl felt a bit guilty about having brought us together. Encouraging—or perhaps forcing—me to go away for a while may have been part of her strategy for dealing with this guilt.

Though all these thoughts percolated in my mind, I rarely had time to do anything but think about them.

I was at home one morning when the real estate agent, Richard Hookey, through whom I thought I had been negotiating the purchase of the house in which we lived, knocked on the door and handed me a notice to quit the premises. This was my first indication that the long legal battle over the ownership of the property had come to an end. In the interim, house prices had increased and now the owners wanted me out so they could sell it for a higher price.

Initially quite shocked, I soon became livid. With two young children I had struggled along for years in that decrepit building in the belief that, once the court case was finished, we could buy it. One of the owners lived just a few houses away and she drove past my front door every day. This woman and her husband were aware of the enormous discomforts we had tolerated, thinking we were just waiting for the sale to go through. Now I felt both deceived and cheated, which made me determined to see justice for myself and my kids.

I still had the deposit I had saved up so desperately, although Mum had borrowed some of it from time to time. She had sold all her little cottages in Townsville, and much of the money she'd received had been drained away by Arthur's vices and excesses. He continued to get into trouble with the police and the courts, as well as with the Taxation Department, for various scams and rorts. When he was threatened with imprisonment, Mum, fearing she'd have no one to drive her around, would bail him out. She had always made a point of repaying me as soon as she could though, and my house deposit remained safe and sound.

I went to see my solicitor, Eric Strasser, still a firm friend after so many years. He was concerned that the passage of time may have somehow negated my claim to purchase the house. He consulted colleagues and I contacted a friend at the University of New South Wales Law School, and between us we came up with a plan of action.

The agreement to purchase had never reached the stage where the owners and myself had signed a contract, but they had allowed me and my children to move in on a rental basis 'for a few weeks' until their legal situation had been sorted out. When the few weeks stretched into months, and I was having to pay bank fees to hold the bank loan I had negotiated, the owners agreed they would pay these fees because the delay was on their part and not mine, and they did so for some time. According to law, this meant that the sellers had acted—part-performance—on our verbal contract, which made it binding.

Eric moved to freeze the assets of the owners and begin a case against them. Despite cautioning me against it, when I arrived home from Eric's office I rang the woman up the road.

'Our solicitor told us we could do it,' she said, referring to herself and her siblings who stood to benefit from their mother's will. 'I wasn't keen, but I had to go along with it. I'm really sorry and embarrassed.'

'Don't be sorry,' I replied. 'Your solicitor told you

what you could do, but he didn't tell you what I could do. We had a verbal contract, and you've broken it. So, my solicitor has frozen your assets and you'll be back in court, maybe for another few years.'

As a gesture of my sincerity and compassion, I agreed, through my solicitor, to a moderate increase in the sale price, and the matter was settled. The deposit completely cleaned out my small savings and, for the first time in my life, I was in debt to a bank. But I also became 'a householder', with all the responsibilities which that position incurs, although I had neither the time nor inclination to celebrate my change of status.

I had, by this time, decided to make a real effort to get organised to pursue the Harvard offer. I visited Evan Sutton at the Commonwealth Department of Education, who enthusiastically encouraged me to apply for an Aboriginal Overseas Study Award. This was a comparatively new program which enabled ten Blacks per year to go overseas for study trips. It had received a lot of criticism from within the Black community though, in part because of the brevity of the study period and the limitations this placed on the ambitions of students. Many felt that the program funded people to go and visit, for example, Native American cultural and alcohol rehabilitation projects, but forced them to come back without either the qualifications or access to the resources to establish anything similar if they had found it to be appropriate. Only one person had ever been funded to undertake a nine months program and come back with qualifications. Evan was eager to discover whether admission to Harvard would prove to be a tripwire that would release the program from its restrictive operation.

I applied, but I also continued to look elsewhere for sources of educational funding. I found none. There was postgraduate funding available to those who had completed undergraduate study, but I hadn't even graduated from high school. There was funding available for people who had certain surnames or belonged to specific families, beneficiaries of trusts set up in this way, but I had no rich relatives or ancestors.

I continued to work while the selection process was moving ahead, and received constant assurance from Evan that my application was being given top, and positive, consideration.

I had earlier given a commitment to MumShirl that I would write her autobiography, and this was an ongoing pressure I felt heavily. The Bardas Foundation, under the stewardship of my friends, Sandra and David Bardas, put up funds to cover expenses incurred during this project. They were to be repaid from the royalties, and I felt obliged to complete the work.

MumShirl knew about the vices of many people, some of whom I considered to be very dangerous, such as a few detectives who were, much later, dismissed from the force for corruption. Aware of this, I had cautioned her not to tell anyone that her autobiography was forthcoming.

MumShirl was too elated to say nothing. Barely able to sign her own name, the idea of a real book with her name on the cover was extremely attractive to her. I arranged on a few occasions for her to come to my house of an evening where, after dinner, I would tape-record interviews. This turned out to be a bit of a disaster as far as writing a book was concerned. MumShirl was not so much an oral historian as an educator, turning each story she told me into some sort of parable. When I would gently remind her that she was being recorded, the material turned into a book, she would immediately revise information she had just given me.

'Oh, yes,' she would counter about a family event which she had just described, 'well, in that case, Aunty Maudie wasn't there and old Joe wasn't there either. They were at another christening party another time.' As well, MumShirl had never read a book and therefore did not know the sequencing of its structure or the sort of information that it should contain. I realised after a couple of these interview-dinners, that all of the work, and not just the writing, was going to be up to me.

While the book would need to be narrowly personal, in order for MumShirl not to lose, by disclosure, the implicit power she had amassed over the years, I thought the personal struggle of her life would stand alone.

We had only just started on this project when MumShirl's brother, Laurie, was suddenly picked up and arrested by the police. We were on a regular visit to him at the Wisemans Ferry alcohol rehabilitation program, for which he was the coordinator, when this happened. With Mum urging me on, I pursued the police vehicle from Wisemans Ferry to Raymond Terrace where he was formally charged. We drove over rough back roads through the dusk, never allowing the police car out of our sight for a moment. We learned later in court that the police alleged Laurie had confessed, and they had written his words into their notebooks, all during that ride. This was patently untrue—it had been dark, and their vehicle's interior light was never turned on at any time. Verballing people was very common in those days, especially

Aboriginal people. It would be many years before sufficient pressure—and the introduction of recording interviews—forced the practice to be stopped.

Laurie had been charged with the murder of a youth who was stabbed to death in the middle of a crowd of people. But he was innocent. In his younger days, Laurie had been a bit of a tearaway, but had carried a gun and never a knife. As MumShirl said, 'carrying a knife would have been beneath him'. In his old age, however, Laurie had completely reformed his ways. He was fostering at least one of the dead boy's younger brothers amongst the many young people for whom he provided a home and guidance at the time of his arrest. Police built a frame around him, tightly enough to get his conviction through the local courts. On appeal to the Supreme Court he was exonerated, but not before he had spent a considerable time in prison and suffered a stroke which left him without speech.

MumShirl withdrew from the book project as soon as Laurie was charged, blaming herself for her brother's arrest. She had let it be known that she was writing her biography, and she reasoned that the police had chosen this means of silencing her, knowing how close she was to her brother.

I proposed that I would write the book without her help, based on things she had shared with me during all the time we had spent together. MumShirl readily agreed.

I took three days out, picked up my trusty typewriter and went to stay at a friend's house. He worked all day and I knew that if the phone rang there it would not be for me. I immersed myself completely in the persona of MumShirl and wrote the book, using her phrasing and her grammatical construction throughout.

At the end of those three days, I called to tell her the book was finished. Then we went to the house of another friend, where I encouraged her to read as much of it as she could, with me just filling in the words she was unable to sound out. For an illiterate person, MumShirl had a very extensive vocabulary, though she was unable to identify many of her words when they were written. Indeed, one of her favourite expressions, which she would shout out if another Black, while speaking at a meeting, used a long word, was 'bourgeois'. She came across only two words in the draft that were not within her vocabulary, so I struck them out. This exercise took another three days. Because she was chronically short of cash, I paid her for her time from the funds I had received from the Bardas Foundation, and obtained from her receipts, so that I could account to the Foundation for how their money had been dispersed. Then I set about trying to find a publisher.

The students at the Aboriginal and Island Dance School, where I continued to teach and work as a voluntary counsellor, were preparing to put on their annual public performance. All the students were to appear in the production, in one guise or another. And all the teachers were asked to contribute a segment to the show. The central story line was to be about a traditional dancer who came down to Sydney to join the school and learn a wide variety of other dance styles including classical ballet, and about the cultural shocks he received along the way as he undertook this journey. The program, then, was rich with possibilities.

There were several traditional youths who had joined the company, and many of us had been either privy to, or involved, in these sometimes traumatic processes and pressures. The teachers of tap, or ballet or jazz, generally chose to use their creative medium to produce drama and humour.

I chose for my presentation a slot just before interval, occurring after the youth had progressed in the school, had been exposed to the wild and loud nightlife of Kings Cross, and become quite a sophisticate, an accomplished performer in every dance style, and fluent in the language, nuance and culture of both tribal and urban life.

My segment opened with the youth lolling in a park, taking his leisure, when he is 'spotted' by a talent scout, a movie producer (very ably played by Kim Walker, in white face, who went on to fame with the Sydney Dance Company). The movie producer immediately zeroes in on his mark, announcing that he will make him a Star. To show his joy, the youth dances and prances in the stage-park. As part of the process towards the creation of this stardom, the producer insists on a photo shoot, during which the backdrop fades out and the youth is left standing alone in a shaft of light. The producer, with the photographers, stands on the periphery of the now dimly lit stage.

The handsome youth in his really neat gear strikes a few poses, camera flashlights pop, then the producer's voice booms out.

'No, no, no. This won't do at all. Look more casual— take off your shoes.' The young man struggles in the light shaft to remove his shoes and socks, tosses them offstage, strikes a few more poses.

'No. The shirt's got to go. Take off the shirt.'

Removing his tie and unbuttoning his snow white shirt, the man's slender but muscled chest and back emerge, glowing with vitality and touched upon by the overhead light, a stunning visual contrast. In this half-clad state, he again strikes up poses for the flashing cameras, displaying the power and sensuous beauty of his fine physique. The producer, however, remains dissatisfied.

'Take off the pants. The pants have to go.'

By now the youth is embarrassed, but feeling stardom might slip through his fingers, he rather shyly removes his trousers. He is left, starkly and almost tragically alone in the light, in his briefs. With a deep breath, he again strikes up what he hopes to be suitable poses from his dance routines.

The producer's voice is pitched with tension and excitement by now, as he cajoles and commands his prey.

'Now, just look more primitive!'

Following this shock ending, during the interval, a man came up and spoke to me.

'I didn't need to look in the program to know which was your piece. As soon as the clothes started to come off, I knew what was happening—and I hated it. But I couldn't stop watching, it was so riveting.'

I had dreamed the scene long before I began to develop it. In part, it reflected my experience, how I had seen white society too often respond to Blacks. When we had achieved in the ways of white people, whether in theatrical or educational venues, there seemed to be an overwhelming desire to force us back, reduce us somehow to a mere primal level, and to strip our souls bare in the process.

* * *

I began to research Harvard and found it to be in Cambridge, Massachusetts, separated only by a bridge from Boston. I located Boston on a map and read notes about it in an encyclopaedia. Apart from the Boston Tea Party, and being held up as the birthplace of American Freedom and Emancipation, the most definitive things I could find with relevance to me was that it was extremely cold in winter and had blizzards.

I felt myself to be heading towards very dangerous ground.

6

Late in 1979, Evan Sutton rang to tell me my application for funding had been short-listed by the New South Wales committee, and sent to Canberra. 'It's a sure thing, so just get ready to pack,' he said, adding that I was top of their list. This certainly cheered up my Christmas, though I had many things left to do.

Aware that success often excites jealousy in others, I told very few people. This is, unfortunately, almost a self-defeating fact in the Black community. I have seen nearly an entire community rise up in anger—through envy and jealousy—at the allocation of a decent house to one of their own. Although people in the Black community often collectively say they want better housing, employment and educational opportunities for 'their people', they don't seem to mean 'any' Aboriginal person. Each seems to want to nominate the recipient. This, of course, leads to all sorts of problems, factions and feelings of general dissatisfaction, as well as an inability to derive joy or pleasure from the success of others.

I did share the news, though, with Hiram Ryan. He was a childhood friend and maybe-cousin, who was working in Canberra and came by to visit from time to time whenever he was in Sydney. It elicited a mixed response. While warmly encouraging on the one hand, Hiram kept lamenting the fact that he hadn't completed all his own educational endeavours, although he had already done business studies and always seemed to me to be doing quite well.

I felt more heartened, however, that those Blacks on the New South Wales selection committee had seen that having someone open the gates to a top international university would be of great advantage to the whole Black community, and had entrusted me with their votes. Still, the list had to go on to Canberra. There a national selection committee would have the final say, based on a range of criteria, such as state distributions, sexual representation, and ensuring that the aspirations of rural applicants were given equal consideration with those from urban regions.

At last I, along with the other New South Wales candidates, was called in for an interview with the national committee, on 29 January 1980. There were only a couple of non-Aboriginal people in the room, and I was assured that they were there as note-takers, that these decisions were actually made by the Blacks who were present.

I explained how I had come to be accepted at Harvard, and how I felt I would be able to share the knowledge I gained with others in the Black community, as well as with the wider community, through the position I held at the NSW Health Commission. The interview was very positive, I thought, with people asking questions and nodding at my answers.

From calculations I had made based on the documents sent to me by the Harvard administration, I worked out that I would need twelve thousand dollars in Australian currency to cover my fees, medical insurance and accommodation costs. The exchange rate was in Australia's favour, our dollar worth about $US1.20. It was the first time in my life that I'd had to be concerned about monetary exchange rates, bringing home to me afresh how enormous was my undertaking. I thought that bringing Naomi with me would perhaps be considered a luxury, and therefore I shouldn't request money for her. I would just budget tightly and we would have to live within those means.

Despite the prospect of these frugalities, it was a huge shock to me when Evan Sutton rang me to say that I had not been chosen to receive the funding. He was very upset, saying he was going to look into the matter, find out more, and get back to me. Meanwhile, he intended to do his own research on where other funds might be found, because he thought my project was of the utmost importance.

It had been a dream to me anyway, I consoled myself. Studying at Harvard was not really going to happen. Still, when I shared this depressing news with the few people I had confided in, they urged me to think of this rejection as a challenge, and not as the end of the world. I had always subscribed to the adage that 'Whatever is going to happen *will* happen' because the spirits will it to be so. But I also knew that it is up to the individual to make sure they are in the right place at the right time, and in a state of readiness. Was Harvard my right place? Was this my 'right time'?

No sooner were the results received than I set out on a letter-writing campaign, casting my net widely and targeting, amongst others, the Ministers for Education, Aboriginal Affairs and Health in state and federal politics. My supporters and I also trawled for information, trying to find out how and why this situation had occurred.

Behind some of the veiled replies, I heard, 'She's not really an Aborigine', though no one said this to me directly, or allowed me to put forward my own position on the issue.

I decided to write to Senator Neville Bonner. On the numerous occasions when we had met over the years, he had gone out of his way to greet me and be effusive in his support for everything I was doing.

To Neville and the ministers I wrote: 'If, as I have heard, this refusal is based on my inability to prove Aboriginality, where should I go to have my blood checked or my head measured?'

From a few I received acknowledgements advising me that my letter had been received, would be looked into, and that a reply would be forthcoming. Of course, in the main they never came.

Seeking to explore what funds might exist overseas, particularly in America, I even wrote to Germaine Greer. She did not know that I had read the article she had written about rape victims and how betrayed I felt about it. I had never raised this with her, so I thought she might be another resource I could tap for information. I knew that she taught at the University of Texas, though I was unaware that this was for only one semester each year, and as my luck would have it, not the semester in which I wrote.

I also wrote to the Reverend Charles Spivey, whom I had met when he was working for the World Council of Churches. He had left the Council and was living in Chicago. In response he sent me, along with his best wishes and news of his work, a short list of executive contacts at the Board of Global Ministries under the United Methodist Church. Time, however, was running short.

Evan rang me with the news that the episode had caused changes in the selection process. The federal committee could no longer re-order the list compiled by the state selection committees. Applicants would be funded on the basis of the priorities set by the states. As I had been the first choice of the New South Wales selection committee, he assured me that in any further selection process I would most definitely be funded. He therefore urged me to consider applying the following year. Evan and I had both failed to find any alternative source of funding outside the province of government.

Neville Bonner, in his reply to my letter, wrote, 'this is outrageous, I will do everything in my power'.

My friend Brian Syron travelled to Canberra and visited Neville on my behalf. Neville kept the appointment, but said he only had a minute to speak. When Brian put my case, and reminded him of his written reply to me, Neville summarised his own position succinctly: 'I am very sympathetic—but this is an election year.' On learning of this, I knew it was folly to expect help from that quarter.

On 14 May, Senator Jim Keeffe, from my hometown of Townsville, brought up the whole question in Federal Parliament. He demanded an answer from Senator Carrick who was representing the Minister for Education. In his reply, Senator Carrick said, on behalf of the Minister for Education, that 'My Department does not have funds available for the assistance of individuals outside established programs such as the Aboriginal Overseas Study Awards Scheme.'

Les Johnson, Opposition Whip, also raised the issue in Questions Without Notice in the House of Representatives. In his reply, Wal Fife, then Minister for Education, informed the House that he was looking for other possible funding, but nothing more came of his efforts.

While this was going on, Geraldine Willesee's father, a retired politician, came to Sydney from Perth where he lived, for a family reunion. Geraldine phoned me to come around to her house and give her father an update on where I was in my search. He was keen and said he would phone friends in Canberra to see what he could do. Before he left Sydney, however, he reported that he was making little progress and was no longer optimistic.

News that I was looking for alternative sources of funds must also have gone out on the grapevine. I received a call from a man somehow associated with the Australian Council of Churches who said he knew me, but I did not know him, which was not all that unusual. A Black face in an otherwise all-white room sticks out a mile, while it is impossible for the Black person to remember every white person who was there. This man told me that the Australian Council of Churches had just received a large parcel of money from Germany to be used for women's education, and urged me to make an appointment to see a woman who was second in charge. He requested that I not give his name as the source of this leaked information.

I made an appointment immediately and turned up at her office with my folder containing, amongst other things, my acceptance papers from Harvard. The woman was very pleasant but jumped in early to tell me that the entire allocation for Aboriginal education had already been spent. We continued to make chit-chat, the woman apologising profusely, lamenting the limit of Black funding in the face of so much need and sympathising with my position, while I wondered how long it might take her to realise I was also a woman.

Almost an hour had passed when she finally said she had to attend a meeting elsewhere in the build-ing, and began to usher me out of her office. Although I was deeply disappointed as I was leaving the build-ing, by the time I arrived home I was angry. Okay, I thought, since this is your attitude I'll go over your heads. I sat down and wrote off a letter to the World Council of Churches in Geneva, stating my purpose and inquiring if they had any funds. For good measure, I also wrote to Paulo Freire in Brazil, whom I had met during his visit to Australia sponsored by the World Council of Churches. Paulo and I had spent a morn-ing talking about a range of things, and I felt sure that he would remember me. I asked him to contact the Council on my behalf, supporting my case. Also I asked if he would send me a letter of reference which I might use elsewhere if his request was not successful in Geneva. I realised, however, that time was by now get-ting short and although I sent these letters express mail, it might be some weeks before I received replies. Would my fortunes turn, and both people be sitting at their desks in the cities to which my letters were addressed?

During this time, Sandra Bardas rang me from Mel-bourne to say that their Sportsgirl stores had brought in a Black American model, Touki Smith, for a series of fashion parades. Touki was coming to Sydney and knew no one, would I have tea or something with her?

Russel agreed to look after Naomi while I kept this appointment. By now, Russel had started seeing a young lady. On the day in question, Russel came home, ran through the house to collect something, and was on his way out again when I pulled him up. Did he remember he was supposed to be looking after his sister? Yes, but his girlfriend's mother was in hospital and he said he wanted to take her to visit her mother instead.

I hissed to Naomi between gritted teeth, 'Get yourself ready quick, child. You'll have to come with me.' Naomi appeared in less than twenty minutes, showered, beautifully dressed, with fresh frangipannis from our tree pinned most fetchingly in her shining hair. In all frankness, I felt like a dag beside her.

My daughter absolutely charmed Touki, who asked if Naomi could come back the following day and spend the weekend with her. She had tickets to see Peter Allen, and they'd hang out together and have a wonderful time. Naomi, of course, drooled and looked so keen that even I couldn't resist her.

Next day, despite the happy ending, I spoke to Russel. Knowing he was in trouble, he sat at the kitchen table with his eyes downcast. I began to lecture him on making commitments and then not keeping them, until he cheekily looked up and told me that his girlfriend had said I would be jealous.

'Russel,' I said, now deadly calm, 'let me tell you something, my son. Girlfriends come and girlfriends go. Even wives come and go. And I *will still be your mother*! I have absolutely nothing to be jealous of. No one will ever take over my position.'

From the look in his eyes I could tell that this truism had hit all his buttons. From that day forward, we have never needed to have any further discussion on this matter.

Evan continued to keep me updated with his efforts on my behalf, and he had been trying to pull strings through the office. His counterparts in Canberra, he said, were very sympathetic but their office, and the government, had no additional funds.

'The government's out of money?' I asked incredulously, and he responded with a small bitter laugh. I had, by then, received a second brief letter from the Minister of Education, saying very much the same thing.

I felt I was running out of places to go when I received a late-night phone call from Naomi Mayers. She was the Administrator of the Aboriginal Medical Service where I had previously worked, and one of the co-founders, with Marcia Langton, Sue Chilli and myself, of Black Women's Action.

'I want to tell you this before somebody else does. I was in Canberra today for a meeting and the Minister stopped me in a hallway and asked me whether I thought he should fund you.' I was unsure whether she was referring to Fred Chaney, then Minister for Aboriginal Affairs, or Wal Fife, then Minister for Education, as I had written to both.

'Hmm,' I replied, hopeful but non-committal.

'I told him no.'

The disappointment and shock were so great that my ability to speak completely left me. Naomi had even been one of the two referees required for my application to the Aboriginal Overseas Study Awards, Joe Mallie being the other. I was in bed, and I swung myself up, threw my legs down over the side, and just sat there with my hand on my head in despair, receiver to my ear.

'You're not an Aborigine. People from Townsville have told me. Your mother even wrote it in the paper.'

'The people from Townsville, who were they, and how would they know?' I replied at last.

'It doesn't matter who they are. They know all about you.'

Do they, I thought? Well, they think they do. I was deeply saddened.

I tried to discern whether Naomi had been drinking. She had occasionally rung me for late chats, a glass of wine in her hand, and I had come to realise that some of the things she had said at these times were not precisely the truth.

'Listen, Naomi, you have known me for almost ten years, and you know I don't tell lies. You don't know my mother at all, yet you would take the word of this stranger to you over mine. I don't understand.'

'Well, why would she lie? Why would she lie to the papers?'

The answers were so complex, rooted in the racism of this country and my mother's desire to escape from the harshness and poverty of her upbringing. I realised, therefore, that if Naomi did not, from her own experience, know about these things, there were no words that I had which would adequately inform her.

'Is this why I didn't get the Study Award?' I asked. Frank Smith, who had been Chair of the national selection committee had written stating that their reason for excluding me had been that the course of study I had chosen to do was not 'sufficiently closely aligned to my professional work'.

'No, I don't think so. I heard that one of the committee members,' she said, naming him, 'told them all
that you have too much.' She gave a short, deep laugh.
Only my most inner-circle of friends—such as Brian
Syron, Lester and Gerry Bostock, and a tiny handful of
trusted others—had been to my house and knew the
circumstances in which we lived, and Naomi was
amongst them. She had even offered me her old stove
and a few items from her own house, after she had seen
the conditions we were living under. And it was a standing joke that I purchased my clothes from the St
Vincent's around the corner from the Medical Service.

'It's your own fault,' she continued. 'You like to live
so secret. Everybody thinks you've got everything.

'But still, people like you shouldn't get any of our
money, we need it for our own things,' Naomi said,
sounding like she had caught me with my hand in her
own purse. This left me quite bewildered. As well she
knew, a whole host of white people were drawing very
large salaries from Aboriginal Affairs, long before any
trickled down into the community, and with very little
benefit flowing to the people in need.

'Now, listen,' she went on, 'if you're going to make
trouble for me over this, I'm going to go to the government and tell them Russel isn't an Aborigine but he's
going to university on Aboriginal funds.'

I gasped with shock at her vitriol and was dismayed
at the baseness of her argument. It was true that
Russel was receiving Abstudy to attend university, but
at my income level he would have easily qualified for
Austudy. The only difference in these programs was
that Abstudy provided funds to enable students to
travel backwards and forwards from their communities
in remote areas, which, living in Sydney, Russel did

not require. Quite a number of Aboriginal students had already switched to Austudy. Russel, though, was amongst those who thought that academic successes generated under Abstudy would help to ensure that the program was maintained, perhaps even expanded.

My deepest dismay, however, was in knowing that Naomi was amongst the very few people with whom I had shared the awful secret of his conception. I took a deep breath and tried to appeal to her better nature.

'Naomi, even though I can't prove I'm an Aborigine, you know I've been treated like an Aborigine all my life. I was put out of school, I've been insulted and abused, and even raped in terrible circumstances because those men thought I was an Aborigine. I have been arrested, and worked hard to bring about changes, a better life for us all. Are you telling me—'

Naomi cut me off. 'Being raped doesn't make you an Aboriginal. Even white girls get raped.'

I was about to drop the phone when, perhaps realising that she had gone too far and sensing my intention, Naomi raised her voice.

'Wait. Wait. Listen, I'll help you. I'll help you raise the money. We can put out an appeal through the Medical Service. You can use our phones. The Black Women's Action account is still active, and we'll keep the money in there. We can do it.'

Dumbfounded, I said, 'Goodnight, Naomi,' and she replied, 'I'll call you on Monday morning.'

The snake opens its mouth and cries soundlessly. I spent a restless night, indeed entire weekend, falling into sporadic short sleeps in which demons plagued me, hearing again, over and over, the voice of the convicted rapist being led off to the cells below the courthouse screaming, 'She's just an Abo, just a fuck-

'ing boong,' and waking intermittently to find my pillow soaked with my tears.

I was still dozing fitfully when the phone rang on Monday morning. Naomi said she would be in the office at ten-thirty, and asked me to meet her there.

We are not 'just' Abos, not 'just' fucking boongs, I thought, and excelling at Harvard would be a very good way to make that point. Did it matter that, in order to prove this, I would have to go along with Naomi's offer, when I really felt like giving her a good smack in the mouth? I had been treated worse at times in my life, though never by someone I had regarded as a friend.

My ambivalence paralysed me, and it wasn't until Russel came to the bedroom door to say he was leaving to go to university, that I climbed out of bed and began to face the day. My daughter was having mid-term holidays, and would have to spend the day with me. Over my solitary coffee in the kitchen, I thought, what the heck, and made up my mind to go to the Medical Service and at least speak with Naomi.

The office was its usual bustling self when I arrived, and Naomi was very businesslike. She greeted me and her godchild, little Naomi, warmly, and it was almost as though she had never said all those offensive things. I recalled Gary Foley remarking once that Naomi was both my 'best friend and worst enemy', but I had never expected these two facets to manifest themselves within one phone call. I said nothing to remind Big Naomi of her spiteful and wounding words, desiring instead to maintain harmony in the godparent/godchild relationship. Naomi said she had located the Black Women's Action bankbook, and told me to use

a phone in the adjoining office if I wanted to make any calls.

I began by writing up and circulating to all those people who had previously been involved, or expressed interest in, our Black Women's Action Group, a pamphlet titled 'A Call for Alms'. After they were posted, I realised that this method would be very slow, we needed greater coverage. So I put in a call to the *Sydney Morning Herald*. I told my story, of being invited to postgraduate school at Harvard without high school or undergraduate degrees, and of being refused funding from the government that would allow me to take up the offer. Initially I was met with disbelief by the reporter who took my call, Carolyn Parfitt. If this was true, however, she told me, it was 'a bloody good story'.

Some checking was needed, but would I come in for a photo?

With Little Naomi for company, we went into the Herald's off-Broadway office, and were taken to a photographic studio. Naomi, playing coy around the men in the studio, kept trying to insinuate herself into the photos they were taking, draping herself over me and being disobedient when I told her to stand back. Eventually, to appease her I thought, the photographer said he would take a couple of shots with her in them if she would step aside after they were done. Fiercely protective of the children being exposed in the media, I admonished him not to use those shots in the article.

Not only was I still asleep but it was also pitch dark on the morning of Tuesday, 13 May 1980, when the phone rang. ABC-Radio, would I do an interview about the article in the paper, which of course I had not yet seen, directly after their AM program? I agreed and rose to brush my teeth and rinse my mouth, anxious to rid myself of that 'just woken up' tone in my voice.

When finally the papers were delivered, I was astonished to learn my story had made front page headlines, and disturbed to see Naomi's cheery face hanging on my shoulder in the accompanying photo.

Mrs Owens had invited Naomi to see a pantomime in the city. She later told me the pair of them had also gone into every newsagency along the way where Naomi 'discovered' the front page picture of herself anew with a piercing shriek.

I was not prepared for the deluge that followed the article's publication. Envelopes with small donations poured into the Medical Service from many quarters, the overwhelming majority from ordinary mums and dads in the suburbs. During the afternoon I took a call from the ABC program manager for whom I had agreed to do the early morning interview. He said that two people had rung, wanting to send contributions. One man, ringing from the Southern Highlands outside Sydney, had initially said he wished to finance the whole project, but had rung back saying he had heard that I wasn't an Aborigine. If the station could confirm that I was, he was still prepared to do so.

I had no idea how the station had head-and-tailed the interview, because I hadn't been asked about this issue during the program. I even felt resentment towards the potential contributor for his attitude.

As well, many obviously poorer people had already leapt up in their attempts to help me raise the money I required. I wanted to acknowledge them, not let the kudos just go to one person who had more. I refused his offer, stating my reasons and inviting him, if he liked, to send a smaller donation and be part of the larger grassroots response.

At lunchtime that day I had raced up the street to buy a sandwich from a nearby takeaway. On the way I was stopped by countless Aboriginal people who congratulated me on my stand, and pressed one- and two-dollar notes into my hand. A few wanted more information—where was Harvard? What did I need? How could they help?

I had arrived back at the Medical Service with promises of hand-knitted leggings, sweaters and scarves from Aboriginal people whom I had informed that Harvard was near Boston, and that I understood it was very very cold.

I thought of the contrast between this unknown white person on the Southern Highlands, making his demands to learn my mother's personal business, and these mainly elderly Aboriginal women, and even some men, who had so warmly embraced the idea of my standing up to the government and going off to seek education elsewhere. Then I knew I was doing the right thing. If I could bring back a degree from Harvard, I wanted the community to feel part of it, to know they had enabled me, that it was ours to share.

At the Health Commission, I was widely greeted and encouraged. People from other floors and other departments came to my desk, to introduce themselves and let me know of their support. The Chair of the Commission, Roderick McEwin, whom I had met at various meetings several times, called me back as I was leaving and gave me his words of support. Momentarily I had thought he might have intended to chide me for speaking to the media without official consent, so when I heard his kind comments of praise for my work and encouragement in my studies, it was hard to wipe the smile from my face.

Still, we had not raised the amount required, and many of my current friends fell in behind me with their support.

Christine Kankindji and her children were sharing a flat in an old building in Paddington with Maureen Morales, and poor as she was, Christine was determined to host a fund-raising cocktail party to help me. I hardly knew anyone there but was gratified to see such a good turnout of support. I was introduced to Maureen's sister, Patricia. She was an elegant woman who I learned was married to Laurie Brereton, a political aspirant for state government, who turned up later. When he arrived, he came almost straight towards me although, of course, I did not know him.

After a few encouraging words about my efforts to

get to Harvard, he said, 'If we [the Labor Party] win in this next election, I'm going personally see to it that Aborigines get equality in the Public Service.' He was so intense that I barely knew how to respond, but I felt relieved.

It was refreshing somehow just to know that someone outside our oppressed group of government employees knew about our situation, that we Blacks were just temporary, without security of income, and excluded from superannuation and any of the other rights and benefits of permanence. I had been working at the Health Commission for five years by this time, and although I didn't often think about our tenuous position, when I did so, it caused me anger, sadness and confusion.

Elaine Pelot, was a white American woman who married a Jewish doctor, and I had been Matron of Honour at her wedding. To help, she held a fundraising dinner, inviting many of her friends. Despite my attendance at their nuptials, I had always felt distanced from Elaine, in large part because of her oft-repeated tales of having grown up with a 'Black Mammy' in America's south and in a family where some relatives, she said, were members of the Ku Klux Klan. I had often wondered if, by befriending me and other members of the Black community, she may have thought she was doing some kind of 'penance'. Still, my mission felt so imperative and I appreciated her support and assistance.

I had for some time been working with Pat Laird, and her husband Kenneth, towards the publication of an anthology of my poetry. Ironically, it had been rejected by my old employer, Richard Walsh, who had moved on from his days as editor of *Nation Review* and now headed up Angus & Robertson publishers. Pat, who ran the small Saturday Centre Press from her flat, had heard me read at one of my very occasional public performances of this nature. She contacted me and asked me to participate in readings she was organising to be held at the Ensemble Theatre. Judith Wright, she told me with great excitement, had agreed to come down from the country and read on the condition that I was also on the program. Flattered by the attention of Australia's leading poet and aware of her lengthy and abiding friendship with another heroine of mine, Kath Walker, I had agreed.

When my news broke in the press, Kenneth was in hospital as he had recently been diagnosed with cancer. This left Pat and me to finish the work. Pat carefully typed up the stencils on her electric typewriter and put them through the press, and all the other work—folding, collating and pasting of pages and covers—was done by hand. Normally the author would purchase completed books from Pat, from those surplus to sales through her poetry club, then sell them on with a small mark-up that would add to the profit of our royalties.

Kenneth suffered complications from his radiotherapy and was dying. Pat said he was so enraged at the treatment I had received that his dying words were, 'Give Bobbi the books. Let's make the bastards eat their words.' So the full income from sales of this first limited edition of *Love Poems and Other Revolutionary Actions* was added to my coffers. Added to my soul was the additional burden of expectation of my success uttered by a dying man.

Love Poems was launched at the Aboriginal Medical Service. The next day, one of the mainstream newspapers captioned their report of the event with 'Black Radical Turned Poet'. The idea that people were supposed to be so simple that they could not be two things at once greatly amused me, especially since, as mother, educator, writer, lecturer and filmmaker, I already had many strings to my bow.

My book initially attracted negative criticism from some quarters, particularly from academics at one of the major universities who thought they owned the bible of what should constitute 'poetry'. When *Love Poems* was highly praised by Judith Wright, however, they fell quiet and the small print run soon sold out.

Muriel Hamilton, who worked at the NSW Health Commission's Aboriginal Health office in Redfern, offered to help me make clothes to wear while I was away. Muriel had previously been a seamstress, and she owned an industrial sewing machine and overlocker. As well, she had contacts in the industry to get patterns and have the buttonholes bound. We had a little fabric left over from some rolls of heavyweight denim which Sandra Bardas had sent up from Melbourne for another project, and I bought small quantities of other material as directed by Muriel. During our every quiet moment, we sweated over her machines, eventually turning out a couple of pairs of jeans, a straight skirt, as well as a pleated skirt with matching vest and colour-coordinated blouse.

Students at the Aboriginal and Islander Dance School, with which I remained associated, put on a special benefit performance to raise funds for me, with the encouragement of Carole Johnson. Kempsey-based Benelong's Haven, an Aboriginal alcohol rehabilitation program under the directorship of Val Bryant, dispatched representatives to attend, carrying an envelope of money they had collected amongst themselves on my behalf. Carol had filled a little purse with American notes and coins ('so you won't be stranded at the airport, unable to even make a phonecall') After the performance, when I was called upon to come forward and be presented with these gifts, I was so moved I burst into tears.

I received a phone call from Reverend Martin Chittleborough at the Australian Council of Churches. Was this, I wondered idly, in response to the publicity or had they received an inquiry from the World Council of Churches in Geneva? As it turned out, the call had been prompted by a combination of both. He asked me why I hadn't come directly to the Australian Council of Churches, and I assured him that I had done just that, as soon I'd learned of the refusal from the government.

As Black Women's Action still did not have the twelve-thousand dollars required, the Australian Council of Churches said they would make a contribution and underwrite my program. They sent a letter immediately to Harvard University to that effect, and advised me that they would make up any shortfall. Reverend Chittleborough suggested I should also contact the Australian Catholic Relief and tell them I had received support from the Australian Council of Churches. This elicited another donation towards our goal.

Much earlier, I had gone to the United States Consulate to find out about the process of applying for a visa. 'Come back just a few days before you want to leave,' I was advised by the Black American man who attended to me at the counter. 'It only takes a few hours to issue a visa.'

With Big Naomi's meticulous care of the bookkeeping,

and her regular updates of how funds were progressing, I soon felt assured that we would reach our target. I returned to the US Consul's office to organise the visa because I didn't want to leave this vital piece of travel documentation until the last moment.

When their office phoned me to come over and pick up my passport, stamped for entry, I felt gloriously happy. This feeling, however, was not to last.

There were dozens of details to be taken care of during my final week, in my work at the Health Commission as well as at home. I had applied for study leave and had been assured of a job to come back to. At home, there were newspaper deliveries to cancel, outstanding bills to be paid, and detailed instructions to complete for Russel to enable him to run the house in my absence. I was concerned about leaving him alone in that dark and leaky house. I was particularly anxious that if water again shorted out the electricity wiring in the ceiling and caused another fire, he might be sleeping and not wake up. Still, apart from impressing on him these dangers, there was nothing more I could do. It just seemed to be one more of the risks I had to take, the sacrifices I had to make, in order to achieve my goal. If I could just get past the next few days, winding things down and packing, I'd be in the air and away. My thoughts did not go any further, I had no comprehension of what to expect after that. I felt I was really stepping out into the great unknown.

Early in the week a message was awaiting me on my desk when I arrived at work, would I please phone the US Consulate? When I did, I was asked to come to their office and to bring my passport. I did so, and there a Black American gentleman, Ken Shivers, who

I learned was vice-consul for non-immigrant visas, requested that we talk in another office adjoining the counters.

'This is quite embarrassing,' he said, 'as I have to tell you that when we sent your visa application to Washington, it was rejected.'

His manner was very friendly and he looked genuinely distressed at having to deliver this news.

'So, what are you saying? That I can't go?'

'As soon as we received word, I telexed them, and impressed on them that this was a very public matter, that your going to Harvard has been on the front page of the newspapers, and their decision should be reconsidered. I am hoping for a positive result. But in the meantime, I'm obliged to ask you some questions and to cancel the entry visa we gave you.'

Oh, my, four days before I'm due to leave, and this is my position.

'What are the questions?'

'Are you, or have you ever been, a member of the Communist Party?'

I almost fell about. I had recently seen a theatrical production at the Ensemble Theatre with a theme around just this type of interrogation. Indeed, 'Are you or have you ever been' may have been the title of the play. I did not think it prudent to burst out laughing, but could not stop a large grin spreading over my face.

'Are you joking?' I asked, thinking perhaps this part of our talk was a lark, a lightening of the atmosphere of gloom which had been slowly descending since our meeting started. Frankly, I thought this particular line of questioning had gone out in the dark ages.

'No. And if you have been a member of the Communist Party, that doesn't necessarily exclude you from entering the United States. But you have to be honest about answering.'

'The honest answer is that I am not, and never have been, a member of the Communist Party. In 1972, we used their offices to roneo off copies of things sometimes, but we also used to use the office of some nuns and even some politicians. This didn't make me a nun or a politician, and it certainly didn't make me a communist.'

I wondered if my photo, prominently displayed on the front page of the Communist newspaper, *Tribune*, snapped at a demonstration in support of Angela Davis, had anything to do with all this. I was going to ask but then decided silence would be a better exercise of my discretion. If his office did not already know about that, it might have been folly to draw it to their attention.

'Okay,' he replied, relieved at getting this part of his duties completed. 'Now, the situation is this. If you will leave your passport here with me until we receive an okay from Washington, then I won't have to deface the visa stamped in your book.' He could see I wasn't clear about this, and explained further: 'A passport with a visa that has been stamped "Cancelled" attracts suspicion at just about every entry point in the world. They want to know why. You want to leave when, Saturday? Okay, leave the passport with me until Friday. We should have it all sorted out by then.'

On my return to work *sans* passport, I started ringing around, trying to make contact with Department of Foreign Affairs officials. I thought a bit of diplomatic pressure might help. As well as promises of phone calls, I was able to secure a letter of support from their Sydney office which I took to the Consulate.

'If it was up to me, I would give you the visa immediately, and I already did,' Ken Shivers reminded me when I saw him. 'It's not me who needs to be convinced, it's Washington. Phone calls have been coming in, but it's not necessary. I'm doing all I can. I genuinely want you to go. I've heard about you, I'm familiar with your work, and I know this would be a great opportunity for you and your people.'

A researcher for John Singleton's program on Channel Ten rang me, inviting me to appear on his show. I had been interviewed on Singleton's chat show before. Despite his negative reputation in the Black community based on racist remarks he commonly passed which were reported in the media, I felt it important to use every possible vehicle to alter the poor image the white community held of the Black community—and his show was just one of them. At the time of my first interview I had been especially incensed by Singleton's statement that he would not hire any Aboriginal models to work for his advertising agency, because Aboriginal people were 'unattractive'. Although he had been forced to retract his statement publicly on another television program, I had taken it upon myself to challenge him on this point and find out whether or not he had yet employed any people of colour. Of course, he had not. It had not been a particularly noteworthy interview, with Singleton apparently making a lot of effort to be civil, even while he was being patronising.

If I agreed to this second interview, I was told, it would be alongside Dr Nugget Coombs and the author Thomas Keneally, both of whom I knew to be stalwart supporters of Black community goals. Between us, I felt, we were bound to be able to score a few points.

On this program, which was supposed to be a discussion of the legitimacy of the Aboriginal claim for land rights, John Singleton used the opportunity to publicly air what he thought he knew of my parentage. 'How can you speak about Aboriginal land rights. Your father was an American seaman, wasn't he?' Singleton asked almost as soon as the short segment began. Though I was sitting with two white males and we were all talking in support of land rights, their entitlement to speak on this subject was not being challenged. Nugget Coombs stepped in and very quietly, very calmly, put Singleton back in his place. He was the old statesman talking to the brash and foolish young man, and Singleton gasped to find himself being spoken to in this way.

As soon as the program crossed to an advertising break and we were to be dismissed from the set, I leapt to my feet and abused John Singleton roundly. I was sick of whatever sins my mother and father may have committed being visited upon me. I demanded to know who his mother and father may have had sexual relationships with, if he could prove his own parentage. Nugget Coombs and Tom Keneally also made their displeasure clear.

David Halpin, a journalist friend, learned of the episode from members of a musical ensemble that had provided the theme and musical segment in the show. They had gone directly to the Journalists' Club after work and told everyone present how pleased they had been to see someone give Singleton his just deserts. David rang me to let me know how others present had responded, and to make sure that I hadn't allowed John

Singleton to undermine my self-confidence and desire to succeed in my mission. I assured him that a twerp like Singleton did not have the capacity to do that.

Aboriginal Health Section employees had planned to give me a 'farewell and good luck' lunch on the Friday before I was to leave, but when the day dawned I had still not been able to confirm my entry into the States. Another message from the Consul's office lay on the desk, and, absent-mindedly thinking it was the same message I had responded to earlier in the week, I shot it into the wastepaper bin. I planned to walk the few blocks to pick up my passport as soon as I cleared everything else I had to do. The Consulate was only open until noon each day, so it was imperative that I do so by then. After that, I would join the staff at the lunch.

The note, containing only Ken Shivers' name and number, somehow beckoned me. I reached into the bin, retrieved it, and dialled the number. It was a direct line to his desk and he answered immediately.

'I'm afraid we received another refusal from Washington overnight. Can you come in and see me this afternoon?'

'But your office closes at midday. I'm being taken to a staff lunch. How will I get in?' I could hear desperation rising in my voice. Was this to be a farewell lunch, or would I still be sitting up here at my desk come Monday?

'I'll leave word at the door for security to admit you.'

'Okay. I'll come as soon as I'm able.'

Although everyone was very amiable and presented me gifts, a beautiful thick hand-knitted sweater amongst them, lunch for me was incredibly tense, and I'm afraid I radiated my stress to everyone. I gulped the food and left earlier than was socially polite, but I think everyone understood. My nerves were as tight as a violin string as I gave my peremptory thanks, warning people not to be surprised if I turned up to work on Monday. Then I sped off down the street towards the Consulate.

'We have sent a last-ditch telex to Washington. It's night over there, so the office is unattended. I'll be putting a man on duty here all night, to sit beside the telex machine waiting for the reply. As soon as an answer comes in, that man will phone me—and I'll phone you. It could be at three or four in the morning, is that alright?'

My daughter and I had been packing and unpacking all week, unable to come to grips with whether we were actually going or not, and here it was, Friday afternoon and we still had no entry visa. I momentarily cursed every demonstration I had attended in an effort to gain freedom for anyone else, Angela Davis in particular. This feeling quickly passed, but I still could do nothing to ease my stress levels.

'Sure,' I mumbled, heading for the door. Turning, tears hovering behind my eyes, I thanked Ken for all the effort he was putting in on my behalf.

'I'm sorry. Stay strong. I'll talk with you later tonight,' I heard as I made my hasty exit.

'Naomi, have you finished packing?' I asked as I arrived home.

Miss Smarty-pants replied, 'Well, have you got the visas?'

'You just leave the visas to me, and finish packing your suitcase. That's all you've got to do—so now do it.' My external bravado was the only thing left for me to sail on, so I was using it.

I completed my own packing, right down to the little gifts of Indigenous Australiana and books which I was taking for my hosts and any others who might render me an important service. Then I waited.

The call didn't come until almost eight o'clock the next morning, and then it was a woman's voice on the phone. My instinctive reaction was to imagine that another negative response had been received, and that Ken, no longer able to share and bear my misery, had arranged for someone else to give me the bad news. But no, a telex had come in from Washington around 5 am, authorising their office to issue me with a thirty-day visa. The woman said she had put off phoning to tell me because she thought I might be asleep.

A thirty-day visa—to study for nine months? Perhaps I was going to be required to renew the visa every month, so the security agents could keep their eye on me, I thought, a little hysterically. I didn't know what sort of powerful agitator I was supposed to be, starting perhaps a second civil revolution at a bastion of conservatism such as I understood Harvard to be.

As the Consul's office only opened from Monday to Friday, the woman said she would wait there especially for me, and would I please arrive at 11.30. So, on Saturday the United States Consulate opened just for me, and as Naomi and I were due at the international airport at 12.15, there was only a very small margin for error.

7

It is 12 July, 1980. I stare out the window in complete bewilderment. Am I really on my way to Harvard?

I'd like to fall asleep, but instead my mind ticks over frantically, trying to come to terms with our departure and make sense of the past few weeks.

It had not been until we were actually at the airport, leaving our few well-wishers to move towards the departure lounge, that the reality of our leaving had struck Naomi. She had burst into tears, and her brother had moved in, himself moist-eyed, and held her in his embrace until she had settled down.

This was to be their first separation for anything longer than a few weeks, a fact which had weighed heavily on my mind. They had always seemed to tease each other mercilessly. However, when Naomi began going alone to stay with my mother during her school holidays, Mum reported that she'd spent the entire time talking about Russel. 'I wonder what Russel's doing now,' Naomi would say at regular periods throughout the day, until Mum became weary and in exasperation said, 'He's gone to bed, he's sleeping, and that's exactly where you ought to be.' Russel, too, had pined for his small companion, and planned activities and surprises for her on her return.

Naomi had taken his attention for granted, especially the protection he extended to her at all times. Living away from him would be a growing experience for her, help her to learn to stand alone.

My ex-husband, William, Naomi's father, had, surprisingly, sent her a few hundred dollars with which to buy warm clothing when he'd learned she was going with me. From time to time, my mother had tried to get me to make Naomi write to him and ask him for money. But, as he had never corresponded with her or even called from year to year to see how she was faring, I had refused. 'Mum, Naomi doesn't have to beg to get her food off me, and she shouldn't think she has to beg to get food off her father. Girls shouldn't be taught that they have to beg off men,' I countered.

When his cheque arrived out of the blue, Naomi had been overjoyed and danced around. She had no doubt missed having a father active in her life. Russel, though, brought her quickly back to earth. Ever the mathematician, he pointed out: 'This cheque represents less than five cents a day over all the years he has never sent you anything. Wake up, Nome, it's Mum who always gives you things.'

My mother's response to the news that I was going to Harvard for nine months was far from supportive. 'You're biting off more than you can chew this time, my girl. You'll come a cropper, you've always been too big for your boots,' she said initially, shades of her talks during my younger years when she had urged me to be satisfied with washing beer-soaked towels and urine-stained sheets in the back of Townsville's Central Hotel. When the article had appeared on the *Sydney Morning Herald*'s front page, she wrote, 'Well, the whole world's going to be watching to see you fall now. I wished you had taken notice of me and shelved this stupid idea. You can only come to grief.'

When this line of argument hadn't worked, Mum had changed tack, coming down to Sydney to personally plead her case. 'I'm an old woman now and if you go away, I'll die. It's time for me to die. So, is that what you want—to be out of the country while I'm lying dying?'

'Mum, it's only for nine months. Do you think you can hang on for just that long?' In response, she had pursed her lips with displeasure. On the eve of her return to Tweed Heads, she said, 'Well, okay, I can see you're determined to go. So give me your address. I'll write—and you make sure you write too.'

'But I don't have an address yet, Mum.'

'I see. You don't want me to write to you. Well, if that's the way you want it—'

'Here,' I replied, scrambling for my diary, 'I'll give you the address of the school I'm attending. Write to me there. I'll let you know as soon as I have a proper address.' The papers I had received from Harvard had explicitly stated that students should not use the school as their address, but what the heck. Overseas students, especially those with persistent mothers, didn't have much option.

Professor Chester Pierce had earlier written that I should plan to arrive in Boston a few weeks before school was due to start in September, so that I could orientate myself and be ready when classes began. I had written to Charlotte Meachem, a Quaker whom

I had met in 1972, and with whom I'd intermittently corresponded since that time, advising her that I was flying through Hawaii, where she now lived. Charlotte invited me to break my journey in Honolulu, and said she would find me somewhere to stay. As well, my dear friend Andre Reese, whom I always called Ande, had moved for a while from Australia back to her home in Los Angeles. And she also invited me to stopover on the way.

I had been reluctant to accept these invitations due to the urgency I felt burning away in my stomach, and because it was always on my mind that anything not directly connected to my work was 'wasting time'. The stresses I had encountered in my preparation for departure, however, had created unimaginable tension. So the idea of stretching flat out on my back on the sands of Honolulu for a few days was enormously attractive, as was the promise of 'hanging out' with an old running friend whom I knew to be a very social creature, capable of having a 'good time'. Naomi was keen to stop in Los Angeles. 'That's where Disneyland is, isn't it, Mum? We've *got* to stop there.' Indeed, I felt Naomi, once she'd visited Disneyland, would have been quite happy just to return home.

For reasons I have since forgotten, our plane was very late arriving in Honolulu. Charlotte's husband was ill with cancer, dying in fact, so she had delegated a young woman to meet us. Even after the plane landed, we continued to be delayed. I was held up initially at the Immigration counter, where my passport and visa were thoroughly inspected. The officer, after an equally long scrutiny of a screen on his counter, waved me through, saying, 'Well, have a good time, Bobbi.' I suppose I shouldn't have been shocked by this, but I was because my passport carried my full name, Roberta. Obviously his computer screen had provided him with this information.

We were further held up at the Customs counter. 'Do you have anything to declare? No. Well, are you carrying gifts?'

'I have a few books in my suitcase, for friends.'

Naomi, who had inserted herself between me and the officer and desperately wanted to be included, to be acknowledged as part of the action, a traveller in her own right, piped up, 'Yes, and I've got lots of Mummy's books in *my* suitcase too.'

Will I, the thought flashed through my mind, just strangle her here and now, or will I continue to drag this loose-mouthed child across America until eventually she drops something into a conversation that will cause us to be sent home or arrested?

Charlotte had found a house for us that belonged to one of her friends. It was wonderful, secure and cosy, with every possible amenity, but instead of being on the beach, it was nestled in a suburb high on a mountain. Each morning when we rose, it was cold. We would dress warmly, catch a bus into town, then have to discard almost all our clothes, the difference in temperature being so great. Instead of my being able to lie sprawled on the sand and rest, Naomi wanted to go everywhere, see everything and do everything. Her energy was boundless, while I had none at all. Still, I traipsed after her as she charged from place to place.

I spoke to Charlotte daily on the phone, and, as she lived at a remote location, went out to visit her just once. She didn't like to leave her husband alone. The young woman whom she had sent to meet us took us on a tour around the island, pointing out volcanoes and other points of interest, drove us to meet a couple of Native Hawaiian friends of Charlotte's, and organised other social events that were suitable for both an adult and a child. I felt the few whirlwind days we spent there were really interesting, this being my first trip to the country, but they were not the rest for which I desperately yearned.

Ande lived in a free-standing duplex in Crenshaw, a suburb in Los Angeles. Her mother, a former beautician and practising Buddhist, lived on the ground floor while Ande, her husband and their family lived above. Ande immediately recognised my exhaustion and organised for Naomi to be largely taken off my hands by other members of the household.

An energetic and feisty woman, Ande and I had formed a close friendship since 1974. I had been introduced to her as a filmmaker by Roberta Flack, the Black American singer who'd been giving a free concert for the Black community at the Black Theatre in Redfern. I had been absolutely thrilled for Ande when, in 1976, just two years after arriving in Australia, she won the Benson & Hedges Award for her documentary *Sunrise Awakening*. She had filmed it at the same theatre around a multi-faceted Aboriginal arts workshop which had been held there. She was a talented and experienced cinematic artist, and had brought to Australia the skills she had learned in Hollywood. However, they had largely been ignored and left to wither by Australian arts funding bodies, which had found it easy to disregard Black Australians in this genre and were not about to cave in easily to applications for funds from a Black American, however laudable her previous successes.

Ande surprised me by arranging what felt like a

never-ending series of 'dates' for me with tall, dark and handsome Black men, all of whom were her cousins. I was dined and danced all over town. Ande herself took me to a party in Nichols Canyon, hosted by Roslyn Heller, and it was obvious she was well known and respected in filming circles. It was at this party that I met Sam Waterson, perhaps best known now for his role in *The Killing Fields* as well as his ongoing position in the television series *Law and Order*. A Yale graduate, when he heard that I was on my way to Harvard, he jumped up with the old school rivalry, dumping on Harvard and asking why I wasn't going to the 'top' school, Yale. 'Because they didn't invite me,' I had replied, neatly nipping his argument in the bud.

Ande had given a copy of my poetry book, *Love Poems and Other Revolutionary Action*, to her friend, writer, poet and broadcaster, Wanda Coleman. When Wanda came around to meet me, I felt honoured to be in the presence of such a talented and eccentric artist, and we got on like a house on fire. Our chat spread out over several hours of an afternoon and early evening, during which time she read to me some of her work and, surprisingly, some of my own which she told me she regarded as great. Suddenly I was startled to hear helicopters approaching. Wanda, however, hardly looked up from a piece she was reading on the policing of Los Angeles. She just kept raising her voice to make herself heard above the noise. At last I could bear it no longer. I leaped up and ran to the window, and saw there, hovering outside the house, just above roof level, two police helicopters. They were so close that their whirring propellers were stirring the dust on the street in front of us.

'That's Los Angeles policing,' yawned Wanda, as I

watched heavily armed men in riot gear on the ground bolting over fences and through backyards. They were being directed in their pursuit from the copters above, just one block over from where I stood.

Good grief, I thought, as I moved away from the window, concerned that I might have been hit by a stray bullet if anyone was to open fire. The thought struck me, however, that I had already been shot at, my flat fire-bombed, and been the recipient of death threats in Australia. If I were to be shot in America, it would at least only be by accident, not purposely directed at me, as would have been the case at home. This small measure of anonymity reassured me, and despite my feeling of ever-present danger, I felt some-how comforted by this realisation.

I went looking for Native American community organ-isations in LA, without a great deal of success. Only two were listed in the local telephone directory under names which would be immediately recognisable. I went to visit the one nearest where I was staying, the other was too difficult for anyone trying to get around on public transport. When I arrived, there was only one young woman in attendance, talking desultorily into the phone for most of the time I was there. I had hoped to find perhaps an art or cultural display, even some pamphlets on organisations or local events. But when I asked the girl she shrugged and went back to the phone. Perhaps, I thought, I will need to get out of the cities to find these American kin, and such a visit will probably take a great deal more to arrange than just catching a bus across town.

The Inner-City Cultural Centre, Ande told me, was a 'must' on my schedule. This time I called first to

ascertain that there would be somebody in attendance
to provide me with information, before I trooped across
town. Los Angeles is a most difficult place to get
around for anyone without a car.

I need not have worried, the place was booming
with activity when I turned up. There were dozens of
mainly young people carrying on all manner of artis-
tic activities. They were drawn, so I was told, from as
many cultural groups as they could attract. The Centre
was a haven, particularly, for people of mixed descent,
and I saw many youngsters with Asian/Mexican/Indian,
as well as black and white, ancestry milling about.

I agreed to say a few words to the students about
what it was like to be in Black in Australia. And all
those engaged in the singing, dancing and acting
classes assembled to hear me. Under the direction of
Bernard (just call me Jack) Jackson, who became a
close friend until his death more than fifteen years
later, the Centre provided a meeting place and opportunity for learning and exposure for many talented
young people trying to break into show business in
this difficult, ruthless and hard-hearted town.

Another friend from yore, Talya Ferro, a Black singer
and entertainer whom I had met in Australia, again
through Ande, took Naomi and me to her house in
Hollywood. She then arranged, much to Naomi's relief,
to take us to Disneyland. In my mind's eye I see Talya
still, in her high-heeled shoes, initially trying to keep
up with Naomi—the child berserk in this fantasyland—
until eventually we just let her have her head and go,
hoping she'd get into no harm. Talya and I sat resting
our feet and sipping cool drinks, and waited for her.

* * *

I had been concerned that, during the three years since I had attended his lecture, I may have forgotten Professor Pierce's face. From his regular and supportive letters, he felt like an old and familiar friend, but would I recognise him when I saw him? And if he failed to meet us at the airport in this strange city, what would we do?

I need not have been concerned because as Naomi and I made our exit from the plane in Boston, he was there. His happy face was so glowing at our arrival that it was impossible to miss him. He picked up our heavy suitcases, which Naomi and I had dragged through all the terminals, as though they were packed with feathers. Then he whisked us into a car and away, home to meet his wife Patsy and daughter Deirdre. They had made space for us in their large basement. We were to stay with their family until I started at school.

'Just call me Chet, and this is Patsy,' he told us. 'Everybody else does.'

It wasn't true, of course. As a Professor on two Harvard faculties, Medicine and Education, an eminent psychiatrist and world-renowned scientist and consultant to NASA, a mountain at the South Pole named in his honour, Chet's name and achievements struck awe and respect into the hearts of almost everyone he came in contact with.

We had barely got settled, creases knocked out of our travel clothes, when Chet took us off to show us around Harvard University and grounds. A long-legged and extremely athletic man, he set a breakneck pace which even the active Naomi had trouble maintaining, much less her slower mother. Chet pointed out Widener and almost every other library on Cambridge campus, the very famous Harvard Yard and Peabody and other museums. Finally, it was time for Chet's favourite treat, hamburgers.

While I was very interested to see all these things, and to be shown how to find my way to Cambridge from Boston, my concern about whether or not I could succeed in this famous place intensified. Chet sat me down on the steps of a building close by the Education School which I was to attend, and tried to allay my fears. I had absolutely nothing to worry about, he said, because I had all the skills required to undertake the work. He praised my writing, my insightful way of looking at things, my ability to express myself clearly. But, I thought, is that enough to get me through here? Or will I, as my mother had predicted, come a cropper?

Naomi was swinging herself over nearby fences, skipping, leaping and dashing here and there, while we talked, and Chet chided me for speaking of her as 'hyperactive'. 'She is not hyperactive,' he said, shades of his psychiatric training, 'she's completely normal.' I told him how, as a baby, Naomi had rocked herself every time she ate until she brought up her food, how doctors had advised me to keep her sedated, advice which I'd rejected. I also described how, later, I'd tried to stabilise her with the Feingold diet but found it impossible because she was too young to comply with its rigidity. Using a single coloured tissue or washing her hands with perfumed soap at school was enough to trigger her off. Chet continued to insist that she still fell well within the range of normal. While I felt reassured by his advice, I was almost despairing about how I would manage her *and* cope with my studies.

It was only in retrospect, when I began to get an inkling of the extent of Chet's commitments, not just around the States but around the world, that I realised the precious gift of his time, support and encouragement, which he had given me. At the time I was too frightened, and perhaps too culture-shocked, to give these gifts the appreciation they deserved.

We were made very welcome at the house. Patsy, as well as taking care of their home, had graduated and been employed as a social worker. She was very friendly to me and the pair were extremely captivated by Naomi, who had a frankness about herself almost beyond belief, as well as an immense capacity to express her joy at life.

I got a lot out of speaking with Chet, and, from time to time, he let me know that he also appreciated talking to me. During one conversation I shared with him how disturbed I often was when, in Australia, white people came up to me in the most unlikely places, such as at cocktail parties, and made what sounded almost like confessions. They would tell me the most base and sickening things about themselves, sometimes about their depraved sexual predilections, at other times about crimes they had committed. I had reflected upon this and come to the conclusion that this was a manifestation of racism. These people rated me alongside perhaps the family dog, in whom they could safely confide because it could never bark back. Chet said immediately that he had exactly the same experiences, and his assessment was extremely close to my own. He felt that these people saw him as being outside their social circle and powerless to use the information against them. What a relief it was to realise these things did not happen to me alone!

On another occasion, when we were all taking a meal together at the end of the day, I asked his late-teenaged daughter Deirdre if she was looking forward to the forthcoming US election in which she would be able to vote. I was shocked to learn that she had no intention of enrolling or of voting, and I spoke to her sharply. 'I have read so much about how many Blacks here have *died* so that you could vote, and you tell me you're not going to bother?'

Afterwards, Chet thanked me for bringing up the subject, for speaking so to his child. He said that children reach an age when they don't take too much notice of what their parents have to say. My outsider's perspective was valuable for reminding Deirdre of her history in a way which he had been unable to do.

Notwithstanding these occasional exchanges, I began to be very troubled, and tried to immerse myself in the minute details of taking care of Naomi. Chet and Patsy, who both went off to work each day, urged us to get out, visit the art galleries, the children's museum, and some of the many splendid things to be seen in Boston. Also, being guests, we had little else to do. But I was unable to rouse myself, to undertake these activities with any enthusiasm. Each morning I would lie sobbing in my bed in the basement, becoming cranky at Naomi when she bothered and cajoled me to take her somewhere, anywhere.

I must pull myself together, I kept saying again and again, worried about what had come over me. It was a long time before I could detach myself enough to analyse the situation. When I did, I concluded that I must have had a breakdown of some sort, occasioned by the stress I had been under in Australia. These early days in Boston represented my earliest opportunity to put down the emotional burdens I had been carrying. They were also the first time in my life when I had no crises calling on my time, no urgent business to take care of, no deadlines for work I was expected to do. I had had no experience with 'leisure time'. I was unable to make decisions about what I might *like* to do, as separate from what I *had* to do. I couldn't cope.

My way out of this depression was to narrow my focus to the task ahead. As soon as it was possible, with the summer break drawing to an end, I began to explore the school and its requirements. I located the housing office, chased up my accommodation application, and tried to badger people in the faculty to find out if there were reading lists for classes I could access so that I wouldn't appear to be too far behind the other students. Other students, I felt sure, had probably already touched on everything we had to learn during their undergraduate study. With no undergraduate study behind me, I assumed that I must be behind. I did not want to appear to be 'dumb'. I did not want the school to regret their decision to accept me.

I was appalled at the dismissive attitude I met at the housing office. They told me that they did not place much weight, and certainly no priority, on the applications from overseas students because many of them failed to turn up. Accommodation for families was in very short supply, there were hundreds of applicants, did I think my case was somehow special? But what of those international students with their children who, like me, did turn up? Had I travelled halfway around the world to discover I had nowhere to live?

I found myself galloping around the Cambridge campus, child in tow, backwards and forwards between offices, trying to sort out the truth from the rumours, of which there were many. I was told horror stories of people who, in desperation, had turned up at the housing office, suitcases in hand, and refused to budge.

They even threatened to sleep there until they had been given a housing placement. With the dicey state of my visa, I felt far too insecure to risk arrest in this way. My visa became another priority I had to take care of. I went to the immigration office in Boston and completed an application to extend it.

I began to meet, and make friends with, staff arriving back from their summer holidays. I found the Education School mailroom and explained to the very friendly Black man who ran it that I had had no other address to give, and if mail arrived for me, would he please hold it? Over time, we grew quite chummy. Perhaps this was because he was something of a philatelist, admiring the foreign stamps on my letters and asking if he could have them. But it was also because it was in his nature to be kind to people who treated him respectfully. He had been in charge of the mailroom of the Education School for much longer than many of the academic staff had been in their offices. There was very little that he didn't know about the running of the place and who was who and what they were up to. His status was such that he was a guest at all the cocktail parties held at the school, where he often shocked visiting professors who struck up conversations with him by telling them he was the mailman.

I continued to receive no joy at the housing office until the Director of Admissions, Mary Murphy, to whom I had gone running several times with my tale of woe, made a phone call on my behalf. The very next time I went to Housing to check availability, which we were obliged to do several times a day, I was informed that a two-bedroom apartment, suitable for myself and my child, in Peabody Terrace, would be ready for me to occupy on the first day of school. Until then, it would have other occupants.

On checking out the complex to locate the apartment, I found it to be a short distance away from the Square, on the Charles River. Naomi was charmed to see squirrels running up and down the trees nearby, no doubt filling their hollows with the stores they require to get them through the long winter months. I asked around to find out the location of the nearest school for her, and was pleased to learn that Martin Luther King Junior School was almost directly across the road from where we were to live.

The first weeks of school consist of Orientation and Shopping, the former enabling new students to find their way around, meet faculty members informally, and take care of numerous tasks such as paying fees, being photographed for the student contact book, library tours, and enrolling in whatever student group one wishes to become a member of. The latter means attending any number of the short introductory presentations given by academic staff to enable prospective students to better make their choices. It was during these two busy weeks that I was also obliged to go dashing around, trying to set up house.

Money was my main concern. I had to be absolutely sure that our little store of funds lasted the full nine months, so everything had to be trimmed. There could be no splurges.

The apartment was unfurnished, so I had a double mattress delivered on which Naomi and I would both sleep until I could get organised. On our first day in the place we scoured and cleaned as best we could. Then I bought a few frozen food items which I could just place in the oven for our evening meals. As

twilight came upon us and I was busy in the little kitch-
enette, I called to Naomi, 'Turn on the lights.' A few
moments later, she appeared in the doorway. 'Mummy,
I can't find the light-switches.' I went to look in all the
logical places, searched the walls, and discovered that
the only overhead light was in the bathroom. All the
other rooms were to be lit by lamps, for which there
were ample electricity outlets in the walls, but we had
no lamps.

Our first meal in our spanking new apartment was
taken with us sitting on the bathroom floor, eating with
our fingers.

Martha Ansara, a filmmaker who had worked with
Essey Coffey on the production of her autobiographi-
cal film, *My Life as An Aborigine*, had given me the phone
number for her mother, who lived in Boston. Mrs
Ansara, looking frail and ill, turned up next day in her
car and drove us around to a few opportunity shops
where we purchased some plates, saucepans and other
kitchen utensils, and an iron. We had tested the iron
in the store and it had become warm. When we arrived
home, though, we discovered that this was all it did,
never becoming hot enough to iron any sort of fabric.
So that was, worryingly, money wasted.

I had ordered a bunk for Naomi, but it would not
be delivered until the end of the week so she had to
continue sharing my mattress on the floor.

I was deep in an exhausted sleep one night when
I bolted awake with a severe blow to the head. I saw
stars, my brains reeling, and all this in the dark.
Naomi, dreaming, sleepwalking, had imagined there to
be a window in the wall behind us, above the mattress, and had leapt up to see out of it. She'd landed,
both feet together on her way down, right on my head.

My cry of sudden pain had woken her, so she stood, an amazed and startled expression on her face, looking down at me. Even awake, she could barely believe that there was no window in the wall, and she was a very shaken little girl.

I got her back to sleep, reassuring her that I wasn't actually injured, just a headache and sore neck. Then I lay awake worrying that if this was an indication that she had begun sleep-walking again, I would have to sleep across the doorway to prevent her leaving the apartment in a dream.

We learned of the footpath sales—where people sell their unwanted clothes and furniture outside their own homes—which are a regular feature around Cambridge. On the weekend we visited as many of them in our area as we could. Using the little sets of wheels we had bought to carry our suitcases, we scurried home with a few lamps, chairs and a bookcase. There seemed not to be too much difference between us, racing around stocking up our necessities for the forthcoming year and the little squirrels racing backwards and forwards with things they would need for their looming hibernation.

School began in earnest. Students had been advised that they were required to take four courses each semester. I enrolled in five. This left me, I thought, with one to fail, if that turned out to be the case, without completely jeopardising my prospects for success. I thought myself very smart for doing this. Later I was to learn that such actions taken for just these reasons are considered part of having been programmed to expect failure. They demonstrate a lack of self-confidence and self-esteem, which, of course, is correct. But how could I have been otherwise?

Walking in Harvard Square one day, just near the Coop, I heard someone call out my name. I was surprised, because I barely knew anyone. Certainly no one knew me well enough to hail me so in the street. I turned, but there was not even a remotely familiar face to be seen. Instead, a Black man, a complete stranger, stood smiling broadly at my confusion, waiting for me to realise that he was the caller.

'I'm Tony Siaguru, from Papua New Guinea,' he said, by way of introducing himself. 'I saw your picture in our newspapers, saying that you were coming here, that's how I knew it was you.'

Tony invited me to visit him and his wife, Mina, at Harvard's Soldier's Field housing complex where they were living with their young children. I was so pleased to meet someone from close to home, and to be able to share news with people who understood the politics and dynamics of what was happening in my part of the world and their own.

The International Students Association had suggested that foreign students should inform their embassies of their whereabouts. I was so angry about everything that had occurred prior to my departure, however, that I refused to do so. Instead, I contacted the PNG Mission to the United Nations, and let them know where I was. Tony, who was studying at the Kennedy School of Government, followed this through for me. Mina was also doing a degree at the Education School. Instead of arriving in September and studying through to June, like the rest of us, the pair had organised to start their work in January, at the beginning of the second semester, then finish in December at the end of first semester.

I was keen to find out how they, coming from an even warmer climate than my own, had fared during the previous winter. If they had already toughed it out without major mishap, I thought, surely I could do so, too.

No sooner had I taken Naomi in to her school to enrol, than she came home with a note from the teachers informing me she was to be amongst the Black students who were to be bussed to another school each day. This was part of the desegregation program. Schools with a high percentage of Black students bussed some of their students to white schools, while those with too high a percentage of white students bussed some of their students across town to majority Black schools.

I went back to the school and said that if they had an excess of Australian students, I would permit Naomi to participate in the program. Otherwise she had a right to attend their school, close by our home, after travelling from so far. Naomi was the only Australian, and fortunately they saw my point.

At the Education School, I was surprised and quite enchanted at the informality between staff and students. We were invited to address the professorial staff by their first names as though we were, in fact, their equals. 'We're all mature people here,' I was told when I queried the practice. The range of people who were in attendance was enormously wide, drawn from almost all corners of the globe and involved in many specialist occupations. And I did not meet anyone who was not in some way a practitioner. While some were in the teaching professions, others like myself were interested in the wider aspects of adult learning.

I attended my classes and tackled the reading lists, spending almost all my time in the library. We had been lent a small television, which Naomi was permitted to watch only during the news and current affairs programs. The condition was that she took notes for me on every news item. I had always been very strict with her access to television, and was not about to weaken our domestic rules and invite total anarchy. Naomi was quite pleased with this arrangement, and her experience in summarising and taking notes has stood her in good stead. I was happy because it allowed me to stay on at the library with my head in books until after seven each night before rushing home to prepare dinner.

Like many people, I suppose, when I arrived at Harvard I thought a library was a place to borrow books, no more, no less. Now I began to see their function much more broadly, as potential repositories of all the history and knowledge of the world. I felt sorry that I had not recognised this before.

While dining with Henry and Elaine Mayer at their house one night some years earlier, Henry, a historian, tried to impress upon me the need for me to start throwing bits and pieces into a box to give, at some later time, to a library.

'What sort of "bits and pieces" do you mean, Henry?' I had asked him.

'Almost everything. Any time you're invited to an official function and you're given a program with your name in it, or a name tag, keep it. If you go to the opera, keep the ticket. You'll be a famous Australian in your lifetime, and where you went and who invited you, how you spent your time, your likes and dislikes, these are the important details about you that modern historians will seek out. So make their job easier, and do your bit to ensure that contemporary Black Australians are not left out of Australia's history as so many have been in the past.'

I had tried to keep copies of some of the articles I had written over the years, but my accommodations had not been conducive to the safe storage of such materials. I had never been to an opera, nor was I, despite Henry's high estimation of me, invited to those sorts of places which had name-tag seating arrangements and so forth. However, my constant exposure to the libraries of Harvard made me think hard and long about how we, as Blacks, were almost invisible in the history of my country. I began to think about the ways I could help to rectify this omission. My squirrelling away of 'bits and pieces', as Henry had called it, started in earnest at Harvard.

In those first few weeks at Peabody Terrace, I was hailed several times as I crossed the courtyard which separated the buildings in the complex and asked by co-residents, mainly by women from the Indian sub-continent, if I was looking for work. 'What sort of work?' I had initially inquired, curious about being approached in this way.

'I am looking for a maid,' always came the reply.

When a notice came around that there was to be a meeting in the Peabody common room of Peabody women, I decided to attend. As the women introduced themselves around the circle, I was surprised to hear, repeated with variations, many times over, 'My name is Jane Doe, my husband is doing a Master's degree at…the Kennedy School, the Education School, the Business School.' It gave me a great deal of satisfaction to be the only woman present at that meeting who could follow up their name with '…and I am doing a Master's degree at the Education School'. The Indian women present were particularly taken aback.

I would later learn that there were other women, scattered throughout the complex, several of whom were Black, who were themselves Harvard students. Perhaps because they were already aware of the composition of these Peabody women's groups, they had not bothered to attend.

After that meeting, no one again asked me if I would be their maid.

Naomi had always had difficulties at school in Australia. On one occasion, when she had been a primary student at North Sydney Demonstration School, I had been called to the phone in the middle of a class I was teaching at the Aboriginal and Islander Dance School. A teacher had told me, 'Come over immediately and pick her up.' When he was addressing the class, he said, Naomi was attentive. But whenever he turned to write something on the blackboard, she upped and moved to any other desk in the classroom, and he had to search the room all the time to find her. It was a chronic problem, but on this day she had been warned twice that if she disrupted the class once more, she would have to go home. She had, of course, jumped up and moved again.

I had spoken to the teacher at length, telling him I was not prepared to see her punished for this behaviour because she was not responsible for the environment in which she lived. Chemicals in the food,

chemicals in the air, colourants and additives in everything she came into contact with—how could he find
her guilty of being over-active when everything around
her only served to over-stimulate her?

Naomi had been to more than half a dozen schools,
mainly because we had had to move so often before
we found a permanent home. When we moved into our
Naremburn house I had, with great difficulty, enrolled
her at a Catholic school thinking she would receive a
more charitable reception. This had not turned out to
be the case. Her first teacher there told the other
teachers what a problem Naomi was considered to be.
Attitudes had hardened against her, and eventually my
daughter had internalised their view of her and her
limitations. She begged me to let her repeat a year
because 'I'm not very smart, Mummy.' The pervasive
idea that, for whatever reason, Black children can't
achieve, which then turns out to be a self-perpetuating
prophecy, was alive and well.

I had agreed with her request to repeat because I
had planned that we would leave for Boston that year
anyway, although I was still deeply concerned and had
attended parent meetings and teacher conferences in
an effort to get these things straightened out. Naomi
had been made very unhappy at school, and it was
obvious to me that she would demand to leave school
the moment she was old enough. This was unless ideological changes were made to accommodate her.

Martin Luther King Junior School turned out to be
a blessed relief. All new students are placed in D-class,
which is only a category and not a ranking, until they
demonstrate by their abilities where in the system they
can perform most comfortably. In the first week, Naomi
came home and told me she had been asked to give

a presentation to the class on Australia. When we unpacked our suitcases, I found that Naomi had brought with her absolutely everything she owned, right down to tiny glass ornaments she saved to decorate her room. I had been annoyed at the time, but now she was able to use her treasures to illustrate her presentation. She staggered off under a load of books, maps and Aboriginal items, some of which I had brought as host-gifts, and came home glowing with pride at being awarded an 'A'.

She moved up in their system and was asked to give a presentation on the entire Pacific. After that she again changed classes. Suddenly, no doubt heartened by the reception she was receiving for her work in social studies, she began to bring home reports of her excellent performance in every subject. Without the awesome burden of having to respond to negative expectations, Naomi flourished. She threw off her depression about school and achieved the marks I had always known she was capable of.

I also came to realise, slowly, slowly, that not everyone in my classes was a genius. Some were no doubt smarter and had more focused book-learning, but my wide experience counted for at least as much as their theory. I was gaining good grades, and eventually I saw that it was not necessary to read absolutely every book on my reading lists, or every book made reference to in those readings. Instead, I learned to read more selectively and, consequently, smarter.

In lectures I sat as close to the front as possible, to hear as best I could, especially with those teachers whose American accents I found difficult. During Shopping Week, I had eliminated from my proposed schedule any courses taught by people who spoke too softly or whom I regarded as mumblers. My hearing wasn't all it could be, and I was determined not to make this difficult program even harder for myself in any way.

The intensity of the learning experience, the book work, and which courses I took at exactly what time, blur in my mind. But many things stand out. Foremost amongst these memories are valuable insights and experiences shared with other students in Conroy Commons, the Education School lunch and coffee room in the basement.

I also spent many pleasant hours with Tony and Mina Siaguru. It was refreshing to be able to make jokes and have them understood without having to explain ourselves to the Americans, who did not understand our points of reference. Still, I knew it would be a mistake to become too dependent on the companionship of Tony and Mina as their tour of duty was quickly coming to an end.

One day I received a letter from my bank in Australia through which I had organised my affairs, including my traveller's cheques, before leaving Australia. It said that since I was no longer in my house, but renting it out, I was required to pay investment, rather than home-owner's, rate of interest for my mortgage. Henceforth the payments would be considerably more than they had been previously.

I was so angry I sat down immediately to reply. On one of my visits to their bank in the process of making my travel arrangements, I had been surprised when a teller had brought over to the counter a file with my name on it. When she opened it in front of me, out spilled all manner of newspaper clippings about me, including the front page article from the *Sydney Morning Herald*. I had been upset by this, but remained silent, wondering if the bank kept files of this nature on all their clients, or just the Black ones.

How, I asked them now, since my son, a student, continued to live in my house in my absence, could they write that my home was an investment property? Russel was going personally to the bank every few weeks to make the regular payments from his student allowance, so why hadn't they asked him? I was affronted that these bank officials felt they could piece together what was happening in my life and within my family on the basis of whatever they read in the newspapers. And that they could make arbitrary decisions related to my house payments. If the increase in the payments had been left unchecked, I probably would have lost the house altogether.

I heard nothing back from them for months. At last, a notice of a reversal of their decision arrived, having been sent by sea mail and taken over three months to reach me. More angst, I thought, and for what?

I joined meetings of the Black Students Union and was also invited to participate in the Native American Program. The latter, to my knowledge, did not hold regular meetings as such. Instead they had their own building and people were welcome to drop by at any time. There were always helpful people on hand and, at times, visitors had access to the Program's resources. Talking to people there I gained a very useful perspective on how to use the experience I was gaining at Harvard. The Native American Program quite aggressively recruited students from around the country, and supported them as best they could throughout their studies. Anyone who received their help was expected to 'give back', becoming mentors themselves once they had learned their own way around.

The Black Students Union, on the other hand, held meetings, although it seemed to me that only a fraction of the potential membership attended. Of those who did, a significant proportion began a rush to change the group, from 'Black' to the 'African-American' Students Union. I listened to several debates about this proposal before offering my own opinion. 'If you go ahead with this name change, do you understand that you will be excluding people like me? Black people from Australia, from New Guinea and the Pacific?'

I was followed outside after this meeting by a young Black man.

'Well, if you keep hanging around with those Indians,' he said, 'why do you want to bother coming with us?'

I was shocked at this blatant display of racism. The Native American friends I had made, who were aware that I shared an interest in both groups, had never indicated they had even the slightest problem with this duality of identity. Indeed, they had encouraged me.

Before arriving in America I had made an effort to read up on the history and contemporary situation of Blacks in that country. I had even included some comparative comments in articles I had written, and published reviews of some of the recent books by Black American authors that had made their way to Australia. I had learned, to my dismay, that many of the most prominent Black organisations, as part of their policy, demanded that the government fulfil a promise it had made to Blacks upon emancipation, of 'forty acres and a mule'.

This subject came up several times in Conroy Commons, when groups of us were talking together, and the reaction from Blacks was sometimes quite heated. Our conversations often went along these lines:

'I'm trying to understand—forty acres and a mule? I have no problem with the mule, but it seems to me Black organisations here are demanding a larger share of what they know the white man stole off the Indians.'

'You don't understand. Our forefathers were dragged here in chains.'

'I do understand that. But *you* are not in chains. You're sitting here in one of the elite universities of the world. You even told me you went to Europe for your holidays during your school break. So obviously you could have gone to Africa if you had wanted to.'

'Yes, but it was our forefathers' blood that built this country up to what it is today. We deserve to inherit our share of this land.'

'Yes, and I have a problem with that, because the last time I heard someone say exactly the same thing, it was a white South African, trying to justify their occupation and ownership of that land.'

Almost without exception, the speaker would then tell our assembled group that his or her grandmother/father or great grandmother/father had been an Indian.

'Then why don't you ever identify yourself as being Indian? Even part-Indian? Do you ever go by the Harvard Indian Program to see how you can help?'

The question of identification and dual identity began to intrigue me, as it did many of the students on campus. And many long and fruitful discussions were held on the subject. Indeed, students even wrote theses on this very theme.

One of my companions was Eber Hampton, a Native American teaching fellow who taught in one of the classes I was taking, Community Psychology, under the stewardship of Professor Richard Katz.

Professor Katz, who by this time had become 'Dick', asked me just a few months after my arrival if I'd be interested in moving from the Master's to the doctoral program. I had discovered, by then, that there was a hierarchy amongst students, with doctoral students virtually considered the princes and princesses of the campus.

What other differences existed, I had yet to learn, and his question had confused me. I knew doctoral students were on campus longer, but how long, and what were they actually doing there?

Dick answered my first question. 'Well, it normally takes between five and seven years, but students can take as many courses as they can handle, if they want, which means they can complete the coursework requirements faster, even in half the time. After that, it depends on how long they want to take to write their theses. Students don't have to be on campus to write their theses, though many do. They can even write them in their homeland, it's up to the individual.'

'Five to seven years? And you're asking if I want to be a doctoral student? Heavens, you've got to be kidding. I'm already concerned about whether I'll be able to survive *this* winter. I'm from a tropical climate, you know!'

My relationship with Dick had not started out too well, so his frequent encouragement and candour always came as a surprise. Some comments he had noted on the first essay I had handed in for his class had caused me to seek him out in his office.

'The content is fine, but your writing style is too journalistic,' he had told me.

I had brooded about this before returning again to see him. 'For the last ten years I have in very large part earned my living and supported my children by my journalistic style. For most of the academic writing I've read, a person needs a dictionary constantly on hand to make sense of it at all, and people outside universities barely read it at all. Are you asking me to change from a style which has earned me a living, to adopt a style that hardly anyone can make a living from?'

We had talked and over time had reached a compromise. As long as I continued to demonstrate that I understood the content of material set for our readings, he would overlook my practice of never using a long word when two small words will do and always writing to be clearly understood. Still, I had wondered whether my boldness and adherence to what I believed had created a gulf I could not cross.

Another friend, Art Zimiga, an Oglala-Sioux and also a doctoral student, helped with my second question, what doctoral students actually did, although his reply didn't offer complete clarification.

'Bachelor students have a "batch" of information or knowledge, Master's students are considered to have "mastered" the subject matter, and doctoral students are supposed to be so familiar with their subject that they can "doctor" it, that is, write down everyone else's opinion, add their own opinion, and put their own name on the cover.'

* * *

Winter descended upon us swiftly. When Naomi heard on the television news that it was due to start snowing at about ten o'clock that night, she pleaded to stay up and see her first snow flakes. I hadn't seen snow either, except at a distance, so we sipped cocoa and waited. Right on the dot of ten, we saw shimmers outside her bedroom window where we were sitting, so we rugged up and ran outside. By the time we reached the courtyard, the specks of snow had grown and were coming down heavily. Naomi shrieked with glee, and we gathered what we could in our hands to take back inside for inspection.

Next day, snow and slippery ice lay everywhere. The air had turned so cold that it hurt to breathe. Marjorie Baldwin, an Aboriginal nursing sister, with specialist skills in midwifery and ophthalmology who had worked with Fred Hollows' trachoma team, had studied in England and been overseas many times. She had pressed upon me her kangaroo fur coat to take to Boston, far more aware than I of what awaited us. I shook it out now, and was glad of its warmth. The coat was a slim link between myself, my community, and my country, and for that reason it was so much nicer to snuggle into its fur.

Out came the leggings and sweaters which had been knitted for me by Redfern and other supporters. None of them were colour coordinated of course, but that was the least of my concerns. With many scarves wound around my head and neck, and leather gloves— a farewell gift from Elaine Pelot—I prepared to stride off along the icy streets to get to school.

Naomi, however, had picked up some idea that, in

order to fit in, she had to wear canvas tennis shoes, the dress code of the early teenage set. How many times that winter I tried to argue with her to have sense, to put health above 'beauty', I do not recall. Still she persisted, refusing to wear leggings or virtu- ally anything she was offered. A few scraps of light underwear, T-shirt, jeans and a light parka flying open, was the most I could ever make her wear.

Winter proved to be the most persistent cold I had ever encountered, but I didn't fare too badly. All Harvard buildings, including our accommodation, are centrally heated, and often over heated. We'd joke that all we should have been required to wear was a big fur coat and a bikini. I recall on Christmas day skidding and sliding over the icy streets towards Harvard Square, where I saw a clock with a temperature gauge mounted on the wall of a building. The clock said 12 noon, and the temperature gauge showed 0 degrees Fahrenheit, the 'warmest' part of the day. I shuddered. The wind chill factor often took the temperature down into the minuses. After experiencing -15 and -20, I decided that the only difference was in the time it would take for a human to freeze to death. Otherwise, piercing cold was just piercing cold, whatever the temperature.

Naomi's first term report came in. Excellent. My marks were posted, I had achieved four As and a B. More relaxed now, I set about choosing my spring semester courses. Another three would complete my Master's degree coursework, but I took four anyway.

Through a mutual friend, I had met a Black Ameri- can couple, Beverly and Robert Glenn. The friend had told me that Robert had worked while Beverly com- pleted her doctoral degree. Now Beverly worked, at the

Law and Education Centre, while Robert was completing his degree at the Education School.

Beverly told me, at our very first meeting, that she disliked children, so when she invited me to her house I didn't go. She rang to press her invitation before finally I admitted to having a child with me. 'Well, bring her anyway,' she said in an off-hand manner, which I later learned was part of her mask.

Having so openly declared her dislike of children, I was surprised to find that Beverly had a whole room absolutely full of toys and games in her extremely elegant house. These were all pulled out for Naomi's enjoyment and amusement. Thus commenced our frequent visits. Beverly was an eccentric but welcoming host, and Robert was ever-willing to leap upstairs and set up the double guest bed so we would stay the night.

One night when we were staying over, we put Naomi to sleep in the attic guest room and continued our talk in the lounge. We were suddenly alarmed by a lot of noise and banging upstairs, and we all bounded up there as fast as we could. We found Naomi, sound asleep, yelling, scrambling around and banging on one of the walls. She woke up as we calmed her, and she looked amazed and startled. She said she was trying to get through the door which she imagined to be in the wall. On the way downstairs after we settled her down to sleep again, Beverly said, 'You know, there used to be a door there, but we closed it off.' Eerie, I thought, very eerie.

Eber Hampton, who drove a pick-up truck more reminiscent of the prairies than of streamlined Boston and Cambridge, occasionally invited Naomi and me along to some local Indian events. One time he packed his tent and extra sleeping bags for us, and took us to the Spring Festival.

It was held in the woods outside Boston. Participants came from all over, and Eber was able to identify the tribes represented there by their many different dress styles.

'Watch this,' he said, with amusement, when the drumming began. Most of the assembly fell into a line and began to dance in a circle, single-file, to the beat of the music. He nudged me. 'The ones still sitting down, they're from the west. In the east we dance anti-clockwise, and in the west they dance clockwise. 'That's why they won't get up.'

He hauled himself to his feet and went over to speak to a nearby group, still seated. 'It's alright to dance the "wrong" way just this once. Come on, no one's going to hurt you,' he said, and taking the hands of a couple, he helped them to their feet.

The air was still quite cold and dancing kept people warm. Before long, every able bodied person had joined in.

A fire had been lit in a small pit and, as part of the festival, it would be kept alight all night. As people straggled off to their campers and tents, the hard core moved in and sat around it, Naomi, Eber and I amongst them. It was the custom, so Eber had informed me, that those who were able to, should stay to keep feeding the fire and share creation stories. We listened to a variety of these stories, all interesting, all very Indian.

There was one extremely dark man amongst the group, with Afro type long hair pulled down into very thick braids. He was Seminole Indian. They were the descendants of slaves who had run away and joined an Indian tribe who lived in the swamps in Florida. He and his slightly lighter companion remained quiet as each person in the circle took their turn telling the creation stories.

A hush fell over the group when the speaker sitting beside them was thanked and it became the turn of the Seminoles. All eyes were turned towards them. They stared ahead into the fire, looking thoughtful but apparently ignoring everyone.

A deep voice, an Elder, spoke. 'It is your turn to tell your story, but if you are ashamed of your stories, the turn can pass on.' At that, everyone in the circle burst into laughter, and the man sat up straight and began his story, and we all listened with attention and respect.

I was delighted at the Elder's sense of timing and teasing humour, so similar to that of so many of my Elders at home in Australia. Despite the cold of the night, I felt warm and comfortable in the company of all these new friends.

8

All my classes were interesting, but the work I took with Chet Pierce that year had the most profound and enduring effect on me. Chet had set out on his career at a time when very few Blacks were admitted into Ivy League schools. Those who were had usually received a sporting scholarship and were not expected to succeed academically. Chet had succeeded in both the classroom and on the sports-field, going on to qualify in medicine and psychiatry, later holding two professorial chairs at Harvard, in the fields of education and psychiatry.

Being the first Black in any field is controversial enough, but Chet had set himself the task of excelling at everything he did. He undertook scientific studies on large mammals, such as elephants and whales, and, when the time came, on the effects of isolation on man and lectured on this subject around the world. Part of his isolation research was undertaken at the South Pole. A consultant to NASA, where his exper-tise on the effects of isolation were particularly relevant, Chet advised on the likely effects of isolation for those involved in journeys into space and ultimately to the moon.

He had also turned his scientific attention to racism, discovering ways to identify and quantify this particular human behaviour, as well as searching for ways in which to eliminate it altogether. He was, for example, a prime mover behind the development of *Sesame Street*. He described this program as a series of advertisements, or jingles, that were picked up and learned by young children in the ghettoes. They spent a lot of time in front of televisions and had previously learned by rote all the advertising jingles for cigarettes, soap powders, and the like. Now they learned numbers and the letters of the alphabet.

In his classes, Chet shared with us the fruits of his labours. In so doing, he peeled back our skin, flaying us with truths that were sometimes painful to hear. Some of the white students, particularly, resented this, and wrote negative evaluations of his classes. These were collated in Gutman Library for prospective students to view, as were all course evaluations. Non-white students largely adored him, though they too were whipped by his words.

'Racism,' he intoned in his quiet, calm deep voice, 'is a mental health disease of national, even global, proportion. It has all the qualities of an epidemic.' He proceeded to justify his statements in medical terms, and rationalise his conclusion before moving to quantify for us some of the ways in which racism manifests. This was indeed heady stuff, and we were riveted in our seats. He had drawn up lists of the behaviours in which Blacks' time and space, and consequently our lives and opportunities, are controlled and contained.

Chet also turned his attention to the many ways in

which Blacks cooperate with their own oppression, presenting us with a list of these as well. Those of us in the room who were Black frequently winced with the truth of his pronouncements, recognising in ourselves and in our friends the behaviours that he was identifying.

One such item on his list, 'Blacks over-disclose', forced me to recall the many times when, at home in Australia, over-disclosure had almost shut down our movement. 'We'll be at Parliament House in the morning, ten o'clock sharp, to demonstrate about this,' someone would publicly announce. Why then were we always so surprised to find, on our arrival, hundreds of uniformed police waiting for us, as well as plain-clothes detectives picking up individuals along the way, and ASIO staff with their cameras set up in surrounding buildings?

Chet's papers, such as that on 'Offensive Mechanisms', which details some of the processes of micro and macro-aggression, will remain sources of inspiration for me for the rest of my life.

In Conroy Commons, Chet's Black students almost ritualistically gathered after his classes to discuss the impact his work was having upon us. There was unanimous agreement that his was probably the most important course we were ever likely to take. It gave us insights into racism and its impact on ourselves and society that we were unlikely to have received anywhere else.

But that's not all there was to Chet, which, even if this had been the case, was still life-saving. His example, as a strong, calm and self-possessed Black man, was also sterling.

In one of the two courses I took with Chet, a young

white man displayed his audacity by starting to jump in and ask questions long before it was appropriate to do so. We had all been told to wait until lectures were finished and questions were invited before bringing up any issues we may have had.

The first time this bright spark interjected, the rest of the class sat forward, interested to see what Chet was going to do. He answered the question, thoroughly but briefly, before pointedly picking up his notes to resume his talk.

The second time, only a few minutes later, Chet faintly scowled at the young man, but replied to the question politely, though coldly.

Insensitive young man that he was, he again interrupted the flow of the lecture. By now we felt that he was actually challenging Chet on several levels, first behaviourally but also on his intellect. He asked a question which had to do with space travel, but which had really no relevance to the material we were being taught at the time.

Chet rocked back in his chair, cast his eyes towards the ceiling, and began to answer the question before bringing his gaze back down to lock eyes with the man. The words he chose were multi-syllabic, mesmeric, and virtually incomprehensible to anyone other than a fellow scientist at his own level, which of course we were not. Neither was the young man. Chet continued relentlessly, while the young man, completely out of his depth, squirmed in his chair and grew visibly smaller and smaller before our eyes. For what felt like forever, but was probably only ten very long minutes, Chet lambasted him by answering his question in exquisite detail. When he had finished we looked around the room to discover that everyone was sitting there stunned.

'Do you know what Chet was saying?' those of us in our Black after-class group each asked one another later.

'No, not a word, but wasn't it mag-nif-i-cent?' to which we all heartily agreed.

Another course which I found very compelling that year was Community Psychology, taught by Dick Katz. In many ways it touched upon aspects of the work I had been doing in Australia, but for which I did not even have names. I thrived on the lecture material, and also on the tutorials held after the formal lectures. So many students took this course that Dick had a cadre of teaching fellows to carry on the themes in smaller groups.

After approaching me to inquire if I was interested in moving to the doctoral program, Dick spoke to me again. This time he invited me to participate as a teaching fellow in his course for the next semester. I was still worried about my ability to pass in my course-work and wanted to reserve what time I had in case I needed it to study. So although I was flattered, if a little confused, I politely refused. As well, I was unsure what I would have been expected to teach. I had been there just one term, which did not seem long enough for me to have learned anything I *could* teach, and I told him this.

'You'd meet with other teaching fellows, and we help you to categorise and parcel up what you already know—that's what you'd teach.'

This astounded me. What I already know? Good grief! How come I didn't know that I already knew something valuable enough to teach at Harvard? The idea that I might have knowledge scooped out of me, knowledge I didn't even know I had, and that it could be labelled and parcelled for sharing with other students was dizzying.

On my arrival at the Education School, I had met the Dean, Paul Ylvasakir. During our first brief conversation we had discovered that we had friends in common in Australia. I later found a note placed in my pigeon-hole inviting me to come by his office to continue this discussion. When eventually I did so, he, too, voiced his concerns that I was in the wrong program. He had sent for my application and read my details out of interest following our first meeting. A student of my obvious experience should have been in the doctoral program.

During my second semester I was sailing through my work with new confidence, born of the splendid marks I felt I had achieved. I had gained all As with the exception of Chet's class. I marked down my poor performance there, B-, to the fact that everything he had taught me was so new and dazzling that I had not yet had time to absorb and analyse it before being required to write essays around the questions. Although not offered here as an excuse, I needed more time to digest and incorporate so much complex—and, for me, emotional—information into my world view.

One day in April, early in spring, Dick Katz approached me again. 'Well, you've survived the winter, so why don't you reconsider what I asked you earlier? You should be in the doctoral program.'

'But,' I stammered, 'even if I were to reconsider it, applications for the doctoral program closed months ago.'

'Not for you, they haven't. And there are others

around this campus who are very impressed with your work, who would support your application. Everyone speaks highly of the contribution you have made.'

I was flabbergasted by this evaluation, especially since in Australia I had been led to believe nothing I knew had any value. It would be hopeless to even think about applying for the advanced degree, though. I had been through so much to get the funding to do the Master's program, I didn't feel I could go through it all again.

Still, in the regular reports I sent back to Reverend Martin Chittleborough, I told him of my good grades and progress, and that I had been invited into the doctoral program. I was surprised to return home one day to find a telegram waiting for me. 'Congratulations on being invited into doctoral program. Accept. Australian Council of Churches will sponsor,' and signed by Reverend Chittleborough himself. A short time later I received a follow-up letter, again congratulating me on my success and pointing out how it would benefit the Black Australian community to have one of their own attaining such a prestigious degree, and urging me to accept.

Nevertheless, I remained unsure. How was my son faring on his own at home? And would he agree to my going away again, this time committing myself to spending several years here? Could I extend my study leave from the Health Commission? Or would I be jeopardising the only job I saw open to me? These questions were central to my decision. Until they were answered I felt I could not make a commitment.

Professor Katz suggested that, since I was so unsure, I should cover all my bases. 'Apply to the doctoral program, and if everything else works out, that pathway

will be open to you. If you are able to return immediately next academic year, the nine courses you have
already taken will be counted towards your degree.'

'I don't want these courses counted towards a higher
degree, I want my Master's degree in my hand to take
home. I can't go home with nothing. If it turns out that
I can't arrange to return, everything I have been
through to get here, and to stay here, will amount to
the fact that I have nothing to show for it at the end.'

'You'll still get your Master's degree in June, and if
you're able to get back here, that coursework will still
count towards your doctorate.'

On this basis, I finally agreed to put in an application, and almost immediately received notification that
it had been accepted. I was so thrilled to think that I
could become one of those campus princesses anytime I wanted. Even if things at home didn't work out
and I was unable to return, I would hold tight in my
heart the feeling that I and others knew I had the
capacity to succeed. But would I get this chance?

There were still end-of-semester papers to get
through, and I couldn't afford to slouch. As usual, I
generated my essays quickly and had them in on time.
Then I began to consider the arrangements I had to
make to go home. Home! The thought was very uplift-
ing. Despite having enjoyed my time at Harvard, I was
looking forward to seeing my son and all my friends
once more.

For the graduation I had to hire a cap and gown, and
there were other expenses involved which I hadn't
budgeted for. We had managed very frugally, my daughter and I, every cent accounted for. Now, apart from
the travel and emergency costs I had factored in, there

was nothing left. After I left Australia a little more money had come in to Black Women's Action from the public appeal we had launched. So I wrote to Naomi Mayers asking her to forward it to me, but received no response.

In my budget I had set aside money for one phone call home during the year. If, as my mother had threatened, she had in fact died in my absence, I would have needed these funds to call and make any arrangements necessary. I was so near the end now that I felt I could use my emergency phone call money to pay these graduation costs.

Throughout the year, many people had written to me and saved me from the depression caused by what we called 'empty mailbox syndrome'. For foreign students and those from more remote places in the United States, the isolation of being so far from the people we knew could only be assuaged, and then only temporarily, by a precious letter—even a postcard—from home.

My mother had put a letter in the post religiously once a week, even if she had no real news. And she always expected a response in the return mail. My son had also stayed in touch, including pages marked for Naomi, which she spirited off into her bedroom to read. Elaine Pelot had been a regular correspondent, saving for me clippings and items of interest from newspapers and magazines. Her fat manila envelopes stuffed with news had kept me up to date on Australian political and social changes throughout the year. Nugget Coombs had written, too. His first letters were tentative, but we soon developed an airmail friendship which blossomed and grew right up until his death. Gary Foley wrote me a solitary but very supportive letter. In his inimitable style, it began: 'It is by sheer coincidence that I write to you on this day', the letter dated April 1.

Dr Paul Wilson, a criminologist with whom I had shared a friendship going back many years, also wrote, warmly and encouragingly. He continued to keep me informed about his work, troubles and travails.

MumShirl, of course, was unable to write, but not long after my departure David Halpin had loaned her a tape-recorder. This enabled her to hold a long one-sided conversation with me, which she recorded over several nights. Unfortunately, when David delivered it in person to me in Boston, he let slip a comment which informed me that he had listened to it first. I decided to discourage MumShirl from using this as a means of communication, and I'd heard nothing back from the occasional letters and cards I sent her, although I was sure she always had one of the many school children in her house read them to her.

By this time I had begun dating a Black American, Dr Don Ware, a cardiac surgeon who, as well as being on the staff at Bethesda Hospital, which I understood to be somewhere near Washington DC, was also Macy Fellow at Harvard. We had found we shared common interests in health, medicine, politics and dancing, and our friendship had grown from there.

Don was a bachelor, and almost his first words to me, after inviting me out to dinner, were, 'Most women I take out to dinner end up trying to get me to marry them,' to which I'd replied, 'Well, you won't have that trouble with me. I have absolutely no intention of staying in America, no matter who asks me.'

Don sometimes rang while driving back from DC, asking Naomi and me to join him for dinner on his

arrival. Naomi refused to go because her idea of a 'real
treat' was a trip to McDonald's. So Don would take her
there first, and allow her to call her friends on the
mobile phone he had in his car on the way. Then he
would drop her home with her goodies and, with the
neighbours keeping an eye on her, he would take me
somewhere where the food was a bit more adult. Don
had been a tap-dancer during his childhood, and loved
nothing better than to go to one of the few Black nightclubs and get down to some serious boogie.

He was an intriguing character, who related to me
many tales about his past which had resonance with
my own. At school, he'd been told by his white teachers and career advisers that, since he was very good
with his hands, he should take up carpentry. Instead,
he had taken up medicine and become a heart surgeon. This meant that he was still very good with his
hands but earned a great deal more money. Racism,
we both agreed.

There was, however, an offside to his personality.
He was sometimes very boastful, though also often
rightly proud of his achievement. He drove an expensive Mercedes sportscar and liked to relate tales of
how white motorists, because of his car, imagined him
to be an athlete or a sports star—never a medical
specialist. He seemed over-concerned about the acqui-
sition of material things. The concept of spiritual
gratification, rather than material reward, did not sit
easily with him. While he appreciated the striving
towards 'selfless deeds' in others, it didn't appear to
be something he aspired to himself. As well, over time,
he became extremely and unreasonably jealous. He
disliked Naomi and me going to stay with Beverly and
Robert, for instance. When it was time for us to leave

for Australia, he jumped in very quickly to say he was driving me to the airport when he learned that Beverly and Robert had already offered to take us.

When his mother flew over from Los Angeles and he insisted I must meet her, I heard the faint peal of alarm bells. Given that I was about six years older than her son, and had been married twice already, I hardly expected her to greet me very warmly. I was surprised, then, when she did. Overall, though, I couldn't help thinking that perhaps my assertion that I intended to return to Australia presented Don with an emotional challenge. Some people yearn for the inaccessible, often without considering whether, if accessible, the object of desire would be their real choice.

Don told me several times that I was 'too familiar with white people' for his liking, that I was not even alert to them when they were around. This made me realise the difference between his world and my own. In Australia, with no Black medical or dental graduates, or funds for capital outlay, we were obliged to go to white people for almost every thing we required—whether it was health treatment, to purchase groceries, clothes or fabric, borrow a library book, or buy a car, keep it repaired or even fill it with petrol. We were all so poor and so grossly outnumbered and out-resourced that we had never had the opportunity to experience any real independence. Consequently, we had been forced to lean towards white people for their services or attention in virtually every situation. Perhaps then, my way of life had become a habit, made more noticeable in America where there were services and information available from the Black community, but I was not in the habit of assuming them to be there nor seeking them out.

I had enjoyed the friendship of many wonderful people during the nine months of my stay and, as my time in America was drawing to a close, I was concerned that I did not have gifts enough left to give them to repay their many kindnesses.

In particular, Native American friends had been an enormous source of support—the students on campus and others in the wider community. One such person, Gkisedtanamoogk, a medicine man in the Wampanoag Nation, had very early extended his warm welcome and friendship. Also, he had ensured that I met many other people who, he felt, would appreciate the things I was trying to achieve and the reasons behind my efforts.

Will I ever have the opportunity, I wondered, to

repay these people? I knew they did not seek material reward, but I wanted in my own heart to feel somehow that the value and indebtedness of their gifts of love had been acknowledged and appreciated by me.

A Native American student with whom I was quite friendly, and who had been working throughout the year on his doctoral thesis, had a sudden fit of nerves towards the end. Fearing that his work might not have been couched in sufficiently academic terminology, he had taken a thesaurus to it, changing more than half the small words to longer ones. The result had been virtually unintelligible, and it was shaping up to be a major catastrophe for him.

He came to visit, his absolute misery filling the small apartment. How could he go back to his homeland people, who were so desperately in need of qualifications amongst their own, he asked, if his work was not passed. And it seemed in all certainty that this would now be the case.

Fortunately I had finished all my own work and had a golfball typewriter, which Chet's friend, John Young, had lent me. So I offered to help put the thesis back into its original form. I had to get him out of my place though, because his tension and distress were more than I could bear. He retired to his own apartment in the building next door, and for the next two days and nights I stayed in touch with him only by phone. He had talked to me about his work before this, so the subject matter was somewhat familiar to me and I was a fast and accurate typist.

At last the big day arrived—Commencement, as the graduation ceremony at Harvard is called. All students gather in Harvard Yard, with proud parents filling every inch of space. Each student is given only two tickets for relatives or friends, so international students really come into vogue at this time. Rarely having relatives or friends outside the school to ask, their tickets are in high demand by others who have more friends than tickets.

When we had all taken the seats allocated to us, a huge black mass of capes and mortarboards filling the Yard, we were instructed to stand. The sky was so blue overhead, and the grass of spring so smoothly and shiningly green. Even the ivy which decked the sur-rounding buildings had been given its annual spruce up for this biggest of all Harvard events. Then, snaking its way through this awesome assembly, came a won-derful spectacle of the most vivid crimson, the doctoral graduates, the princes and princesses of campus, had arrived.

I breathed deeply with the intensity of the moment. In that short hushed time, when we all craned our necks to catch a glimpse of perhaps friends and acquaintances we knew to be amongst the splendidly attired doctoral graduates, the thought really struck me: I could be one of them.

My next thought was of how great that colour would look on me. I could not drag my eyes away from this show of pomp and ceremony. Up on the stage, the formal proceedings got under way, with presentations by students especially selected for the honour, con-gratulatory speeches by the Harvard President and others, and the conferral of an honorary degree on a woman who had made a most significant contribution to American cultural life, Leontyne Price.

We disbanded, each school's students then gather-ing in the adjoining smaller Yards for the individual degree presentations. There we were sorted into the order in which our presentations would be made. The Director and staff from the Native American centre came towards me as I stood towards the back of the long line which had been formed. 'We know what you did, and we thank you,' they said, referring to the student I had helped who was also to receive his degree.

I spotted Robert, looking extremely handsome in his robes, the first time I had ever seen him in other than casual clothing, and Beverly, beaming her pride from the audience. Naomi sat with Australian friends, Phil and Martha Mollison, and their son, Sky, who came along for this part of the ceremony.

The past nine months whizzed through my mind— trips I had made to New York, walks I had taken in areas famous for their autumn leaves, the mountain of books I had read my way through, and more, all the friendships which this ceremony denoted to be at an end, or at least an end to this phase. I was both happy and sad on the day.

At last it was my turn to go forward, to be kissed on the cheek by Paul, congratulated by Associate Dean Blenda Wilson, and to be handed that large flat red envelope containing the fruit of my year's work.

At home, later, I could barely contain myself for wonderment, teasing my degree out of the red envelope, gazing upon it, putting it away, only to repeat the process. It was so hard to come to terms with the reality of achieving my aspirations of having more than the servant's life, which had been mapped out for me as a Black child in Australia. I was sitting in Cambridge with my very own Harvard degree in my hands.

* * *

I had arranged for us to leave on the weekend following the graduation, and our suitcases were all but
packed. The son of a fellow student had agreed to pick
up furniture which I wanted to store, and borrowed
pieces had been returned. The apartment was looking
really bare.

Don came by the next evening—he had been kept
busy with the presentations at the Kennedy School—
to take me out to a celebratory and last dinner before
our departure. At the restaurant I was approached by
two elderly Black women.

One woman spoke. 'I want to congratulate you, dear.
I saw you yesterday but I didn't get a chance to get
near you.'

Complete strangers to me, they told me that they
went every year to Harvard graduations, counting Black
heads, approaching and congratulating each Black student, making sure that the Black students were aware
their achievements were being noted and appreciated.

'But I'm from Australia,' I said, feeling perhaps I was
getting praise to which I was not entitled.

'A Black is a Black anywhere. Go with God,' the old
woman said as she walked away smiling.

9

We arrived back in Australia uneventfully. I received a letter from my mother immediately upon my return. 'I hope you are not getting too big for your britches, my girl,' she wrote, and I was glad that her admonitions were moving further up my body. It had been my boots she'd been concerned about last time. But what would she say when I told her that I planned to return to Boston, and give her another chance to go off to the Hereafter in my absence? It wouldn't be long until I found out, because she also announced her intention to come to Sydney the following week.

Russel was withdrawn and forlorn. He had not enjoyed the lonely routine of coming home to an empty house each day. We had even been away on his birthday, which had fallen just a couple of weeks before we had arrived home. I tried to make it up to him, having brought gifts and holding a late-birthday family dinner. It wasn't hard to see, though, that he considered this to be a consolation, rather than first prize.

Living on his meagre education allowance and studying full-time, he had not been able to involve himself much socially, cooking his meals each night with just Catso for company. On one occasion he had treated himself to a tin of pink salmon, opened it then left it on the kitchen table while he went to answer the phone. When he'd returned, Catso was licking her whiskers, having completely consumed the centrepiece of his evening's meal.

He had gone to Tweed Heads to visit his grandmother during his vacation, and taken Catso with him. Catso had never been a traveller. She had once torn her claws out on the carry basket I had used to bring her to the vet to be sterilised. From then on, she bolted if she heard a car engine start up.

Russel had left her loose in the car during the long journey. In return, she had scratched him constantly on the neck as she tried to scramble over his back and out through the small gap he had left in the driver's window as they sped along. Still, she looked none the worse for it, sitting happily licking her paws at the sight of us all once again gathered in the kitchen.

I went back to work immediately. We had very little money and I had to start earning once more.

Naomi pleaded not to go back to the nearby Catholic school, and having witnessed the difference in her that attendance at a more reasonable school could make, I agreed to her requests. Instead I enrolled her in a state high school. I was appalled, however, when I went for her admission interview.

'Naomi will have to go down to a lower class,' we were told, in response to the information that she had been living in America.

'Naomi attended school in Cambridge, where she

was doing fine. As a matter of fact, she was doing excellent.'

'School there is not the same as school here. She will have to go down.'

Naomi was none too pleased either, when she discovered that neither her teachers nor her new school chums were interested in her overseas experiences and observations. A few of the children eventually asked her in the playground, 'What's Disneyland like?' But they treated anything else to do with her time abroad as though she had merely been sick at home in bed for a year.

I renewed my old acquaintances, going around to visit them one by one. Naomi Mayers apologised for not having answered my letter requesting funds—she had, she said, already disbursed the rest to other people who had wanted funding to do things. When I asked for more details, what sort of things, she said, 'Oh, conferences and the like. You know. They come up all the time.'

Reverend Martin Chittleborough warmly welcomed me, beaming at me as I walked through the door. Yes, the Australian Council of Churches would honour the offer he had made for funding to see me through. Did I have any idea of how long it might take?

At the Health Commission, my close associates, Marian Simon, Nola Roberts and Bob Jones, were happy that I had returned. When I told them I had been accepted into the doctoral program, they took it with very good grace. They assured me that for a project so important to the Black community, and to my personal development, they would wholeheartedly support my application for additional study leave.

In the state elections which had been held in my

absence, the government had turned over, and Laurie Brereton's commitment to permanency for Black employees had been instituted. I was jubilant—equality in the workplace at last—though I had no idea of how this would impact on me.

As part of this process of gaining permanency I was required to have a physical examination, which included a chest X-ray. Fears stemming from the brutal manner in which I'd been dragged off by police from my home in Townsville for compulsory TB testing flooded my mind.

My friend Marjorie Baldwin had, some years earlier, invited me to a barbecue where I had met her soulmate, Dr John Thompson, or 'Thommo' as he is affectionately known. In chatting with him between his duties of turning the steak and sausages, I learned that he was a thoracic specialist. So in fits and starts between cooking and eating, I had related my tale of horror about my experiences in North Queensland, that I'd been forced to submit to tuberculosis testing for years and how police had come to get me, even during my pregnancy, to haul me up to the hospital.

'What year was this?' Thommo asked pensively. When I replied, he bolted off for another turn on the barbecue.

Returning a short time later, he told me, stammering and obviously embarrassed, that he had been in charge of the Thoracic Ward at Townsville General Hospital during this time. Had I not received three letters each time, asking me to come to the hospital for an appointment?

'No, no letters.' He loped off again to wave his cooking utensils, deep in thought.

Later, 'Well, where did you live?'

'In Stanley Street. In the cutting.'

'That explains it then. Everyone knew that's where the Blacks lived, and the staff probably thought you couldn't, or wouldn't, read the letters.'

I could see he was stung to the quick as his past complicity in the racism which had been part of everyday life in North Queensland during this period was becoming clear to him. Now, through his relationship with an Aboriginal woman, he had been growing aware of the pain that had been inflicted upon individuals for no reason other than their colour. Our conversation was no doubt another harrowing step for him in this process.

'I signed the police warrants,' he admitted. At that, it was all we could do to stop ourselves from bursting into tears and holding each other, as the shock of these revelations stunned both of us. Marjorie was one of my close friends, and he was Marjorie's lover. Something soul-building had to come from all this, for all our sakes.

I told Thommo that I had not agreed to a chest X-ray since this time, and felt I never would again. He said he would get my files and X-rays down from Townsville and look after me himself. Nothing so terrible would ever happen to me again.

The friendship between Marjorie, Thommo and my family has grown close since that event. When Russel began studying at New South Wales University and could find nowhere to park his Gemini Grasshopper, Marjorie and Thommo invited him to leave it in their yard, which was close to the campus.

Now I contacted Thommo again, to see how the Health Commission's demand for a chest X-ray could best be handled. He wrote them a letter, advising them of his specialist qualifications and that I was in his care. Although there were a few raised eyebrows within the Commission's clerical staff, this must have been effective. After I completed the rest of the medical requirements, I heard nothing further in this regard.

At the Aboriginal and Islander Dance School, I found that a white woman had been brought in to take my place, teaching the literacy classes and maintaining the little newspaper we had put out. She was on the payroll. I was taken aback by this because the work I had done for the School had been on a voluntary basis. Carole Johnson sought to appease me by informing me that the work I had commenced with the students had proven so valuable that it had enabled her to then seek funding to ensure its continuation.

I went to visit Joe Croft, at the time a working partner at Coo-ee, an Aboriginal arts and crafts shop in Paddington. Joe, a friend over many years, had helped me to get a parcel of gifts ready when I'd first departed for Harvard, throwing in discounts and cut-price items from the shop to boost my meagre store. He had once intimated that he was privy to some aspects of traditional knowledge. At the time, I had not had any reason to explore this with him, and thinking perhaps his knowledge was limited to 'men's business', I decided that it was no concern of mine. Now, however, I confided in him the problem of Beverly and Robert's inability to conceive, and he said to leave it with him. He knew of some traditional practices but needed time to decide on the most appropriate one. He would also start putting together another parcel for me to take back to Boston.

* * *

MumShirl was ecstatic when I turned up at her door. She pushed gawking children aside and came rushing to hold me to her breast. 'When,' she said, 'can we go out to celebrate?'

I thought I would arrange an outing to coincide with the receipt of my first pay. Then we could go to a very cheap place as I was anxious to save as much money as I could.

A publisher had been found for the book I had written for her, Heinemann Publishing in Melbourne. Nick Hudson, the managing editor, got in touch and said he was coming to Sydney to speak with MumShirl and me about its format and forthcoming release. He chose the Golden Ox for our dinner meeting, an expensive restaurant in Regent Street, Redfern, and put together a party which included Sydney-based people associated with the company.

When MumShirl arrived she had a relative with her, and we had to draw up an extra chair to the reserved table. After she had sat down, MumShirl looked around in an agitated fashion, and soon the door opened and more of her relatives trooped in to join us. They too drew up chairs and tables were rearranged to accommodate them. After Nick Hudson's querulous look, to which I replied with a shrug, I whispered to MumShirl, 'How many more have you got coming?'

'Only one more. She'll be here any minute. It's my party, we're celebrating *my* life, and we're also celebrating your return...' she turned her head and announced to the table, 'from Harvard with a Master's degree.'

As if that were not enough, MumShirl called, 'Waiter, waiter, bring...' indicating Nick, 'that man the wine list.'

Nick was gracious in defeat, and, following his example, I relaxed to enjoy the evening. Nick ordered several wines to go with the meal, one of which came in a long thin black bottle.

MumShirl called the waiter.

'Do you have any more of these bottles out the back? Empty ones? My prisoners make sets of glasses out of these.' Then she demonstrated to all at the table how the bottoms and tops were cut off with a glass cutter, and joined together again in a different formation to become sleek long black glasses.

The waiter scrounged around in the garbage and set aside all the bottles he could find. Then MumShirl decided we would all have to drink enough of that particular wine so that her prisoners could make two half-dozen sets from the empties she intended to take home.

I think everyone was completely gob-smacked by her, and they all ate and drank up as she'd ordered them to do. A merry party was being had by all, when she turned to me and said loudly, 'Well, now that you've got your degree, show them all what you can do.'

I looked at her blankly. I mean, really, I had no idea whether she expected me to do card tricks, leap up on the table and dance, or merely dazzle people with a verbal display. Fortunately the moment was interrupted by the waiter wanting dessert orders.

I began to dread having to tell her that I was returning to Boston, and chose not to do so that night.

Nick, very moved by MumShirl's larger-than-life personality now that he had met her in person, was even more keen to get a move on with publishing her book, and asked me to provide some photographs for it. MumShirl insisted we include a group photograph taken on Erambie Mission just outside Cowra, MumShirl's childhood home, to mark Coronation Day, 12 May 1937. I contacted. Robert Merritt, author of *The Cake Man*, which had been staged at the National Black Theatre, and contracted him to help identify the people in the photo as the Merritts were also from Cowra. I would pay him with the residue of the Bardas Foundation funding for the book. I thought it would take him a week at least to travel there to do the job, but he was back the very next day, task completed. He was extremely happy to pocket a week's wages for a project he had been able to finish through his family's knowledge and connections without even leaving town.

When I went to collect MumShirl to take her to the photographic studio for some further shots, she was already preparing a list in her mind of things she wanted us to do together in the future, including drives in the Health Commission car to country prisons.

'Mum, I know you're not going to be happy about this, but I'm going back to Boston. I've got a chance to become the first Black doctoral graduate in this country, and I'm going to take it.'

'You've met a man over there, and you're going to get married and stay there,' she replied, her face crumbling and bottom lip quivering. I had rarely seen her so upset except when she attended a death or a funeral.

'No, there's no man, no marriage. I just want to have a go at something that's never been done before, and I know I can make it.'

'But you've already got the degree. You said you'd bring it here to show me.'

A thought flashed through my mind. With MumShirl on one side and my blood mother on the other, both objecting to my leaving, this project was not going to be easy.

'That's the one I went over to get, and yes, I've got it. But there's an even higher one, and if I had it, people would have to call me "Doctor".'

'Oh, like Fred Hollows and old Nugget [Coombs]? Well, that would be very fancy.'

'This isn't about being fancy, Mum. It's about showing that Blacks have got what it takes, but that we haven't had opportunity.'

I could see MumShirl grappling with these ideas but also becoming increasingly unhappy.

'Well, who's going to help me while you're gone?' she asked plaintively.

MumShirl had always managed, one way or another, long before she'd met me. She had commandeered assistance when it wasn't voluntarily forthcoming. As she often said, she had 'robbed Peter to pay Paul' whenever that seemed the only way. Although she had come to rely on me a great deal over the years we had worked together, I still knew she'd manage.

My mother lobbed onto my doorstep, down from Tweed Heads, as promised. She admired the snapshots which had been taken at my graduation (the portraits by the school's official photographer had not yet arrived). When I shared my news with her, her reaction was anger. 'You run away and leave this little boy,' she said, referring to my towering university student son, 'and drag this little girl all over the world. I don't know what you've got in your mind.'

'Yes, and you'll be dead again before I get back, I know. Can we skip the arguments? No Black person has ever had this opportunity before—and I'd be crazy not to take it.'

'You'll be sorry, my girl. Sorry you spoke to your mother like that, and sorry you don't know your place in this society. Whoever heard of the sorts of things you keep putting your hand up to do?'

'Precisely, Mum. If I have a chance to go first and don't take it, there may not be a chance for a second and a third. If I go and I'm successful—and I know I will be—then I'm going to make damned sure there's a long chain of graduates who follow me.'

'Don't swear at me, young lady,' she huffed as she walked from the room. I would have laughed aloud if I hadn't sensed how frustrated she was at not being able to force me to obey her will. I had grown up under the rain of my mother's expletives, of which 'damned' would have been her very mildest oath. She tried to struggle through the rest of her visit without reference to my plans. I, however, broke my own resolution not to harass her further about my parentage by bringing up the subject in what I hoped might be an oblique manner.

'Mum, is there any point in my looking for records of the person you've said is my father while I'm in America?'

I received a question in response, typically Mum. 'Will you be upset if I say at this late stage that the answer is no?'

'I'm not upset. As a matter of fact I've been read- ing all this cultural stuff which says children normally take their identity from their mother.' Mum peered at me with a most suspicious look, not knowing whether to be pleased or if this was another of my 'tricks', as she called them.

'Now, we both know you've told me a lot of coverups in the past, trying to have me believe your parents and grandparents were Scottish or Irish, but many of the bits and pieces I've picked up from you and from Aunty Glad have made me think that what you've told me in the past has not been exactly true, or, at best, only partly true. How can I take my identity from you if you won't even tell me what it is?'

I had settled myself down comfortably and companionably in a chair beside her at the kitchen table, trying to establish a setting in which she could feel trust and perhaps, at long last, break her silence and confide in me. I was even using the least accusative form I could think of with which to approach this thorniest of all her sides. She stared at me from behind her spectacles in the long silence that followed my question, and I could see her eyes dart into a hundred places before she drew herself up to reply. When she did, I didn't know whether to burst out laughing or cry.

'You won't be happy with this answer either, dear. There is Scots and Irish floating in here,' she said, indicating the blood pumping through the veins in her old and spotted hands, 'but if you go back far enough, we're White Russians.'

With that pronouncement, Mum pushed back her chair and fled once more into the sanctuary of her bedroom.

I continued to sit for a while, alternately holding my head in my hands in despair, and chuckling at her nerve. White Russian indeed. So much for taking my identity from my mother—I could already imagine the startled and sympathetic looks I would draw if I proclaimed myself to be a White Russian. Delusional, people would whisper.

The very idea forced me to recall a young, very dark-skinned girl whom I had taken in to live with us for a few months while she got herself sorted out. After a few evenings spent talking with her, she had suddenly spoken to me in high dudgeon. '*You* think I'm Aboriginal, don't you? Well, I'm not. I'm white.' I had been taken aback. She had gone on to give me, in the face of enormous evidence to the contrary, the basis on which she had decided upon her whiteness.

It had, therefore, come as no great surprise to me when, a few months after she left my home, I learned that she had been hospitalised for attempting suicide. She repeated the attempt several times, and complicated her life with drug use. It was only some time later, after she had come to terms with her Aboriginality and blackness, that she recovered and began to build a reasonable life and future for herself, given the restraints imposed upon us all by racism.

Following this attempt to pin my mother down once more, I sighed and went on being who I had always thought I was anyway. I would waste no more time chasing my mother's phantoms, who she said she was, who she said my father was. It all felt so futile and unnecessary. I would look in the mirror every morning to ensure I was still who I was yesterday, and the day before, and I'd be very surprised if I ever saw a White Russian staring solemnly back at me.

I received a number of phone calls from the media following the publicity about my return to Australia. During one, a live-to-air broadcast with a Perth radio station, I was asked: 'Do you feel that now you have received a Master's degree from Harvard that you'll be acceptable to the Australian public?'

I was shocked. 'Does every Black person in Australia have to have a Harvard degree to make us acceptable, equal even, to the most poorly educated white? Is that what you're asking?' I stormed back, impatient with the crassness and the absurdity which lay behind his racial-superiority line of questioning.

Heinemann's intended to hold MumShirl's book launch as soon as the publication was ready, which was after I had returned to Boston. Nevertheless, it fell upon me to choose a suitable venue and draw up an invitation list. I chose Murawina, an Aboriginal preschool program in Eveleigh Street, because of its ease of access—right at Redfern station—and centrality of location for the Black community. I felt it was important that a book about the life of one of the Black community's Elders should be highlighted to the children of the area, giving them, perhaps, incentive to want to learn to read.

A Sydney-based Heinemann representative tippytoed around the venue, and rang me with his reservations. For over ten years the media had promoted the area as black and unsafe, and he feared white people attending the launch might be attacked. I tried to reassure him that this was extremely unlikely, that the mood of the community would be very high around this event, but the hesitation remained in his voice.

I rang Nick Hudson to discuss the issue. Wherever MumShirl and I had decided, he assured me, was where it would be held. He said he would make catering arrangements for about twenty to thirty people, advising me that normally only the family and interested friends turned up to these events. 'But MumShirl has more than a hundred relations in Sydney, and

there are hundreds more who regard her as "family",
and that's not even counting her friends,' I argued.

'Well, how many do you reckon is a fair thing?' he
asked.

'Five hundred, at least,' I replied.

I finally got him to up the number he was prepared
to cater for, though it was still not as high as I would
have liked. I was sure he was beginning to wonder
about the expense, though he didn't mention it.

Finally, I asked Brian Syron, with his theatrical flair,
to jump in and stage-manage the event in my absence.
He said he would be delighted, and was abuzz with
ideas even before we had finished our conversation. I
said I would leave it all to him, he was to go ahead
and do anything he liked.

MumShirl grew agitated about the book being
released while I was not even in the country. Couldn't
it wait until I came back?

'Why, Mum? There's something worrying you, isn't
there?'

'Yes. What if someone gets angry about something
in the book? Who'll be there to answer the questions?'

'Angry? Angry about what? Laurie's out of jail. The
police who set him up in the frame, they've already
been exposed in the Supreme Court, so they're not
likely to say anything. Who's going to get angry about
what's in the book?'

'Well, the Queen. She's a nice lady and I didn't mean
to offend her by having that bit in the book.'

In *MumShirl*, there is an episode about how, on
being invited to lunch with Queen Elizabeth II, she
arrived to discover a huge crowd milling in an enormous dining room, the tables laid with numerous
glasses and many sets of knives, forks and spoons at

each place. Intimidated and alarmed that she would not know which glass or piece of cutlery to use, MumShirl had asked for directions to the toilet—and then just kept walking, right on out the back and away.

'Mum, if the Queen reads your book, I will be very, *very* surprised. The chances are zero. And, if she did read what happened at that lunch, she would not be angry. She probably doesn't like having to have lunch like that either.'

'D'you think so?' she asked, relief rising in her eyes, but still the shadow of doubt troubling her.

'Mum, believe me. Thousands of books come out every year, and a lot of them say very nasty things about the Queen. I'll bet she doesn't read any of them. If she were to read your book, we would be very flattered—but the truth of it is that she won't.'

There had been many times when MumShirl's naivety had been touching, and it had often been difficult for me to predict what was likely to trouble her. Although encouraged by my reassurance, she made me promise to come back to Australia immediately if the Queen's lawyers threatened to sue her. I smiled to myself as I told her that I'd be happy to take full responsibility.

Pat Laird, whose Saturday Centre Press had published my *Love Poems and Other Revolutionary Action*, was pleased to learn I was returning to Harvard. She told me she had been very lonely since the death of her husband, Kenneth. As I had shared with her some of the trials I had encountered through having to take care of Naomi and also study, she said she would love to have Naomi stay with her. She would be company, an interest for her, another person in her home. She had a small second bedroom—would I please, please, trust her to do this?

There had been occasions in Cambridge when other parents had tried to undermine my authority in regard to Naomi. Some even went so far as to phone me when I had refused to allow my daughter to join a group of children who were going to somewhere called 'a haunted house' at midnight on Halloween. At twelve years old, I felt Naomi was too young to be out without someone I personally knew and trusted at this hour. I had heard stories about maniacs who put sewing needles and pieces of glass into apples and sweets which had then been given to children as Halloween treats. The woman who rang, a parent herself, was abusive on the phone. 'Everybody is going,' she told me, repeating the chant that my daughter used whenever she wanted to get her own way. 'Everybody is *not* going', I told the woman firmly. 'I am not going,' I hadn't been asked, 'and Naomi is not going either—and that's final,' I said, before hanging up.

I had been disturbed then to realise that the sort of behaviour I was used to, and the support I would normally have been able to rely on in a situation like this in Australia, was not available to me in Cambridge. Another mother in Australia, I felt, would have merely said to my daughter, 'Well, it's a shame perhaps, but you've got to do as your mother tells you, dear.' Certainly I had never before had the experience of a mother ringing to challenge my authority over my own child.

Pat's offer was, therefore, very attractive, and with Russel living only a short distance away, I felt Naomi would be alright there for nine months. Finding a safe place for her to stay in Australia would free me to immerse myself in the books and take as many courses as I was able in order to shorten the time I would have to spend away to complete my doctorate.

Reasoning that I would not need to be in Cambridge for the full Orientation Week, I continued to work until the last moment at the Health Commission. I wanted to amass as much money as I could, because I was sure that, as a family, we were going to need it.

Russel was acquiescent but obviously not happy with my plans to leave him alone for yet another year. I overheard him telling one of his friends on the phone, 'Mum's going off again to America.' From his tone of voice I suddenly realised that he had no concept of what it was I was doing there, how I was spending my time. He imagined me to be having a wonderful time from which he was being excluded. Naomi's version of her months away was not about study and books, but about the games and events Chet had taken her to, places she had seen, things she had done, and, of course, Disneyland. No wonder he was feeling a bit left out of it all.

As well, I would miss his next birthday, his very important twenty-first, so as soon as I had enough money set aside, I bought him a return ticket to Boston to use during his own university holidays in December. This shifted his focus, gave him something to wonder and smile about again. He began to ask about Boston, the long plane journey, stopovers, and everything else to do with undertaking a trip of this nature.

When I went to pick up the parcel of things Joe Croft had put aside for me, I found in it boomerangs, posters, small cultural gifts and a whole heap of other valuable stuff. Gary Foley, employed as Director of the Aboriginal Arts Section of the Australia Council, had also given me some posters and other items. With this collection I realised I would be able to organise a display in Boston about Black Australia to draw attention to my community's situation.

Martha Ansara had given me a print of the film she had made with Essey Coffee, *My Survival as An Aborigine*. Essey told me I should leave it over there permanently so that the vital information it contained could be made available to anyone who wished to see it.

Joe also had a small brown-paper packet waiting for me in which, he said, there was a special item, something similar to a bullroarer. My friend, Beverly, was to whirl it in the presence of her husband, and this would be sure to solve her infertility problem. I was not to be within earshot of it, he continued, unless I too was hoping to hear the patter of little feet. I did not share with him the unlikeliness of this happening. I had had the keyhole surgery of tubal ligation some years before, when I'd been advised that these procedures were reversible. It was a cautionary measure against ever again being subjected to conception through rape.

To apply for another student visa I had to supply a form from Harvard which had been posted to me. In desperation when it failed to arrive, I rang the Dean, Paul Ylvasakir. I was sure that the form must have been sent by sea mail. Now it was too late to send another, even by airmail, and have it arrive in time for me to leave at the appointed hour. Paul came up with a solution—he would have someone take a new form to the airport and send it over by pilot's pouch. I only later realised what an expensive exercise this was, for just one sheet of paper.

The form arrived, delivered right to my door, and I

rushed into the US Consul's office. My friend from the previous year, Ken Shivers, immediately came out to greet me. My visa would be ready next day. Even though things were still hectic, they were certainly going a bit more smoothly than they had the year before. Why, I still had three days to spare. I was therefore surprised to receive a phone call the next morning requesting me to come immediately to the US Consul's office.

I was again shepherded into the interview room. 'Did anyone come to see you while you were in Boston?' asked Ken, a little tight-lipped.

'Anyone like who?'

'You know who I'm talking about.'

'Oh, you mean those guys in the trench coats with their hats pulled over their faces? No. They didn't come. No one did. And when I went to extend my visa, and pulled my papers out of a Harvard envelope, I had no trouble with the Immigration Office there either.'

'Well,' he said, more to himself than to me, 'I wish they would fix up their end of the business instead of leaving everything to me.'

'The answers, in case you have to ask me your questions again, are still no. I am not now, and have never been...' I said jokingly, at which point he gave a small laugh.

'Okay, by tomorrow, I promise. And I'll give you a multiple entry visa, though you'll still have to bring your student forms in before you can travel.'

He was as good as his word, even giving me a familiar pat on the shoulder as I was leaving. He had been delighted when he'd learned that I was going back to do the doctorate.

I added his name to the list of people to be invited to MumShirl's book launch.

Too soon, then, it was time to go. This time, however, I had a fairly good idea of what I was letting myself in for, and my resolution was to get stuck in and finish my studies in the shortest time I could possibly manage.

10

As busy as I'd been before I left Australia, I had forgotten to let any of my friends know my arrival information. So after a flight taking almost twenty-four hours, there was no one to meet me. I gathered my suitcases, lead-heavy with all the cultural items I was carrying and, hauling them onto a trolley, headed for a phone.

Fortunately, my first call was answered. It was Sunday morning, Beverly and Robert had been invited to a barbecue that afternoon. Jubilant at my arrival, Beverly said, 'Jump in a cab, come on over. You can have a rest, then we'll all go on to the barbecue.'

Even before my head hit the pillow, I was out like a light. When I woke, it was dark. I saw a light in the stairwell which told me someone was still up, so I stumbled down the stairs and looked at the clock. Good heavens—the barbecue was well and truly over. Beverly heated me a plate of soup, then I staggered back upstairs and woke again about ten o'clock Monday morning. I realised I had slept through twenty-four hours.

* * *

All the rooms at my first choice for Harvard graduate accommodation, the Cronkhite Graduate Centre, had gone. But staff at the housing office said they could place me somewhere on campus, since I was alone, since I was a doctoral student. I was allocated a dormitory room in Child Hall, far across campus from the Education School. I knew I would regret taking it once winter arrived and I had to plough through knee-deep snow across the Yard, but beggars can't be choosers. We were permitted to paint our rooms, even given rollers and regulation paint to allow us to do so, and I did.

That evening I returned to Beverly's and, finding both her and her husband at home, I drew out the little parcel that Joe Croft had given me for them. Beverly was delighted with the gift, but even more so when I told her its purpose. She was, of course, sceptical, but with enormous gusto threw herself into whirling it, then made Robert have a turn, before she took it up again. The deep mystical drone filled and warmed their house. Later, they delivered me and my suitcases to Child Hall.

Dick Katz was immediately pleased to see me. Would I be a teaching fellow for his class this semester? he asked. I had made up my mind to do my doctoral studies under the supervision of Professor Courtney Cazden, in the department of Teaching, Curriculum and Learning Environments, or 'TCLE: pronounced Tickle', as it was affectionately called. Although I desperately needed the money the position paid, I felt I should concentrate on getting courses under my belt to count towards my degree. 'Perhaps next year,' I suggested. I was surprised then when he asked me if I would at least give a lecture to his whole class in the hall during this academic year, and I readily agreed.

The new batch of Master's students included a wonderful Black American woman, Donna Reed. Donna was Boston, born and bred. A single mother of an early adolescent daughter, Donna lived in an old apartment building in Dorchester. There is a bus which runs from Harvard Square, through Central Square, over the Charles River, and straight past one side of the Boston city centre, which I had taken occasionally. If I stayed on that bus, Donna told me, I would find it ran about the same distance again, and I'd be deep in the Black area of the town. I did so, in her company, and against the advice of some of the local students, and found myself in an area not too unlike Redfern, with its shuttered doors and derelict buildings. Donna and I often laughed that the distance between Dorchester and Harvard was about the same as the distance between the Black community in Australia and Harvard.

Donna's story was unique. She had gone to a ghetto school, where she'd become infatuated with some young man who was not a student but who had encouraged her to stay at school and to learn Spanish. She'd been depressed when, on her graduation from high school, with Spanish one of her best subjects, the man had made his intentions clear. He wanted her as a runner for a drug syndicate with which he was involved. His outfit could now advance because, with her language skills, she could go direct to the dealers in South America and they could cut out the middle man.

Donna, instead, went on to college, taking preschool education. After that she had set up her own small child-minding facility in her apartment where she looked after and taught the children of mothers in the ghetto who needed to get out and work.

Recently, however, the US Government had brought in new regulations, which required even people who ran small childcare operations such as hers to have a Master's degree, so she was forced to close down. The work had been a labour of love for her rather than a lucrative operation, and Donna went onto welfare.

The previous year, the government had also created a plan to get women off welfare by offering to pay school fees to enable them to better themselves. Armed with this information, Donna, quick as a flash, first got herself admitted to Harvard and then went to the welfare office and demanded they pay her fees. The women she dealt with at the welfare office were aghast at her audacity, not having such high credentials themselves, but there was nothing they could do to stop her. Donna had identified a loophole and exploited it, but it was quickly closed. The likelihood of another welfare mother from Dorchester going to Harvard completely disappeared.

Donna pointed out the irony of her studying at Harvard. 'I used to crawl around the floor doing finger-painting with all those little Black kids, and show them how to tie their shoelaces and do up their buttons. I have to get a Harvard degree now, so I can go back on the floor and do finger-painting.'

Donna became my close companion, although how she ever managed to organise herself remained a mystery to me. Her fees were covered, but her welfare cheques did not go far, and she was forever trying to get bus drivers to accept food stamps for her fare because she had no money with which to get to school. On occasions when she arrived for classes flushed and hyper, I knew she had come on the train and then, small roly-poly person that she was, somehow climbed over a high fence to avoid going through the turnstiles because she had no ticket.

Donna's life had been quite frightening. She, too, received no support from the father of her child and fended for herself in the tough neighbourhood in which she lived. After some classes, when she was 'flush' as she called it, we would go to a nearby eatery where she loved to have an Idaho potato. Although a short little woman with a definite tendency to be overweight, Donna was a keen dancer and performer, and well connected in the local theatrical scene. Despite all her hardships, she had a quick wit and a keen sense of humour, which made it a delight to spend time in her company.

Donna shared with me her troubles, of which there were, and had been, many. The previous year, she had been a victim of rape and, perhaps because I was a sympathetic listener, felt sufficiently comfortable to talk with me about it.

At the time, she said, she and her daughter lived in a first-floor apartment in a building adjoining a row of shops, almost opposite a subway station. One night a man entered her bedroom window, armed with a large knife, jumping over from the awning of the store next door. Donna had been in bed reading, her daughter asleep in the next room.

In response to my quizzical expression, Donna continued: 'I said, "Oh, do come on in, honey. What would you like me to do for you?"'

'What!' I burst out, shocked and dumbfounded.

'I had my twelve-year-old child in the room next door. What do you think I should have done, scream?

That would've only woken her up—no one else would have come. I didn't want him to know she was even there—or we might both have been raped and killed.'

'Okay,' I said, feeling very chastened. 'Did you call the police when he had gone?'

'He finished what he'd come to do, and was threatening to kill me if I told anyone, so as he was going back out the window, I said, "You come again, honey, anytime you want, hear me?" I knew he would just go over to the subway station for a while, lounge around, and wait. So, I call the police, they come, take a report, then go. Then he comes back and kills both of us so we can't give evidence against him.'

I was shocked by her low-key narration of this incident, which I found particularly chilling and appalling. 'So, did you do anything?' I asked, wondering how she coped with this life.

'Sure did,' she said brightly. 'I moved. I moved out the very next day, went to stay with my sister for two days, then got myself a new place. It's much safer where I am now, ain't nobody can get in.'

Donna took me once, when she had her rusted old car running briefly, on a tour of some of the nightclubs in her area. She wouldn't allow me to go into the toilets alone, in case anyone was in there shooting up. She said she was ashamed of 'her people'. At one club we saw all these 'pretty Black men', as she liked to call them, with their hair straightened and slicked down, dressed to the hilt in their finery. She pointed out an internationally famous boxer, whose name I have forgotten, but who was wearing 'fine threads' and a wide-brimmed hat as he stood breasting the bar. We made our way to a table to sit down and have a drink.

Soon, the wide front door opened and two policemen walked in, replete with big side-arms on their hips and silver handcuffs dangling from their belts. There was a noise like thunder in the room, clearly audible above the loud music, before a perfect stillness settled. The police walked through the place, studying everyone at the tables, then spoke briefly with the bartender before leaving.

'What was that noise?' I asked Donna when the place started to pick up again.

'That was everybody's pieces being dropped on the floor.'

I looked at her questioningly. She was obviously talking about guns.

'If you not carrying it, it's not yours. Police find some big ol' gun on the floor somewhere near where you sitting, honey, it's not yours and you've no idea how it got to be there. Musta belonged to the people who were sitting here before, them ones just left.'

Donna loved to hear stories about Australia. She had never met anyone from Australia before, barely knew where it was on the map when I met her. The more she learned, the more she wanted to visit, even come over to live. She read everything she could get her hands on about the country and culture of Blacks in Australia. The more she learned, the more frequently she lamented, 'I've always known I was borned in the wrong place. I'm an Aborigine, dropped by accident in the wrong part of the world.'

Donna, who had only once been as far as New York, suddenly developed a deep yearning to travel—but only to Australia. She wanted to see Uluru, which she grew to regard as the centre of the universe.

* * *

A few years after I left Harvard, Donna was diagnosed with cancer. She wrote to me constantly. On hearing that she was dying in hospital, I sent her a tiny envelope containing a pinch of red desert soil from Uluru. It had come from a small parcel which had been given to me as a 'thank you' for supplying funds to enable some Aborigines from the Centre, but living in Darwin, to attend the Uluru handover.

Immediately this soil was in her hands, Donna's condition stabilised and she went into remission. That very afternoon, just six hours after she had received it, she was allowed out of hospital. For the next six weeks, Donna danced and lived 'the high life', as she wrote in her letter to me during this period, and performed her poetry and sang at a number of public functions. She also wrote that she credited the Uluru soil with her 'miracle'. At the end of this time, Donna relapsed and died very quickly.

Another Black woman also often joined us, Deloise Blakely. Deloise was also a character, with a most unusual background. During her early days at school, she had come into Conroy Commons, put her hands on her hips, and announced very loudly, 'My name is Deloise, and I'm from Harlem!'. This gained the attention of everyone in the entire place.

It transpired that Deloise was not actually a Harvard student. She was enrolled at Massachusetts Institute of Technology, which was not far down the street, and she had cross-registered to do some classes at Harvard. Somehow, she had managed to get one of the scarce dormitory rooms, and became a room-mate of mine in Child Hall. At other times she lived in New York.

Deloise had been a nun for many years, before losing her religious calling and then having a child. She commuted constantly between New York, where her child lived, and Boston in order to attend school. I went with her once to New York and stayed with her in her tiny apartment, which she kept darkened with thick shades. This was to keep external noises and the like from distressing her infant child who was suffering from some severe handicap, the name of which was never made clear to me. I thought perhaps it was Down's Syndrome. Certainly, the child kept up a level of moaning throughout all its waking hours, and was severely mentally handicapped. Deloise had a woman living in who cared for the child all the time, so that she could study and could go about her business.

The building she lived in was in bad repair, and had, I understand, been boarded up by the authorities. However, Deloise had led a tenants' revolt. The result was that the people who originally squatted in this derelict building took over its administration, became responsible for its repairs, and to all intents and purposes, according to Deloise, they 'owned' it.

We had, against my better judgment, caught a late train from Boston to New York, arriving around two o'clock in the morning. When I suggested we should catch a cab to Harlem, Deloise wouldn't hear of it. 'You got money for a cab?' she asked me brusquely. I nodded, wide-eyed with fear from the thought of riding the New York subway at that hour and willing to sacrifice whatever it took to avoid it. Deloise whooped, 'Right—so we eat tomorrow', and dragged me down to the underground platform.

On the cold and dark streets deep in Harlem, I was sure we would be hit for the overnight bags we were carrying, if for no other reason. I positively tiptoed, anxious to make no sound to draw attention to our-selves, two women walking alone on the footpath, or sidewalk as they call it there. Deloise not only stamped her feet loudly, but she stirred every sleeping body in each doorway as we passed.

'Hi, there, Freddy. You still got that cold you had last week? Izzat you, Charley? Well, you go on back to sleep. It's just Deloise, passing in the night, okay?'

I could barely believe our good fortune when we arrived at her apartment building intact and still carrying our overnight bags. Deloise, however, was completely unfazed—it was something she did all the time, and usually completely alone.

Next day Deloise took me, again on foot, around the neighbourhood, introducing me to alcoholics, drug addicts and pimps. She also brought me into a con-vent so that I could meet nuns with whom she used to work.

When it was time to return to Boston, we were again walking to the subway with our bags when Deloise spotted a tough-looking youth with a huge ghetto-blaster on his shoulder, coming towards us. We had heard him coming long before he swung into view. I had been told a great deal about these anti-social brothers, gathering in doorways, playing loud music, blocking the streets, and attracting a lot of negative public and police attention.

'Hey, yes, you there,' screamed Deloise, gesturing wildly. He seemed to point towards one of the knobs of the ghettoblaster with one long thin finger, and the noise level dropped several decibels. Then he pointed the same finger at his own chest.

'Me, you want *me*?'

Deloise nodded vigorously. He sauntered towards us.

'Carry mah bag,' said Deloise. 'I'm a grown woman and you is a youth. So you be polite now, you hear?'

The youth took her bag immediately and began walking beside us. I could see ahead of us people moving out of our way as we approached them, he looked so tough and his music was still loud. Then he looked me up and down and made me an offer. 'I'll carry your bag, too, if you'll take this?' he jiggled the ghettoblaster. 'It's very light, sister,' he added when I seemed reluctant to trade.

It was light, much lighter than my suitcase, and his face broke out in a grin as we made the exchange. Suddenly I noticed that everyone was jumping out of *my* way and turning to glare at *me* as we approached the subway entrance. So, I thought, whoever is carrying the boombox is the baddie, eh?

When I next visited Beverly, I was delighted to learn that she had taken her tests and was pregnant. Robert grinned like the proverbial Cheshire Cat, but Beverly was very apprehensive. She had been this far before, several times, and each time had been devastated by miscarriage. That explained the roomful of toys and games she had set up in her house and had shared with Naomi.

While I'd been home in Australia, I had asked Russel to be my representative at the launch of MumShirl's book, and to prepare a short speech to deliver on the night. Perhaps he would even pick his sister up from Pat Laird's house, I asked, and take her so she wouldn't miss out.

I was unprepared for his brief phone call a few weeks

before the book launch. 'Mum?' he said when I picked up the receiver, and then, 'Nobody can look after her better than I can.'

'What are you talking about, Russel?' I asked, thoroughly perplexed by his defensive tone and words.

'I've brought Naomi home. I'm looking after her now. She'll be alright with me. I'll make sure she eats properly and comes straight home from school. I won't let her out of my sight.'

From twelve thousand miles away, there wasn't a lot I could do about it. I assumed there had been some clash of authority with Pat over something to do with Naomi, which had occasionally occurred even between Russel and me. Given the circumstances now, whatever they were, Russel had sorted it out the best way he knew how.

Russel was an excellent cook, very particular about eating only healthy food, and a fitness enthusiast. He had been almost a guardian angel to Naomi ever since she was born. After I became used to the idea of him taking care of her, I realised that if I had asked him to look after her, he would probably have felt it to be just another imposition I was laying on him. But this way, looking after his sister had been his own decision, and he was anxious to prove to me how responsible he really was. As well, recalling how lonely he had been in the house all by himself, I knew they would be company for each other.

Another phone call a few weeks later, and both the children's excited voices came clearly over the line. They had just come from MumShirl's book launch and wanted to share their high with me. Brian's stage management had gone wonderfully. He had organised the Wiradjeri matriarchs of MumShirl's age group to take centre stage, to participate in the speeches, and be presented each with a bouquet of fresh flowers, Brian's own personal extravagance.

Brian told me that the participation of the matriarchs had played a big part in the launch's success. MumShirl's story was, in so many ways, also the story of their generation. That's why he had felt they should have their share of the limelight. Not only had they embraced the book, but they'd brought with them all available members of their own large extended families, hence the big crowd. The only down side, he thought, was that the publishers had brought so few books to sell, just a couple of dozen, which had caused great disappointment to many.

Russel's speech had been brief, made to a packed room. He complained too that, although he'd arrived very early, every available copy of the book, *MumShirl*, had already been sold.

I later learned that a thousand people attended the launch. The event, planned to be held from five-thirty to seven-thirty, had rocked on until dawn, with the local Black singers and musicians taking advantage of the assembled masses to whip up a party and turn on a good night. At the height of the evening, police had even had to ban vehicular traffic from the street to ensure everyone's safety, because not everyone was able to crowd into the Murawina building and instead milled in the street trying to hear the speeches going on inside.

My joy at the news I had received while at home in Sydney, that Blacks could now become permanent in the Public Service, was short-lived. I received a letter from the Health Commission—part of my obligation

as a permanent public servant was that I should contribute to the superannuation plan. Would I please
therefore sign the enclosed documents and forward my
cheque for more than a thousand dollars to fulfil their
requirements to effect my change of status. After that
I would be required to make regular payments as my
share of the contributions to this plan.

A thousand dollars? Where would I get an extra
thousand dollars or so to send them? This was my
second year without an income, and I was looking
towards several more. I was living on the smell of an
oily rag anyway, with the little money I had earned
through my holiday work being eaten up by council
rates, taxes and small domestic repairs. I had thought
that permanency would somehow benefit me. Now I
felt that it was more likely to force me to abandon my
study plans and go back to work in order to make these
payments. Sick at heart, I wrote back that it was
absolutely impossible for me to pay at this time,
would they please advise me what that would mean
for me?

During each of my study years, I suffered intermittently
from bouts of depression. I struggled against the often
suicidal thoughts which had lain just under the surface of my normality ever since the trauma that had
occurred in my youth. I had taken courses in psychology and counselling, partly in an effort to find a key
to dealing with these dark moods which so frequently
descended upon me. But everything I had learned had
convinced me that only expressing and ventilating my
feelings and talking about the event and its consequences, could heal me. However, this was a therapy
which, largely for my son's sake, I felt I could ill afford.

I did not trust therapists to honour their obligation to keep such personal revelations confidential. Besides, my silence was such an ingrained habit by this time that I thought I would never be able to break it.

My psychological problems seemed to manifest themselves physically. Since the birth of my son, I had, several times, experienced pain in my lower back, especially when I was emotionally stressed. This weakness in my spine had been exacerbated, although they denied liability, when a Health Commission car issued to me had a roof so low I had to slump in the seat to avoid hitting my head on the ceiling.

At Harvard, this back problem recurred. At the clinic, I was referred to a physiotherapist, who told me I would need to change the way I walked to try to relieve the tension that built up at the base of my spine.

'Wiggle when you walk. Really *move* those hips, up and down, and from left to right, as you walk,' she told me, swaying across the surgery to demonstrate.

'Hey, no way!' I replied. 'If I were to walk on the street like that, I'd have every potential sex maniac within coo-ee using "provocation" on my part as an alibi. Marilyn Monroe might have got away with it, but film stars have a battalion of bodyguards. And look where walking like that got her—dead!'

The physiotherapist was insistent. 'You walk like you're trying to disappear, with your tail tucked in, your shoulders hunched in, there's nothing out there of yours at all.'

'Oh, excuse me. I thought you were just going to give me heat therapy or something like that.'

'I am, my dear, I am.'

My way of trying to deal with the depressions which triggered these episodes was to force myself to keep busy and focused on events that lay ahead. My son's pending arrival during his Christmas vacation was one such major event. My heart pounded with eager antic-ipation whenever I thought about it.

On my return to Cambridge, I had seen Don, who had kept in touch with letters and postcards during the three months I had spent at home in Australia. Something quite indefinable, however, had triggered my alarm bells, and I always pleaded pressures of study to avoid spending time with him. Once, when he had rung me from Bethesda Hospital to tell me he was driving back to Boston, I had gone to a friend's house nearby to stay the night. On my return to Child Hall next morning, all the students on my floor com-plained that my phone had rung non-stop throughout the night, keeping everyone awake. I wished then that I had anticipated this and unplugged it. But it had not occurred to me that Don's possessiveness would go quite that far. On another occasion, he turned up in the hallway, having convinced someone to open the door of the women's dormitory to admit him. Then he argued loudly and pointlessly with me for hours into the night, and I became afraid of him. I was concerned that a man in his esteemed position had been pre-pared to jeopardise his career and appointment at the university by trespassing into the women's quarters to accost me. What else might he do?

Fortunately, the answer was not much. Then I began to worry, as I had on a few previous occasions, whether the speed with which fear rose in my heart stemmed more from my earlier experience, when I'd been raped and an attempt had been made to murder me, than from any immediate threat. Still, I reasoned, I couldn't afford to let my guard down. It made more sense to move away from relationships that generated fear than to deal with the question of the source of the fear itself.

During my ruminations about fear and its effects, I was invited to a social gathering at a friend's house in Cambridge at which a dozen or so women were present. While we were chatting, two more women arrived, one of them so obese that her friend had to help her to walk. She took up the greater portion of the lounge, and the rest of us rearranged ourselves, and some sat on the floor. I was the only Black, as well as possibly the oldest woman present, and remained seated on a straight-backed chair which I prefer, next to the grossly overweight young woman on the sofa.

When our host served coffee and cookies, the conversation turned to, of all things, diet. As I had learned from experience that the problems of being too thin don't rank very highly in such discussions, I didn't join in. Instead I felt quite uncomfortable that this conversation was allowed to continue in the presence of a woman of such gigantic proportions. It seemed almost an affront.

After listening to different women speak about how they were carrying on their individual battles with the bulge, I was aghast when the woman beside me spoke up defensively. 'I am this size on purpose. Of course it's not nice, and it's certainly not fashionable, but I was raped when I was younger and looking like this, I'm sure I will never be raped again.'

'You made yourself so fat to avoid being raped?' One of the younger, brasher, women incredulously voiced the reaction, I suppose, of most of us.

'Yes. And I wear no makeup, and I'll do anything I have to in order to be as ugly as I can. And if a man was to come at me now, ugly as I am, and still have bad intentions, well, I'd pee in my pants. And that's only if I couldn't squeeze out Number Two. I've read up everything on how to stop men, and I'm prepared to do whatever I have to.'

This woman's response to having been raped repulsed me, and tears sprang into my eyes as I listened to her. Here, I thought, is an extreme response to fear. At the same time, her method of trying to gain some degree of control over her life and feelings of fear had had the reverse effect. In any situation, she was so obese that she would require assistance, even to rise from the lounge, and certainly she would be unable to run if she wanted to escape. By the preventative method she chose to adopt, she had handed over any quality of life she might have hoped to enjoy to whoever was her rapist. I wondered if she realised she had given up her life voluntarily.

This woman's words echoed in my mind. Perversely, perhaps, she had established an extreme against which I could measure my own response. I had already worked my way through a range of 'possible' responses to immediate danger, taken lessons in karate, weighed up situations before walking anywhere, all those sorts of practical things. From time to time I had been forced also to consider what long-term consequences can arise from having been the victim of men. I decided that a delicate balancing act was required, each situation, every relationship, every social invitation, every step outside my own front door, getting its own tailored evaluation.

Still, I'd concluded, I was not prepared to hand rapists my life. To meet someone who had, for all intents and purposes, done just that was very disturbing.

Although I had never been able to look at the world in the same light again after having been a victim, I did not wish to stay a victim for life.

I began to accept invitations to social events from a man I met at an Education School cocktail party, Kenton Williams. Kenton was from West Virginia and had a broad southern accent and many rustic expressions, which amused me no end. 'Hot dog!' he would exclaim at new or surprising information, drawing out the 'dog' so that it sounded like 'd-a-w-g', reminding me so much of MumShirl who used also to pronounce 'dog' in this way.

Kenton was then the Regional Director of the Department of Health and Human Services. He already had a doctorate, but was undertaking another Master's degree at the Kennedy School of Government. Separated from his wife, he lived in the Soldier's Field Harvard housing complex. He said he was very much looking forward to meeting another 'Black Orstralyian', my son.

Russel and I had made all the necessary arrangements for me to meet him on arrival at Logan airport. At an ungodly hour of the morning, though, his crisis call woke me. Calling from a public phone box, he told me he was in New York. The airline that was supposed to take him had ceased flying to Boston since his ticket had been purchased four months before. This left him no way to get to Boston. Staff at the company's flight desk had told him to go across town in a bus, which he could catch outside the terminal, and get on the shuttle. Apart from the few coins he was using to ring me, he had no cash and there was nowhere open to change his traveller's cheques, even if he knew where he had to go.

'Russel,' I told him, 'you go back to that desk and

tell the person working there that you have just flown halfway across the world, and that they are responsible for you getting to Boston. Be firm. You have a ticket in your hand which clearly states their responsibility.'

'Yes, Mum,' he replied in a tired, unenthusiastic tone.

'Oh, and Russel,' I added, 'it's alright to raise your voice. You hear me?'

'Yes, Mum,' he again replied, sounding a little more encouraged.

A few minutes later the phone rang again. 'Mum, I'm calling you from the phone on their desk. They're going to take care of everything for me, make sure I get where I'm supposed to be, and I'll be arriving at eight o'clock.'

Relieved at the resolution of this drama, I went to the dorm kitchen, made a coffee, took a shower, then rang Kenton. He had promised to accompany me to the airport and drive Russel and his suitcases back to Child Hall.

At the airport, as we stood waiting for the passengers to disembark, Kenton asked, 'How will I know him?'

'Oh, he'll be the one wearing no coat,' I replied. I had advised Russel to dress warmly but, knowing he had little concept of the bitterly cold climate of Boston in December, I had a good idea what 'warmly' would consist of in his mind. As well, he didn't own an overcoat.

Russel's face split into an enormous grin and his eyes lit up when he saw me through the crowd. We embraced, a warm hug, before Kenton handed him a scarf, beanie and mittens he had brought to lend him for the duration of his stay.

'What are these for?' Russel inquired as we gathered up his luggage and walked the short distance to the car. 'I won't need these.'

'Keep them anyway, just in case, okay?' I cajoled him.

Kenton delivered us to Child Hall and went on to work. I had earlier approached every student on my floor and asked if they had any objection to my son staying in our dorm. They were clearly delighted at the prospect of the additional security of a young man living amongst us, as we had all read of a spate of on-campus murders that had taken place in women's dorms in universities in Florida and other states in the south. More than one woman, going home for the festive season, had offered her room for his use.

Russel used the bathroom on the floor below, which was one of the men's dorms, to shower and dress, after he had given me the small gifts he had brought me from home. 'Breakfast, a bit of a walk around part of the campus to show you where I'll be, then into bed for a rest, get over your jet lag, okay?'

I took him to a tiny corner diner nearby, where customers sit up to the counter and can get breakfast all day, two eggs, any way, toast and coffee, for little over a dollar. It was his first taste of the life he'd seen portrayed in Hollywood movies, and he was plainly pleased.

The short walk to the diner, however, was also his first real exposure to the cold. As we had to backtrack to go to the Harvard campus, he said he wanted to go by the dorm so he could pick up the beanie and scarf. He brought the mittens, too, 'just in case'. Although he said he felt awkward, clumsy and 'goofy' in them, he soon discovered, as we all do in that climate, that warmth precedes glamour any day.

Recovered from his jet lag, he began to come to classes with me. Sitting attentively throughout, he said he was surprised to find he already had a basic understanding of almost every subject discussed.

I introduced him to my friends on campus. The Dean, Paul Ylvasakir, spoke to him in his office and later caught up with me. 'He is so bright,' he told me, 'we could easily find a place for him here.'

'You mean graduate school? He hasn't finished his undergraduate course yet.'

'He has a maturity beyond his years. Have you ever listened to him?'

My mind flashed to the 'did/did not' arguments he had had with his sister, and I replied, 'Yeah. Many times.' I brushed those thoughts aside, recognising that he had come a long way since those years. Besides, I was his mother and in my company Russel always felt safe to voice his uncertainties. That, I realised, was more a reflection on the closeness of our relationship than on his development. The problem of seeing him as others saw him was peculiarly my own.

I passed on Paul's comments, but Russel assured me that he would prefer to finish the studies he was undertaking in Australia. After that, he'd see.

At the dorm, he was a big hit with the young women on the floor. Raucous twittering always told me when he was in the kitchen, being plied with cups of tea and treats by these women who competed with each other for his polite attention.

He began to venture further afield, going out to different places with friends to whom I had introduced him. We went one morning to have breakfast with Kenton and his son at his apartment, both of whom stood around six and a half feet tall. We had the full American works of ham and eggs, orange juice, followed by enormous stacks of pancakes with cream and maple syrup. On our way home, Russel told me that he had felt dwarfed in their company. 'Mum, I'd be tall too, if you'd fed me properly when I was younger.' This turned into a blazing, though brief, row. I had done everything humanly possible to keep that child fed, without help, all those years, and his reproach was like a red flag to me.

Did he think Americans ate like that all the time? 'No, it was a special occasion, you were coming to breakfast.' Kenton had done everything to turn his invitation into an event Russel would remember.

On another occasion, we were talking with friends when one of them, in passing, asked Russel where he was staying. 'With Mum,' he replied, matter-of-factly.

'In the women's dorm?' she had continued, a tone of incredulity in her slightly raised voice. Russel looked at me, his face frozen in anger.

We were barely outside the building when he turned to me. 'How come you didn't tell me it was a women's dorm?'

I had assumed he would know. But I realised that he had spent his entire life in the company of women, his mother, his sister, his grandmother, Mrs Owen, and all my adult women friends, so he thought nothing of being the only man in a large company of women. Therefore he had completely overlooked all the clues which might have told him something about where he was staying.

His displeasure didn't last long, as the treats continued and the dorm-mates continued to vie for his company. He no doubt realised there were benefits after all, and he never brought the matter up again or demanded to be moved.

We were invited to Christmas parties, New Year parties, and family get-togethers all over town. We even went to New York where, at a fellow student's family house where we arrived unannounced, two more seats were cheerfully added to the already brimming table. We were made to feel extraordinarily welcome, as though we were doing them a favour to attend. Later, in an enormous basement especially decked out, there was dancing and even a hired barmen to attend to the thirst of the guests. Russel drew me aside. 'Mum, this is so inspiring. Each one a professional,' he said, waving his hand towards the beautifully attired bunch of Black doctors, medical specialists, lawyers and others so obviously successful in their fields, 'and not one white person in sight.'

We had, of course, been to all-Black parties in Australia, but poverty and unemployment were the norm, the common factor. I thought, God, I wish every Black child in Australia could see this, feel up close the possibility of pursuing a successful career, and be inspired and heartened enough to shake off their despair and chase their dreams.

Too quickly Russel's time with me passed. As I put him back on the plane, this time to Los Angeles where he had arranged to spend a few days with Ande, sadness descended upon me. Fortunately it did not stay too long. Russel had experienced the reality—the cold, hard work and personal sacrifice—of my time in America. That made his visit worthwhile and, as well, I had passed the 'hump'. I visualised each of my study periods as mountains to be climbed over, the first few months being the hard slog of loneliness, settling in for the long haul, and marked my calendar with the halfway mark. Once I reached that date, I was over the hump, and from there on, life was a downhill slide towards the airport and home.

11

Back home once again in June 1982. Confident now of completing the required coursework during the following academic year, I took up my duties with the Health Commission. A new Director had taken over, Dr Tommy Gow, and he asked me how best I felt I could use the skills I had acquired while I was away. I reflected on this and put together a training program in mental health and counselling techniques, assembling the most relevant pieces from all the courses I had attended on these subjects, to share this information with the Aboriginal Health Workers.

The program was to be run through weekly sessions held in the Redfern Health Commission building in George Street. Its success, I felt, could be measured largely by the response from the Aboriginal Health Workers in attendance, who had been turfed into the work of helping people without any real training.

I gave a session on non-directive counselling—enabling the clients to work through their own problems, come to their own decisions and assisting them to go in whichever directions they chose—with practical demonstrations and exercises in how to go about this. During the session several Health Workers broke down and cried. Muriel Hamilton was amongst those women who came to a sudden and painful realisation of her predicament. 'I've been doing things wrong all these years,' she told me. 'No wonder clients run away from the women's refuge—they didn't make the decision for themselves to go there. I did. I see it now.'

Elaine Walker, who was an exception and had been encouraged to take a number of training courses at mental health venues including Callan Park Mental Hospital, came up to me later to tell me that of all the courses she had attended, mine was the one most culturally relevant. It had hit all the big issues and addressed the differences between the needs of the mainstream and those of the Black community, and given practical and down-to-earth advice as well as supervision in using the information. I was mightily pleased.

It was time, now to put into motion my own special agenda, that of ensuring a line of Black Harvard graduates.

I considered people I knew whom I could approach, and who I thought would have the stuff it took to get through the study program. There was not just academic ability to consider, but also determination, guts, and the likelihood of their being able to maintain their enthusiasm through the long period of cultural and geographic isolation.

Finally I thought about Norma Ingram, or Norma Williams as she was at that time known. I visited her when I learned that she had left Murawina, the

Aboriginal preschool which she had founded. Here was a woman of substance, who had put her nose to the grindstone of work and survived immeasurable setbacks. She had taken the fledgling 'feed the children' program from its makeshift mobile home in a park, through to the Shepherd Street premises in Chippendale, made available by Leon Fink. She had weathered the political jungle, red tape and runaround until the Black childcare program was finally established in its own premises and became renowned as one the best of its kind in the whole country.

When I spoke to her, Norma was without direction for her future, and listless in a way that affected her domestically so that when I knocked on her door, I found that her house was in chaos. She lived in a tiny cottage in Eveleigh Street, Chippendale, the street outside her door littered with broken glass and debris. Since I had left to go to Harvard, she told me, she had been assaulted. Some fellow had climbed over her back fence and struck her on the head with a lump of wood, smashing her spectacles.

Norma felt the same way about her work at Murawina as I had about the Health Commission before I'd embarked on my studies: that she had done a good job but exhausted the extent of her personal knowledge. Each year had become an unsatisfying copy of the previous one, so she had resigned. Her marriage to Gary Williams was over and she didn't know what to do next to get on with her life.

Emotionally, Norma was stuck in a rut, and not a very nice rut at that, and did not seem to be coping well. Her accommodation was less than salubrious, she felt in danger in her own house with just her children for company, and her prospects for improving her situation, she suspected, were low, probably non-existent. I talked about what I had been doing at Harvard, how much I felt I had learned, and about the courses that would be available to her if she thought she would like to have a go.

The more I spoke, the more animated Norma became. She found tea, borrowed milk from a neighbour, and we settled down to yarn. 'You really think I could do it, eh?' she asked me a dozen times.

'Norma,' I replied, 'you could do it, you could get into the Master's program at Harvard and succeed. But you've got to be sure this is what you want, because it will be very hard to get there, and even harder to get through. But yes, if you set your mind to it, I think you certainly can. Look at all the things you've already done, setting up the preschool from nothing, and turning it into the great program it has become. Don't underrate yourself just because everyone else in this country does. When you get to Harvard and tell other people what you've already done, they'll be blown away. True.'

'But—it's very expensive, isn't it?' she asked, with a gesture around the room to indicate how little she had.

'If you make up your mind you want to go, and you do everything you need to do to get ready, I promise you I will raise the money. And when you come back you can help me raise the money for the next one. What we want here is a chain, a lot of people all helping each other to get through, until we have so many degrees under our belts that success becomes a norm for the Black community.'

Norma smiled, the seed of the idea already taking root in her mind. She would enrol in teacher training here, upgrade her study skills, get a bit of essay writing behind her. There was no hurry, I told her, I'd be back in a year to check out how she was going.

I had made a commitment which I intended to keep. If Norma turned out not to have what it took, including the support network to have her young children cared for in her absence, I would keep looking until I found someone who did. The money? Well, I had proven, through my fund-raising efforts on behalf of the Aboriginal Medical Service and with my own studies, that there was goodwill out there. People were willing to assist when they saw someone trying to have a go. I realised fund-raising to send 'Blacks to Harvard' might end up being a much higher barrier to have to jump, because educating people to understand that there must be equality at the top of the ladder as well as at the bottom was not something that had been attempted in Australia before.

Evan Sutton, my contact of old at the Education Department, rang to say he had someone he wanted me to meet. Peter McKenzie had been a successful applicant for the Aboriginal Study Awards and would be studying art at a university not too far from me. I met Peter and was surprised to learn that it was only after he had been successful in his funding application that he looked for a university to attend. He obtained a book of American universities which ran courses corresponding with his needs. Starting at the top of the list making applications for admission, he had struck it lucky early in the alphabet and would be attending Clark University, which was not too far from Boston. Could he contact me upon arrival?

* * *

Russel and Naomi had fared wonderfully in my absence, with Russel hardly allowing his sister out of his sight. So many of my friends told me that 'whenever you see one of them, you see two.' Russel had taken her everywhere with him, even sitting her up between himself and his current ladyfriend when they went to drive-in movies.

Still, she remained unhappy at school. Shockingly, she told me she was again repeating a year, and again at her own request. I was deeply concerned about this internalisation of the attitudes of her teachers, reflecting back at her their belief that Blacks could not achieve scholastically. As well, I learned that the eruption between Russel and Pat Laird, with whom I had left her the previous year, had not been merely a minor struggle for authority. Pat said she had been completely unable to cope with Naomi and had felt relieved when Russel had whisked her away.

I decided then that the burden of responsibility for Naomi's care should rightly be upon me, and that I'd take her back to Cambridge with me. It was never a possibility that her father, though he had re-married to a woman with children of her own, might care for Naomi, even for a short period. He had neglected his only blood child for so long that we had never felt him to be there for her. Russel was moving towards his final study years, his work load heavier, and he needed a bit of peace and quiet. If it took me any longer than I anticipated to finish my own studies, I told him, we'd rotate the responsibility for Naomi between us, year about, a suggestion to which he readily agreed.

Although an irregular correspondent, I received word from Beverly that her baby, a girl, had been born, and she and Robert had named her Dana. This was

happy news, which I shared with Joe Croft when I went to visit him at the arts and culture store. Joe smiled, a little smugly I thought, before passing completely over the subject and leaping ahead of me. 'When are you leaving to go back? I'll have you another parcel for you when you're ready to go.' Joe was a real sweety.

The Dean had made sure that all the papers required for my student visa were prepared in advance, and that I carried them with me this time rather than risk that they might, once again, be sent by seamail. Ken Shivers at the US Consul's office was beginning to feel like an old friend, and he came around the counter to greet me warmly. I had arranged for him to be invited to MumShirl's book launch, and bless my soul if he hadn't gone and had a wonderful time.

He told me about his reception immediately. 'MummaShirl,' as he called her, 'came right up to me

with her arms outstretched. She grabbed me in a bear
bug, and said, "You're the nice guy who made it possible for my baby to go to America." Then she took me
all over, introducing me to folks, and I was made mighty
welcome, felt right at home.' He seemed very pleased
to have made this connection into the local Black community, and I really liked hearing how he had been
made to feel appreciated even though I wasn't there.

Naomi and I were soon on the plane, winging our
way back to Boston. I had decided to return a few
weeks early, to settle in before school began. Kenton
had suggested before my departure that I'd be more
comfortable in an apartment, the bathroom next door
instead of down the hall, and the refrigerator a secure
place to leave food. Aware that I didn't have the
necessary documents to be able to rent off-campus,
such as a Social Security number and local references,
he had said he would be happy to share-rent with me
and would look for a place in my absence. So we
arrived to find we had somewhere to live, a fair way
out, at Fresh Pond. It was a little bare, although he
had already moved some of his own furniture in.

Naomi took over the spare room that I had hoped
to use as an office in which to write my thesis. I
enrolled her at Rindge and Latin High School, a bus
ride from where we lived but only a short walk from
the Education School which I attended.

The Dean, Paul Ylvasakir, was again pleased to see
me. Knowing that I worked at the Health Commission
all the time I was home, he warned me again against
jumping straight back into study. When I told him
Naomi was with me, and that we were living in the
Fresh Pond high-rise buildings, he picked up the phone

and called one of his friends who ran a private sports club almost across the street from our building.

'There's a nice swimming pool, sauna, playground, even a kiosk, and it's yours anytime you want to use it,' he said after replacing the phone. 'I've arranged for you and your daughter to have a month's membership free. By that time, school will have started, and it will be beginning to get too cold for you hot climate people to think about swimming.'

Oh, what bliss. Naomi and I wandered over there for a few hours at a time, several days a week. Although I could convince the body to veg out and soak up the rays, my mind continued to race, turning over every aspect of all the things I was trying to achieve by coming so far and being in Boston. I was reminded anew of the weight of responsibilities I felt I was carrying.

I was girding my loins for this penultimate assault on the workload for my doctorate. There were things I needed—tranquillity, a place to study, a desk upon which to assemble my work and write, and some form of relaxation. I settled on dealing with the most physical of these requirements first, hoping the rest would flow from there. I asked Kenton to drive me to the nearest timber yard, or lumber yard as they call it there, where I bought wood, glue, screws and screwdriver, a saw, putty, sandpaper and varnish, then went home and built myself a solid work desk. Although it dominated the room, the desk was big enough for the borrowed electric typewriter, my books and files, and some space left for looseleaf work.

Liz Fell, a long-time friend who worked at the Australian Broadcasting Commission in Sydney, had visited Harvard to make inquiries about the Neiman program for journalists. During her stay, she had introduced me to Phil Stone, a professor at the School of Science. Phil and I continued to meet socially from time to time, and once we had discussed spinal problems. Now he offered to lend me a rocking chair, similar, he said, to the one President Kennedy had used for his bad back. I was disappointed when he brought it around as it was in such poor repair, but this too turned into another hands-on project of the type that always helped me stay grounded. I stripped the woodwork back and painted it royal blue, bought cane which I soaked until it was soft in the bathtub, then wove a new back and seat before making bright cushions with which to finish it. I now had both my workspace and my 'relaxation'.

I had agreed to be a teaching fellow in Community Psychology for Dick Katz's class this year. I had anticipated being able to complete all my coursework requirements and teach simultaneously, though I knew that making sure Naomi was where she was supposed to be would prove a strain.

Professor Courtney Cazden was my adviser, and when we were discussing the program I planned to undertake, I told her that I intended being a teaching fellow for Dick. 'Well, there's no reason why you can't be a teaching fellow *and* earn academic credit for doing so,' she told me.

Teaching fellows hold down paid positions, so the idea that I could earn cash and academic credit was extremely appealing. I went to see Dick, signed the required papers, and told him that Courtney had said I should also arrange with him to have the experience entered on my academic record. 'Well, I don't know if I can do that. I've no idea how I'd mark that sort of work,' he replied.

Back to Courtney's office. 'Well, now you go and tell Dick that if you are still teaching at the end of the semester, then obviously you've passed.'

Courtney, who stood a good few inches shorter than me, was the most practical and highly organised woman I met on campus. She had became a good friend to me and later visited Australia a number of times.

Teaching fellow meetings were held in Dick's office prior to holding classes, and I made enduring friendships with the people with whom I worked, Rebecca Reichmann in particular.

Rebecca had a most interesting background and a wonderful perspective which she shared with me. An American, as a child she had travelled on a student exchange program to a remote location, Alor Star, in the rice bowl region of Malaysia. There, the local children hid behind bushes and giggled at tourists as they walked past, whispering amongst themselves about these big 'ugly white Americans'. Rebecca joined them, hiding in the bushes and whispering too, and felt herself totally accepted by the children with whom she played.

On her return to America, Rebecca confided that she took a good look at herself in the mirror and became disturbed to find that she was, in fact, one of the big 'ugly white Americans'. As soon as she had finished her schooling and was able, she ran off to South America, to another remote location, where women were valued for the hard work they had to do. Rebecca, being bigger and taller than the local 'nut brown women', worked hard in the fields to win their friendship and respect. After a while, though, and despite the acceptance she had won, she realised that it didn't matter how long she stayed or how hard she worked, she would never become one of the nut brown women that she so yearned to be.

Returning again to the United States, she consciously availed herself of all the privileges accorded to white Americans, and was in the process of completing her doctoral studies at Harvard. Meanwhile, and as her colour and status allowed, she joined the Boards of various agencies which, amongst other things, allocated funding to global projects. In this capacity, she participated wholeheartedly and, she said, when the other members of the Boards looked around, they never saw that they had a little nut brown woman sitting there with them. Consequently she had been able to ensure that the needs of the people whom she cared about, the nut brown women of the world, got their fair share of consideration and funding.

Although we received training for the teaching roles we were about to play, I was anxious about the whole procedure. I was quite used to getting up in front of an audience of strangers, giving a presentation, fielding questions and then walking away. However, I was nervous about this, my first experience of teaching an all or majority white group over an extended period, and being in the position to grade them. I felt unable to share this aspect of my anxiety with Rebecca or with her friend, Virginia Gonzales, both of whom had considerable experience as teaching fellows.

For quite a few of the students, too, a Black woman in front of the class was a novel experience. In the early stages I was uncomfortable with this role reversal, and noticed discomfort amongst some of the scholars. Was I transferring my nervousness? I wondered.

One evening, shortly after I had begun taking the class, I was approached in Conroy Commons by a white student from my group. He had wanted to ask a question in class, he said, but had decided not to do so. I invited him to sit down and tell me why. He had not been able to think of a way to frame his question, which was something to do with minority group response to stress, that would not offend me. We discussed his query, and I was able to answer and relate it to the readings, and he went off quite happily. His parting remark, 'I didn't want to get marked down, that's why I didn't ask you in class,' was edifying, and I thought it over for quite some time.

With reflection came the realisation that I, too, had struggled throughout my life, white teachers in front of me, to frame questions and comments in ways that would not offend them. So it was probably second nature to me now. Their grading of my ability to frame questions and answers in ways that supported the views they already held on matters such as race, and not my knowledge or academic curiosity, were often the criteria which decided my future. It was the same now with some of these students, who were concerned that I might misuse the authority with which I had been entrusted.

I noticed that not all the white students in my group were similarly restrained. It was soon easy to spot those students who had had Black teachers in the past and were comfortable with the arrangement, or those with Blacks in their social circle with whom they had developed rapport and a mutual respect. One such young woman, in particular, turned out to be the niece of Jerry Lewis, well-known comedian, who had come to Harvard from California to undertake her Master's degree. She spoke frankly about her uncle, the serious and private person who contributed much of his time and money to particular charities concerned with medical research for children. She said how difficult it had been for her to reconcile his public persona, as a pratfalling comic, with the man she knew and admired for his kindness and humanity. It had only been when she could see his stage work as something he did very successfully for a living, as a job, that she could make sense of her enigmatic kinsman.

There were just a few Black students in my group, but not all of them were comfortable with a Black in a position of authority, either. One, a part-time Master's student whom I had known the previous year, came to me after hours and said, 'I don't know what to call you this year.'

'I'm the same person I was last year. What did you call me then?'

'Yes, but you weren't grading my work last year.'

'I don't grade essays on the basis of what anyone calls me, in class or here at Conroy Commons. What you put on the page after you've done the readings and what knowledge you bring to bear on the question, that's what I'll be looking at. If it would make you feel better, you can switch groups—or I can have a second marker look at your paper if you're worried I may be unfair.'

'Oh, no. I want to stay in your class. It's so interesting. I just feel a bit strange, that's all.'

'Well, get over it. You didn't come to Harvard to be taught by Blacks? I can understand that. I don't condone it, but I understand it. We've all been brainwashed to think Blacks don't know much. I have trouble with the idea that I might know something sometimes too.'

The little extra money I earned from this part-time

teaching position eased my financial burden to the extent that I felt I could participate in a few off-campus social activities. Rebecca, Virginia and I went downtown one day to spoil ourselves by having a facial at a large department store. Never before had I had such a luxury, and I was quite excited at the prospect.

The beauticians took us each to separate cubicles, where we had couches upon which to lie and covers to protect our clothing. My face was whisked clean with a square of cotton wool, then a tiny mask was placed across my eyes to protect them from a steam machine which was run over my skin before I was left sitting in this steam environment for a few minutes. Soon a soft white towel was used to mop my face and a dollop of cream was applied, before the clothing protection was whisked off me and I was directed back into the lobby to pay.

Is that all there is to it? I wondered as I sat there alone, waiting for Rebecca and Virginia to join me. We had all been ushered into our cubicles at the same time, so I thought that my wait would not be very long. Five minutes passed, then ten, then fifteen, during which time the manager came by and saw me sitting there by myself waiting on my friends. I began to realise that, whatever the full beauty treatment was, I had not received it. My joy at having come on this outing was replaced with deep disappointment and embarrassment. The manager, too, realised I had been given short shift by my operator and came over and offered me a free manicure, no doubt as a gesture of apology. I declined. If the white women—and they were all white women—who worked in this salon were so concerned about touching the skin of a black woman, they should have put up a sign saying so, and saved me from having to pay for a service I so obviously did not receive.

When Virginia and Rebecca joined me, I stood up and left with them, and we were well and truly away from the salon before I shared with them what had happened. They had received twenty more minutes of indulgence than I had been given, and they became very angry on my behalf.

'No, I don't want to go back. I'll just never do it again,' I told them as we wandered between the counters making our way towards the front door. I was tearful with the emotional pain of the experience and unable to summon up the energy even to go back, as Rebecca and Virginia were keen for us to do, and demand a refund of my money.

Meanwhile, at her school, Naomi was discovering that Americans were more open about all manner of personal things than was the case with Australians. One day she came home so upset she was on the verge of tears.

'Mum, do you know that kids here introduce their brothers and sisters as "step-brothers" and "step-sisters". A girl actually introduced me to a boy today who she said, right in front of him, was a "half-brother". Really! Can you imagine that?'

I had, of course, heard these expressions in Australia, but only rarely. They certainly were not terms used in our family and I understood Naomi's shocked response.

'I would never call Russel my half-brother,' she said tearfully, 'and I'd be really hurt if he thought I was only half his real sister. You don't think about us like that, do you, Mummy?'

Putting an arm around her shoulders to comfort her,

I assured her that she and Russel were both my babies, both from that special place under my heart.

'How can they do that to each other, Mum? Put up a wall like that between themselves. How can they be so hurtful?'

'Perhaps they're used to it.'

'There will come a day in their lives when they're sorry,' she said, insightfully and defiantly. 'My brother is the closest person to me in the whole world, and if he thought I was only his half-sister, he'd probably take a step away from me—and then he mightn't be there for me when I need him. Oh, Mum, how can people be so stupid—and so cruel?'

This event had opened up a Pandora's box for Naomi, an exploration of the relationships between people, the love they have for each other, and how they demonstrate that love.

Not too long after that she again came in after school and mused around me. 'Mum, did you tell Dad it was alright if he didn't support me? All the other children of divorced parents get money from their Dad.'

'No, I didn't tell him it was alright,' I said shortly. This was an area I didn't want to get into with her, remembering how William had threatened to disclose to Russel the true nature of his birth if I pursued him for child support, even for Naomi. The very idea caused me enormous pain, and I did not want to reveal any of these things to her merely because some children at her school had set her thinking.

Still, I could see, although she hadn't said so, that Naomi felt she had a right to her father's support. The standard of living for our family had been compromised, we had lived hand to mouth all these years, going without and never having enough money for things we often needed. The way Naomi had expressed her concerns made me feel that I had been complicit in some way.

I determined then that, on my return to Australia, I would, belatedly—but not too late—go to the courts to try to get for Naomi what was her due. Russel was already a man, and I would not include him in my attempt for child support. I reasoned, therefore, that there would be no questions raised about him, as would have been the case had I applied to the courts earlier.

A child has a right to the standard of living that can be provided by both parents. Naomi's right, I understood, had been subsumed and consequently negated, first by the criminal circumstances of her brother's conception, and, mixed up in all that, by her own father's desire to wield the love he knew I had for both children in a way that would benefit him financially.

I felt skewered by the circumstances that had overwhelmed my life. They had so often forced me to take options that I felt to be in others' best interest but which had left us all somehow deprived. We had all paid dearly for the crime that had been committed against me—a crime which had had resonance for all of us through all these years.

I wept bitter tears every time I thought about all this, and often felt suicidal under the burden of my grief. Why had no one ever tried to help us? I sometimes wondered. but no sooner had this question formed in my mind than the answer quickly followed: perhaps because I hadn't been able to tell anyone, and those whom I had told had, in the main, betrayed me.

For weeks then, whenever Naomi saw something in a store she wanted, or asked for money for the movies or a treat which I could not afford, I spiralled into such sorrow and depression that she stopped asking. When I noticed this, I felt an additional burden of guilt.

Is there no end to this pain, no way I can work myself out of this complicated situation? I'd fret as I lay in my bed at night.

I became fatalistic. All pain passes—or else you die. I had read this somewhere, and it seemed right for the occasion. If I didn't die—as indeed I had not—then what was left for me was work. Tunnel-vision, that's the key, I reassured myself. Hit those books, study hard, concentrate on work, there is always another meal to be cooked, another load of washing to be done. If I can just keep going, one day I will look around and maybe the pain will have gone.

Fortunately, there were other distractions. Peter McKenzie, whom I had met in Sydney, came up several times from Clark University to visit. I found myself often quite cross with him. Living on his Aboriginal Overseas Study Award, he frequently turned up with boxes of winter shoes and boots, clothing and other items, barely able to stagger under his new purchases but without a penny in his pockets.

Kenton was paying off awesome debts he had amassed before I met him, and Naomi and I were living on a very tight budget as our money had to last the full academic year. but we had discovered an eatery in nearby Fresh Pond shopping complex where they served food cheaply yet maintained a nice ambience, and we occasionally went there. When Peter arrived, usually to stay the weekend, he could never join us to eat out there—unless I was willing to treat him.

We once had a very loud argument in a bus as we travelled from Fresh Pond to Harvard Square. Peter had convinced himself that the Aboriginal Overseas Study Award system was completely merit based, and that the committee's selection of him meant that he was somehow intellectually superior. Yes, he had a relative working in Canberra, and yes, he was on good terms with some of the people involved in the process, but no, he had been selected on merit alone.

I had already had similar discussions with a few of the Black Master's students at Harvard. It seemed that they were unaware of the history of collegiate integration, and also felt that their admission meant they were the finest brains in the land. I'd had the good fortune, much earlier in my time there, to talk with people who had been active in bringing about changes, even on Harvard campus, to force schools to admit both women and minorities, and to bring in quotas as a means to ensure their continuing participation. But this, these people had assured me, was not equality. It was perhaps a bridge to equality of opportunity in the future, but should not be mistaken for the existence of equality in the present. Had the Black Master's students with whom I had had these discussions presented themselves for admission a few decades earlier, they would not have been admitted, no matter how clever they thought they were, or were even able to prove they were. And just because they had been admitted now did not necessarily mean much more than that the quota system was in place. Equally as bright Black students whose applications were received after the quota was filled were less fortunate, not less smart.

On the bus, Peter's increasingly loud demands that I agree he had been chosen wholly on merit irked me. I sat staring out the window at the bleak buildings we were passing on this drab day until I could take it no more.

Turning to him, I said in a quiet and cold tone, 'Peter, if, as you say, the Awards are based on brains alone,' he perked up hopefully as I spoke, 'then how come the Australian Government would fund you to go to Clark, which most people in the country have never heard of, but would not fund me to go to Harvard?'

He was deflated. There was no answer, and I didn't expect one. From then on Peter was more circumspect in raising questions of this nature with me.

Despite our various disagreements, Peter and I cooperated to a remarkable degree in trying to raise awareness within the institutions in the area about the existence and situation of Blacks in Australia. Peter, a skilled artist, designed posters for several of the exhibitions I held at Northeastern University and other venues, and arranged for me to go to Clark University as a guest lecturer. He also took many photographs of me, at work, studying, writing, and used them, mounted and framed, as part of his study portfolio. When he had finished his work, he presented them to me as a parting gift.

On my bus trip to Clark University to give a lecture a curious thing occurred. I arrived early at the country line bus station, and indeed was the first person to board the bus. I took a seat about two-thirds down the aisle and the handful of people who followed took seats in front of me.

We were not far along the highway when a quite tall Black man came up from behind and, standing in the aisle, leaned over to speak to me. I was really surprised because I could have sworn the bus had been empty when I boarded, and certainly no one had walked past me.

I didn't understand the man when he spoke, though his voice was certainly loud enough for me to hear.

'I beg your pardon,' I responded, leaning towards him to better catch his accent. He repeated his words, but I still could not understand what he was wanting from me. I continued to ask him to repeat himself, which he did, and eventually he tapped the folded beret he was carrying in his hand on the top of the seat beside me for emphasis. I still did not understand his thick accent, but by this time I had picked up a slight air of desperation in his voice.

After repeating himself four or five times, he turned on his heels and went off towards the back of the bus again.

When he left, I kept replaying in my mind his words and his actions, trying to make sense of what had occurred. The bus pulled up at several stops, and more people came on board, until it was quite full.

By the time I reached my destination I had worked out, more or less, what the man had said to me and what his actions had meant. He had wanted either money or my ticket, and from the crease in his folded beret had protruded a small dull grey pipe which had made a muffled metallic sound when he tapped it on the top of the seat.

Two or three people from Clark University met me, and immediately asked, 'How was your journey?'

'I think I was held up,' I replied, my legs trembling from the realisation. 'Or, I would have been—if I'd understood what was being said to me.'

'Yeah, well sometimes people get on the bus and they haven't got a ticket.'

I watched the bus draw away and saw the man looking at me sulkily through the rear window. 'He'll have
trouble when it's time to get off, which is when they
collect them.'

Perhaps Puerto Rican, the man had been enormously
unlucky to have chosen for his mark someone who was
so unfamiliar with his accent, and he with mine. He
had seen me struggling to understand him and then
guessed from my own accent that I didn't have a clue.
The gun in the beret, as by then I was sure it was, was
no help to him, either. I concluded from this experience that sometimes it is a help not to understand
what's going on.

Usually if I was going to New York I would catch the
train, but once I went there by bus. Several hours into
the journey a Black man had leaned from the seat
behind to speak to me, but this one I could understand.

'What you got in your bag, Momma?' his voice
sounded suddenly in my ear.

I looked around, startled. I had a small overnight
bag at my feet, as I was to spend two days with a girlfriend, Mickey Smith, in Harlem. The man was of
indeterminate age, somewhere between thirty and
forty, I would guess, mouth unsmiling, eyes a-glitter
and something of a sly expression on his face.

'What are you talking about?' I demanded sharply.

'Oh, come on. Mommas 've always got food in the
bag. I'm hungry. You must have a candy bar. Won't you
share your food with me, Momma?'

'Well, you've really lucked out. If I'd known this bus
trip was going to be so long—and we weren't going
to stop anywhere—I probably would have brought

myself something to eat. But as it is, we both have to starve.'

Outside Harvard's campus, America, for me, seemed to consist of a whole lot of disconnected vignettes. All of them added a little something to the perspective I formed about that country.

Naomi's first semester at Cambridge Rindge and Latin High School went reasonably well. I would supervise her comings and goings, make sure she was always home on time, and keep food on the table. Often, though, I was too busy with studies, preparing for the class I was to teach, and researching and writing my thesis proposal to have time to really listen to her.

The high school consisted of five different high schools all within one large complex. Naomi had been placed in one of the experimental, rather than traditional, schools, where, I was assured, there were a good many international students.

After school hours, we seemed to carry on a running war between us, with Naomi straining to be allowed freedoms that I felt to be beyond her years. I knew I couldn't keep her locked up indoors all the time, but as our apartment was on the twenty-second floor, I didn't care much for her to play in the grounds. Our building was one of two identical high-rises, separated by a fence. It was privately owned and managed, while the other had been sold to public housing.

Naomi, when she was permitted to play outside, was always to be back in the apartment by the time the 5 pm news came on television. One day she came in a little early, her face ashen, and switched the television on even though it was not yet time for the news.

Shortly after a news bulletin came on: it transpired

that older youths often gathered in the carpark of the building next door, and on this day, an argument had developed. One boy had pulled out a gun and shot the youth with whom he had been arguing. Then, taking fright, he looked around and saw that many people in the vicinity were staring at him. So he fired the gun off repeatedly, killing a woman who was taking groceries from the boot of her car, and wounding several other bystanders, before bolting off. When this news came on the screen, Naomi began crying. She and her friends had heard the first shot, run to the fence to see what was going on, and, so I suspect, had been lucky not to have collected any of the other stray bullets.

I was aghast, this was not the sort of life I wanted for her. I was trying to build a better life for us all, get an education, and hopefully help to resolve some of the problems of racism and inequality that existed in my own country, so children like my daughter could have opportunities which had never existed for me.

From then on I determined to watch her as closely as I could. I eavesdropped on phone conversations she had with her friends, and met as many of them as was possible. Increasingly I became disturbed about the influence America was having on her and discussed this almost endlessly with some of my friends.

Many students at her school were the children of international scholars and staff at the universities, colleges and institutes in the area, but there were also a lot of local children. The majority of international students, it seemed to me, were white, and the school largely drew its Black student body from around the local area. While the friends Naomi chose from amongst her classmates were not exclusively from the

Black student group, a great many seemed to be so. At first I had been pleased about this. However, I had to reconsider my response when I learned that some of her companions were the younger siblings of dealers, pimps and prostitutes in the area.

When I complained to my friends and associates that Naomi could always tell me the current code names for street drugs, even though they were changed weekly, I was told to wake up to myself, this was 'real life'. Parents shouldn't expect to be able to protect their children from knowing these things.

I remained unconvinced. Knowing the street names didn't mean my child would necessarily end up taking drugs. But not knowing them would be an additional hurdle for her should she even think of moving in that direction—a hurdle I would have liked to see remain in place.

There was one more incident, a fight at school between boys, which I never got to the bottom of, but the upshot of all of this was that I decided to take Naomi out of school. This move almost completely divided my friends.

On one side, a whole host of friends fell in beside me, championing my stance and voicing their willingness to assist me with her education. I was given information about the Home Schooling Movement, which I learned to be one of the fastest growing movements at that time, where curriculum was developed for situations such as ours. However, I decided that the four months left of our States-side tour of duty was not really long enough to worry about formalising the fact that I intended to take over her education myself.

Other friends came to me with proposals, which

included taking Naomi for a day to their workplace and allowing her to familiarise herself with what specific jobs entailed, such as receptionist, secretary or computer operator. Others said they would arrange for her to visit private schools in the area. Chet came by often to pick her up and have her accompany him to presentations he was to give around town. I set up a schedule which included periods of reading, writing and maths each day, as well as learning typing, note-taking and filing. This may not be all that her schooling should consist of, but it was certainly preparing her for the real world of work. Also, it gave her confidence and experiences which I felt schools often failed to provide.

Naomi and I grew closer during this period. We coordinated our study and work so that we could watch 'Hawaii-Five-O' together each afternoon as a sort of relaxation period. I also obtained a month's free entry into a women's exercise class at a nearby gym, and we would go there to leap up and down and roll around on the floor, with Naomi being far and away the most energetic of us both. I felt this would at least do for 'sports' until we made it back home to Australia. Kenton also took her ice-skating, so she was kept fairly active and did not long lament the fact that she was missing mainstream school life.

An Australian election was looming in the future, and enough time had passed for my rage at the Australian Government to have subsided to a low roar. So I contacted the Australian Consulate in New York to make inquiries about voting. I received a warm welcome from Jeff Dixon, and subsequently from Adrienne Jones, and everyone proved to be very helpful. This was in contrast to my previous experiences with Australian officialdom.

Throughout the entire time of my studies in the US, and despite having an addiction for following global news, I saw only two news items on television concerning Australia. The first was about a drought in country New South Wales, during which kangaroos came into Dubbo and were filmed drinking from hoses in people's gardens. This had struck me as a sort of exotic trivia piece, news for when there really was no news.

The second news item was the election of Bob Hawke as Prime Minister. It was even carried as a small article in the *Boston Globe*, headlined, 'Australia Moves to the Left'. My memory of Bob Hawke was of him, some years earlier, turning up, very late and almost falling down drunk, to a lunchtime rally at Sydney Town Hall organised by the Teachers' Federation. He had been detained at an extremely long lunch with mining magnates, even though his fare to Sydney had been paid for by the Federation. This caused me to reflect quite negatively on what the media regarded as the 'Left'. At the rally we had sweltered in the noonday heat waiting for the key speaker. The crowds eventually drifted away back to work and the organisers had complained loud and clear about what they thought of Hawke's behaviour. People were even more disgusted when, after his stumbling arrival, he had refused to speak until a young man bearing a sign 'No Nuclear Hawkes' was removed from the crowd.

I was disappointed at the political changes that had been occurring in my country, where the Labor Party could take on board as a leftie and its party leader a man who had obviously been in bed with mining company heads, and for whom reservations about the danger of uranium mining on Aboriginal lands were not an agenda item.

Letters from my mother continued to arrive regularly, but I was growing concerned about her. Nothing major, just small things caused me alarm. She had always been fastidious about writing, priding herself on her spelling ability and keeping a dictionary or two always to hand, habits she had ingrained into me as a child. 'The object of writing is to be *understood*,' she had forever insisted. and I smiled to recall letters she had sent back to me over the years with words circled as misspelt, notes in the margins, like a frustrated teacher wishing to ignore the fact that I was over thirty years old.

Now, occasionally her paragraphs petered out, as though she had lost her train of thought while writing, and had not bothered to reread her missive before mailing it to me. Once I received, on two consecutive days, very brief almost identical letters from her. Apparently she had forgotten that she had written the first.

I awoke one night with a sick feeling in the pit of my stomach and my mother's image foremost in my mind. It was almost as though she had sent me a telegram or I had received an ominous message from her in a dream. I was unable to concentrate on my work all day, and the fact that the mail brought no epistle from her heightened my distress. It had been more than two weeks since I had heard from her, a most unusual situation. Still, my funds were always in such short supply and there had been a couple of unexpected expenses with Naomi's health, so I felt I couldn't afford to phone home. That was a cost I had decided I could only incur if there was a genuine crisis. A feeling of unease did not amount to an emergency.

During the evening Kenton became annoyed with my moping and lack of concentration, and he just picked up the phone and dialled my mother's home. When it was answered, he passed the receiver to me.

'Mum?'

My mother's voice came down the line, crystal clear, though shaky, over all those miles. 'A terrible thing has happened, Roberta, and I have just this minute walked into the house. We've been away. We were coming back along the inland road, the New England Highway, and when we were high on a mountain a big wind came up and blew the caravan we were towing right over the cliff. It dragged the car almost over the cliff, too. We almost died.'

Mum's voice trembled and was interspersed with an occasional deep sob.

'Are you okay?'

'All our things are gone. The caravan split open, broke into little pieces. The clothes and everything else we had in the caravan, they're scattered all down the cliff and there was no way we could get to them.'

'But you—*you're* alright? You weren't injured?'

'Sick and shaken. I don't think I'll ever recover. But— how come you're calling now?'

'I have no idea, Mum. I felt all day that there was something wrong, that you were trying to send me a message.'

'I did, dear. When I thought we were going over that cliff, that I was going to die, I thought I would never see you again and I cried out to you. Sounds silly, I know, because you're so far away and there's nothing you could have done even if you'd been there. But I'll be alright now, now that we've arrived safely home and I've heard the voice of my most far-away child.'

Who to thank for these premonitions, I wondered, as I lay in my bath, letting the warm water wash away the tension I had accumulated throughout this very stressful day. A vision of a thick coiling snake rose up before my eyes, a bush snake who had seen the catastrophe that had almost robbed my mother of her life. I sighed with relief. 'Oh, I am being looked after,' I whispered aloud to myself. Somehow I knew straightaway that I was where I was supposed to be, doing the things I was meant to be doing.

By this time I had become a bit concerned about the direction my work was taking, and I was keen to finalise the last few stages. I had heard from the Australian Council of Churches that funding to enable me to finish had almost run out. They would keep their commitment regarding fees and accommodation costs, but there would be no more money available for me to travel backwards and forwards to Australia. This caused me to panic and struggle against sinking into another depression. I had planned my abstract on the understanding that my thesis would be on the subject of Black Australian education. Without a research program and the input of people in Australia, such a thesis would be impossible. I feared that I would have to develop a proposal about a more accessible, but far less relevant, American-based subject.

As I was plodding wearily through the basement at the Education School one day, a tiny sign on the noticeboard caught my eye. It was an advertisement for a competitive travel fellowship, created to honour the memory of one Peter B. Livingston, administered by the Harvard Medical School, Department of Psychiatry.

I made a copy of it and took it around to ask friends what they thought.

The fellowship represented the only chance I had left to write my thesis on my chosen subject, Australia. If I could only win it, I thought, I could use the prize to go home, travel quickly around Australia interviewing the people I regarded as experts, then return to compile and analyse the data the journey had generated and write my thesis.

No one I asked about the competition seemed very enthusiastic, and Chet gently cautioned me. 'Schools normally award prizes to their own students,' he said, pointing out that the advertisement emanated from the Medical, not the Education, School, and he was surprised that it had been displayed on the Education School noticeboard. I went home from our meeting a bit disheartened. Chet held positions in both the Education and Medical schools, and I felt sure he knew exactly what he was talking about.

I scoured the noticeboard again, hoping that there might be a similar fellowship on offer from the Ed School, but I was unhappy to find there was not. So, I reasoned to myself that night, I am without options. If I don't apply for the fellowship, I'll be unable to go home. If I do apply and am not successful, I'd still be unable to go home, but at least I would have given it my best shot.

I wrote up my application, outlining the tack I wanted to take with my thesis, illustrating how certain common words, such as 'incentive', 'achievement' and 'community', are loaded with the values of whoever is using them, and how they are then not understood in the same way by people who do not share the same values. I delineated the power relationship implicit in

the government's use of these words and its relationship with minority constituents, who also use the
same words. I explained how individuals representing
both speak to each other without understanding,
always to the detriment of the most needy people who
have the most to gain. I also detailed how I would use
the funds to further this research, if I were successful.
This project took me two days, after which I posted
my application and crossed my fingers for good luck.

Over the next few weeks I received two surprise
phone calls, both early in the morning.

The first came from the Dean of my school Paul
Ylvasakir, just after seven. He had received bad news
overnight, and had sat up waiting until this 'reasonable' hour to call me. One of his nephews, a champion
skier, had just died in Switzerland—from a drug over-
dose. Apart from his wife, whom I had met very briefly
at a function, I didn't know any of Paul's family, so I
was extremely surprised by his call.

'I wanted to tell you this,' he said, 'because you
were almost the first person who came into my mind
as soon as I heard the news. I have to tell you—when
you took your daughter out of school, to keep her away
from drugs, I thought you were being, um, naive. But
suddenly, when I heard that this lively and lovely boy,
my nephew, just over twenty and never, to my knowledge, involved with drugs, died in this way, everything
you had been saying made sense. Drugs do not respect
people. My nephew was not a poor boy, not a Black
boy, he was a very comfortable white boy, but we all
thought he was a man. Now, he's just a dead white
boy.' I could hear his tears over the phone and I had
no idea how to comfort him, so I just let him talk.

'Taking your daughter out of school, it might not

work, but it was everything that you could do. You did everything that was in your power to do. Me and my family, we stood back and hoped our boy would find the right way of his own accord. What a loss. I know now we didn't do everything we could do. We didn't have a clue about this...' he tapered off, leaving his sorrow hanging in the air.

'I feel sure your nephew would not want you to feel responsible—'

'In the American way, I'm not responsible, but the way people were before this, oh, we're responsible alright. We were his family.'

'Paul, don't blame yourself. It's easy for me. You know the boiling frog theory? Well, I wasn't here while the water was getting hotter. I arrived to find the water hot, couldn't help but notice it and had to get my daughter out. It's a tragedy that, like so many other Americans, I guess, you didn't feel the climate chang- ing, but you can't blame yourself for that.'

A long silence followed during which I could feel Paul agreeing with me, although he didn't say so, then, 'Listen, I'm sorry. I didn't mean to go on like this. I just wanted you to know you've done the right thing, and how much I admire you for it.'

There was little joy for me in Paul's statement, the cost to him had been too high. I had never regretted my decision to remove Naomi from school, to shield her to the extent that I could from the culture of sex, drugs and violence which seems to permeate so much of American society. Australia was her 'real life', where the overtness and frequency of these things was so much less. It wasn't that Australia had none—I was well aware, from my own experience, that violence and sex lay close to the surface in Australian culture, too.

Through my work at the Health Commission I already knew the extent and likely growth rate of our drug scene as well. I spent the day sadly, reflecting on all this, and in sympathy with Paul and his family.

The second call, just a week or so later, took me completely unawares. An unknown, soft and cultured male voice asked, 'Roberta? Roberta Sykes?'

'Hmm,' I agreed, non-committally.

'I am ringing to tell you that you have won the Peter B. Livingston Fellowship.'

My mind spiralled out of control. Is this a joke? Who is this man? What's happening here?

'Roberta—are you still there? Did you hear me? You've just won the Peter B. Livingston Fellowship. Don't you have anything to say?'

'I'm...uh...speechless,' I croaked.

'Ms Sykes, that's completely unlikely,' he replied, humour dancing from his voice.

He continued chatting a little while I steadied myself, before asking me to attend a celebratory lunch. There were two winners, he said, myself and another student, a man from the Medical School. We were to meet at an expensive restaurant, and I wrote down the date, time and address. I knew my mind wouldn't hold these details, I was trembling and too over-flowing with joy.

12

I was assured now that I would be able to complete my thesis on the subject of my choice. With little to do apart from take care of Naomi and attend to her schooling, I had some time at last in which to reflect upon the kaleidoscope of experiences and impressions which I had amassed on my road up to this point.

Naomi and I had made many friends and had entertained many visitors during our time in the States. I recalled now the time when my friends, Sandra and David Bardas, from Melbourne, had called to say they were coming up from New York and would like to have dinner with me. I understood this to be their first visit to Boston, and Sandra had heard of a famous restaurant, Joyce Chen's, that they were keen to try. Would I meet them at their hotel?

When I arrived, Sandra was waiting in the lobby. David had been delayed and was upstairs freshening up and would join us shortly. Meanwhile Sandra and I were to go into the bar and have a pre-dinner drink.

I had scrubbed myself up and was wearing the most

respectable of my small selection of clothes suitable for the evening. Sandra was her usual fashion-plate self, dressed in a pale blue patterned outfit, which I instantly admired.

We found the bar and had settled down into the plush upholstered chairs when a crisply attired waiter approached us, his lip curled at the appropriate angle. Bending towards us he whispered, 'Madam, I regret that I am unable to serve you.' I was shocked. Was this racism I was encountering in the five-star hotel? But no. He continued, 'We are not permitted to serve anyone in denim.'

Sandra and I both looked at her gear, and yes, under those diamantes the fabric was indeed denim. Beneath his gently sneering eyes, we made our way to the door. Outside, Sandra said quickly, 'I'll run upstairs and change. Wait for me.'

I grabbed her by the arm. 'No you don't. I intend to lunch out on this for years—about how I got chucked out of a fancy hotel for being with a rich Jewish girl who didn't know how to dress.' We both cracked up laughing and just stood around giggling like foolish schoolgirls until we were joined by David.

At the restaurant, we caught up with each other's family news as well as the situation in Australia. Since arriving in Boston, I had sent their family Christmas wishes, using one of the Black nativity scene greeting cards I had been thrilled to discover there. Sandra told me she had produced the card at the dinner table and one of her children had eyed it curiously, a Black family gathered beside a gift-laden Christmas tree.

'Why has she sent us this Black card?' her child had asked. 'Does she think we are—?'

'We send her a white Christmas card every year,

don't we?' Sandra had responded. She went on to enlighten her brood. Surely, she reasoned, their reaction to receiving a Black card, which the children had regarded initially with surprise and wonder at its inappropriateness, might be akin to my own reaction at having received only white cards all my life. She had used the opportunity to set them thinking about how racism might sometimes be taken for granted.

During our dinner, Sandra and I began talking about the advancements in technology while David visited the men's room. When he came back, we were talking about computers, which, although I'd had only a little to do with them personally, seemed to be the way for the future. Although unable even to consider the purchase of one myself, I was urging Sandra to buy one.

'What would she need a computer for?' David inquired as he settled back into his seat.

I tried hard to think of a reply. Although politically active on behalf of the Black community, Sandra was primarily a home-maker. She had talked to me occasionally about her desire to write her family's history, but apart from that I could think of nothing that would make a computer an imperative in her life.

'She could use it for storing recipes,' I piped up, an idea that had come to me like a brainwave, but which would later haunt me.

'Hmm,' David said, obviously completely unconvinced.

Over time, Sandra and I both bought our computers. Sandra turned a room of her house into her 'computer room', from where she has coordinated a host of projects including major demonstrations by fashion designers against uranium mining at Kakadu National Park.

Two Aboriginal dancers, Lillian Crombie and Michael Leslie, also came up from New York to visit. They were studying and performing with the Alvin Ailey Dance Company in Harlem. They had been students of mine at the Aboriginal Dance and Skills Development Program, and I was really pleased to see how successful they had become, winning scholarships to travel so far. As I had no room for them at the time, Kenton had made space for them in his lounge room.

Their visit gave them the chance to touch base with me again, hear all my news and share theirs. We felt ourselves to be the only Black Australians on the American eastern seaboard. So it was appropriate that we should spend time together and discuss the strangeness of the environment in which we found ourselves and our responses to it. As well, they told me, the trip to see me was a very welcome respite from the rigours of dance training. They also wanted to see Cambridge, and it provided a very different view of American life from what they had become familiar with through living in New York. We spent a happy few days together, Kenton being amused to have three Black Australians chatting rapidly in his apartment in an English he claimed he could just barely understand.

Not all my visitors were so pleasant. During my first year Germaine Greer had contacted me, explaining why she had not been able to respond to my letter inquiring about funding, and advising me that she was coming briefly to Boston. Would I be interested in coming to a dinner? She said there would be someone there she thought I ought to meet, Professor Dana Chandler.

I was already quite friendly with Dana Chandler, who

was the Director of the African-American Arts program at North-Eastern University, and we had plans underway for an exhibition of Aboriginal protest posters and other cultural material. Still, I thought it would be a nice evening and decided to attend.

The meal was very pleasant and included lots of fare which I could not otherwise afford. As well, I had the opportunity to chat with Dana and meet some other white people.

Afterwards Germaine organised for someone to drive me back home. There were several of us in the car when I asked if she had received the copy of *Love Poems and Other Revolutionary Actions*, which I had included with my letter.

This question seemed to trigger Germaine off. She

roundly berated me about my publication, scornfully saying 'You call *that* poetry? It's not poetry at all.'

'Well, Judith Wright seems to think so. She wrote to me several times and told me herself that—'

'She's a better expert than me?' Germaine's voice was harsh and shrill, and I was embarrassed that she felt she could talk to me like this in front of a carful of her white friends. I had never seen before what I'd heard described as a 'Greer tantrum', but this time I was the recipient of both barrels.

Well, I wonder what caused all that, I mused to myself as I made my way across the courtyard to my building. Perhaps I said something that offended her earlier in the night, but screaming at me on the way home about my poetry made no sense at all.

It was no surprise, indeed somewhat of a relief, that I did not hear from Germaine again. Years would pass before I was to gain an insight into the subliminal reason behind the behaviour she exhibited that night—which had far more to do with racism and its myriad manifestations than poetry.

Over the next decade I was, sadly, to discover that many of the mixed-race friendships, particularly with white Australian women, which I had thought of as being mutually supportive, were regarded by the other person as a way of patronising me. My attendance at Harvard, I realised, threatened this view they had of themselves and these relationships inevitably broke down. This was to be a hard lesson; white Australians, in general, have no history of dealing with Blacks as equals, a problem which, to this very day, has not been overcome.

During the time that Naomi spent in Cambridge, she had maintained her own relationships with people at home by writing letters and sending postcards. Once she became a teenager, she often kept these activities quite secret from me. I knew about them, of course, but girls of that age like to exercise their independence. One of the ways in which they do that is by keeping secrets and rationing out information as though it were currency.

I was therefore surprised when Naomi told me that Mrs Owen was arriving in Boston to see her. Mrs Owen had grown from an occasional babysitter when Naomi was five years old to something akin to a grandmother-by-proxy. I knew Mrs Owen to be thrifty, always living on a tight budget and saving her few cents, but that she would save up to come halfway around the world to visit Naomi, well, I was fairly blown away by that.

A genuine and enduring affection had sprung up between her and the children, particularly Naomi, who had often stayed over at Mrs Owen's house for no apparent reason, other than, I thought, that Mrs Owen made her cakes and treats, and gave her the little attentions which, time-wise, I could not afford. Because of her kindness, I had encouraged the children to include Mrs Owen on our family Christmas gift list.

I smiled when I dropped Naomi over to the motel at which Mrs Owen was staying so that they could spend time together. I was grateful for the normality that her visit injected into our geographic isolation, and appreciative of the financial cost this visit must have incurred. The world, I thought, is a small place when people determine that it will be so, as Mrs Owen had obviously done. Naomi, however, took it all in her stride, seeing absolutely nothing unusual in someone who cared about her travelling so far to be, so briefly, with her.

During my stay I had taken very few trips around, the budget not running to much. Bernard Jackson, from the Inner City Cultural Centre, whom I had met in Los Angeles, accepted a short contract in New York and sent me a plane ticket to come down and visit him. He had been intrigued that someone he knew was actually going to Harvard, and he said he would welcome the opportunity to chat, since we were now only a few hundred miles apart.

I found Jack, as he preferred to be called, to be one of those philosophical and learned old men one is rarely privileged to meet in this life. Had he lived in the Black community in Australia he would have been regarded as an Elder.

Our meeting took place at a time when America was making a great to-do about another space mission. I had learned from scientists working at Massachusetts Institute of Technology and elsewhere, with whom I occasionally socialised, that the US Government seemed to be moving towards the development of space mansions, places where the ultra-rich would go to live, free from the pollution they had created on this globe as they had amassed their riches. Those of us, the majority left on earth, I thought, would be the proles, servicing these mansions and living in nasty conditions created by global warming and toxic emissions. Manned space ships were the first step towards developing space taxis, and other experiments were under way to explore the feasibility of completely recycling and self-sustaining mini-communities, which could exist in bubbles with artificial climate control.

I shared my concerns with Jack as he was one of the few people I knew with whom I could discuss these ideas. 'What also bothers me,' I said, 'is the complete

absence of Blacks in these programs. Are we all destined to be proles?' I had previously asked Chet Pierce,
whose job as a scientific consultant at NASA, I understood, was to make the final selection of astronauts,
why no Blacks had been sent into space.

'Black candidates have been eliminated, for one
reason or another, long before I ever get to see who
the finalists are,' he had informed me. 'Each crop starts
with several hundred, and some don't make the physical, others can't stand up to weightlessness, others
might not have the right mix of skills—all sorts of reasons. When I'm called in, there are perhaps only half
a dozen left, and they are all white by this time.'

'The Russians have already sent a Black man into
space, a Cuban,' Jack told me. 'There was not a word
about it in any of the American papers, of course.
Cubans lined up on the beach and danced and waved
as their satellite was going over, and it was even in
the Cuban newspapers on sale on the newsstands. But
then, you don't read Spanish, do you?'

'Jack, if Australia had had its way, I wouldn't be able
to read English, much less Spanish. No, Australia is
so monolingual, I'm ashamed to say. But perhaps
things will change in the future.'

'Hey,' I said, jubilant with the information Jack had
just shared with me, and happy to have a fellow traveller with whom to chat about the big questions of our
universe, 'did you see a movie called *The Spook Who Sat
By The Door*?' Based on the book of the same name by
Sam Greenlee, the story was about how the FBI had
continued to exclude Blacks long after compulsory
integration had been brought in. Eventually one agent
came along who was so able that, in the prevailing
political climate, he could not be ignored. The FBI had

attempted, as had been the fashion in those days, to put him, the only Black candidate they had ever let enter the Bureau, in a glass office so that everyone could see they had a Black on board, but to give him a job just working the photocopier. Instead, the Black agent had amassed a bank of organisational skills and taken these out into the streets where he put together a Black army, based on FBI methodology. With it he threatened the establishment, using their own weapons, unless equality of opportunity became a reality.

'Yes, and read the book,' replied Jack, 'but I'm surprised you have. Doesn't seem like the sort of thing that would be readily available in Australia.'

'No, but we have our ways.'

'Yes, and what we need now is another spook. Someone who will get us into the space program, ensure we don't all end up as proles. You'll see,' Jack continued prophetically, 'the US space program will put a dog and even a white woman up into space long before they consider a Black man.'

Later, when the Black community organised a demonstration in Washington DC to support the call for the declaration of a national holiday to honour Martin Luther King Junior, I along with hundreds of other students, Black and white, jumped on the train to attend. Here was a man whose influence had extended much further than the shores of the United States, and whose assassination had shocked the world. I wanted to take the opportunity to see and feel for myself the solidarity that his name engendered, and I was not at all disappointed.

From my vantage point high on a hill overlooking the square, but unfortunately out of earshot of most of the speakers, I could still sense the excitement and feeling of quest. Thousands of Americans of all races and all religions gathered, shoulder to shoulder as far as the eye could see, to demand that the nation should honour this great man.

Around me sat many families, far enough away from the centre of activity to protect their young children from the milling crowd, yet hoping to ensure that these youngsters would remember their participation in this as part of the struggle for equality. The segregation signs, marking out water fountains, toilets and schools as being either for Black or white—but not both—had long since disappeared, though not without bloodshed and great loss of life. But there was tacit acknowledgment, by the appearance of such a great mass of people, that racism was by no means dead.

I had witnessed many things during my time in Boston that I had found quite remarkable. At an award presentation held by the National Association for the Advancement of Colored People (NAACP), I had seen an audience of Blacks weeping with sympathy when the parents of a white youth, who had lost his life defending a Black stranger whom he had seen being beaten up by a group of white men, was presented with the association's highest award. On another occasion, I had been talking with friends at a Black restaurant when Michael Dukakis called in. He was running for some political office, having earlier lost his governorship. As he made his way around the room, chatting and shaking hands with each of us, including all the staff, it was obvious that the Black vote, even here in the north, was a sufficiently motivating incentive for political leaders to wish to court it.

So, struggle with it though I had, I'd found it difficult

to make patterns emerge from North American race relations. A Black woman told me wryly that desegregation laws had forced the integration of buses, schools and workplaces, so that Black and white now spent their weekdays together, but that voluntary segregation was still the practice of the land, on the Sabbath, when each group trooped off to their separate churches. 'The Lord cannot be very pleased,' the woman had told me. I mused over this as I contemplated, and tried to make sense of, the enormous mixed crowd that had gathered there to honour a Black man on that memorable day.

The chasm between groups of people, and the search for ways to overcome it, continued to attract my attention in many other ways.

Shorty O'Neil, an Aboriginal colleague, was based in London for a year as part of a community effort, which was continued for some time, to try to maintain a presence in the United Kingdom and Eastern Europe through which to heighten awareness of Black Australia's problems.

Though I had met him only briefly in Australia, Shorty wrote to me often, long letters of his trials and tribulations, which stemmed from his isolation. He was a classic 'character' in no small measure. He was determined to maintain his 'Australianness' yet to also somehow, by whatever means possible, get his message across.

He wrote to me, initially, of his desperation in that cold English winter. Shorty, like me, had spent most of his life in Australia's torrid north, so I could empathise with his plight. Despite his poor spelling and often complete absence of punctuation, I found the imagery he shared with me in his letters about his current life extremely compelling.

He was not, so he told me, able to give up wearing his rubber thongs, because his feet were so hardened from going barefoot that thongs were the most he could tolerate. He also had very little money, certainly not enough to spend on warm clothing. Instead, in his little flatette, which did not enjoy central heating, he put on all his garments at once, clothes over his pyjamas. He then looped cord and belts around the little single-bar heater, his only source of warmth, so that it dragged along behind him as he walked around his place to make himself a cup of tea.

Then quite suddenly, his fortunes seemed to briefly improve. He wrote to me that he had been to Europe, where he had socialised with the landed gentry and sat drinking and chatting over several days and nights with a baronet. As I deciphered it, his letter in part read: 'The Europeans are more open to learning about our situation than the English. Probably this is because they don't feel it was their ancestors who are responsible, and they are free from guilt so they can accept it more.'

Not long after that I was asked if I could meet up with an Aboriginal delegation arriving in New York City. From there we were to be bussed to the home of the Six Nations, at Oonandaga, in upper New York State, before being taken to Washington DC for a conference on Indigenous peoples. While waiting in New York for the arrival of the group, I was invited to attend an exhibition about Black Australia.

Imagine my surprise to see coming towards me in this salubrious setting a vaguely familiar face. One quick glance at his feet, wearing his trademark thongs, and I recognised him immediately as my London correspondent!

Shorty had brought with him a large Aboriginal land rights flag, and as other delegates came out from the plane after their long journey, we held it aloft and they fell upon us with glee. This was a particularly exciting event for me, being with so many of my countryfolk. For so long I had been the only Black Australian on the entire east coast of America. Although I only knew some of the delegates slightly, and many of them not at all, we immediately fell in together and soon we were singing and making jokes as we were driven to our destination.

The Six Nation Indians welcomed us solemnly and took us into their homes. Their community appeared comparatively isolated, but they were not immune, so I was informed by my hosts, to the problems of alcoholism and alcohol-related violence faced by Indigenous communities everywhere. For this reason, a couple of wonderful Indian women took it upon themselves to accompany me wherever I went, and I can only guess that the same consideration and courtesy was extended to everyone else in our party.

Those of us who were not too exhausted were driven around the grounds and proudly shown the herd of buffalo which the Indians were reviving. Their traditional food had been almost made extinct by the white man, and this was one of the many ways in which they were going about their cultural revival. When the herd reached a certain size, a young pair was given as a gift to other tribes who were without any buffalo, so that they could also begin to breed their own herds.

A long ceremonial building had been built from solid wood, and stood majestically at the centre of their complex. It was here that we gathered during the days and in the evenings for many warm welcomes, introductions and cultural presentations. In honour of our visit, the Indians had slaughtered one of their precious buffalo, and we were treated to a range of foods containing this meat. It was not difficult to tell from the trouble they had taken with their preparations how much they appreciated that our delegation from halfway around the world had come to visit them.

In our party, as well as Shorty O'Neil, there was Pat Dodson, still a Catholic priest at the time, Yami Lester, Barbara Shaw, with traditional people from the Kimberleys and, as I recall, also the Centre, to complete the group. There were also one or two Balanda, though their names escape me.

Our visit being concluded, we were taken via an inland route to Washington DC, along a highway which provided us with a tremendous spectacle of autumn foliage in many earthy hues. I had already seen a little of this deciduous treat, so different from the countryside I was used to. Shorty told me that it made him feel uncomfortable to see the trees dying like this, even though he knew they would come alive again in spring.

We had barely reached Washington DC when I came down with a severe cold and fever, and had trouble keeping up with all the presentations and social events that had been planned for us. I felt a bit guilty to be missing things. Yami was also not feeling too well and some of the traditional people in our party felt obliged to stay with him in his room and keep him company. Yami, who had been blind since his childhood as a result of exposure to the Maralinga bombing in his traditional homelands, said he had not enjoyed the trip. He had been unable to see the things we saw and to him, the travel had meant just a great deal more noise than he was used to after the quiet of his Central Desert abode. As well, he was unable to identify all the sounds about him or make out what these unfamiliar sounds meant. I was suddenly struck with an understanding of what life outside the perimeters of home must mean to a person without sight. This knowledge was frightening to me because my mother's mother had been blind and my own mother had been seeking out specialists to deal with her increasing blindness. Would my own world shrink as time passed, or would technology and medical advances come to my aid in the future and save me?

Another time, I was approached by Native American friends to ask if I would be willing to chair the international panel at a conference they were hosting at the Harvard Law School. When I agreed, they told me they would be back in touch with me shortly.

The conference dates drew near, and I was becoming concerned that I had heard nothing more when I received a phone call. 'Do you,' a man asked after introducing himself, 'wish to pull out? We would understand if you do.'

'Why would I want to do that?'

'Have you had any death threats?'

'What! What are you talking about? Death threats? What sort of death threats?'

'Well, there's been a bit of trouble. I thought you may have heard. Jewish students around the school have been objecting to the conference. They put pressure on the Dean of the Law School to try to make him ban the conference, said the Jewish alumni would stop giving money to the school. The Dean's withdrawn from opening the conference, but he hasn't banned us from going ahead. Are you still prepared? Can we count on you? There's probably going to be a demonstration against us. Will you mind?'

Well, this is a strange turn of events, I thought, when Jewish people demonstrate against Native Americans.

'What's this all about?'

'It's your panel, actually. The international session. We've invited a representative from the PLO to attend.'

'Oh, okay. That makes a bit more sense. But no, you're the Indigenous people of this country, and you've a right to invite anybody you want to your conference. I'll be there.'

The day dawned, and I was due at the Law School at 10.30 for my briefing; my panel was to begin at midday. As I was making my way through the Yard, some Indians whom I did not know hailed me.

'Come back in an hour. We're running an hour behind schedule. Security's been holding everything up. There's been a bomb threat and now they've got metal detectors on the doors and everything.'

'Oh, okay,' I replied, and wandered over to a nearby coffee shop in Harvard Square to kill some time.

Exactly an hour later I again headed around through the Yard. At the front door to the Law School, a demonstration was in progress and Security was keeping the demonstrators from blocking the door. The protesters were orderly, I can say that about them, as they marched around in a circle with their placards, although I was really annoyed to see anti-Indian signs being held high in the air.

As well as using metal detectors, Security were searching people at the door. I identified myself as the Chairperson and was immediately whisked upstairs to a room where some of the participants on my panel were already seated. Harvard detectives, coats off and shoulder holsters with guns on display, lounged around, gazing out the window, checking the halls and answering the door when anyone knocked. Those panellists who had arrived seemed very relaxed and were making jokes about what we might expect. I was introduced to the group and we began to make plans about how to run the agenda.

All our eyes turned when a sharp rap on the door announced the arrival of the one person still missing, the PLO representative. A very young white girl, slender and attractive though otherwise quite nondescript, entered, with an armed escort provided by Harvard preceding her.

'Uh, you're from the PLO?' I asked her, quite amazed that such a to-do was being made over someone so seemingly innocent.

'Well, I'm an assistant at the PLO Mission to the United Nations, and I've been sent up here to represent the Mission today,' she replied with a typical mid-western American accent. I almost fell about laughing.

'Have you been to the Middle East?' I asked.

'No. I just work at the United Nations Mission. I don't know what all this fuss is about. I'm an American.'

None of us present, we found as we talked amongst ourselves, knew what the fuss going on outside was about either. A young American woman arrives to talk about the policies of an agency which has accreditation status at the United Nations, and the Jewish students decide to take offence?

The hall where we were to give the presentation was very formal and imposing, and we were accompanied on our short walk through the building by our armed guards. It all felt very strange.

Still, the panel ran smoothly, with me opening and introducing, acting as time-keeper, and summarising and closing. I was also required to advise the audience during my opening speech that, under the circumstances, we could only accept questions in writing following the presentations. None of the panellists raised anything that I regarded as controversial. I suppose I would not have necessarily objected if they had, but the goals for equity and equality of participation in international relations and affairs were quite standard fare.

Later, some Indian friends and I went off to have a drink, leaving the demonstrators still circling outside the Law School.

'You're the only one, then, who didn't personally receive a death threat,' I was informed by one of my smiling companions. 'We had posters all over the school. I think they scoured the student enrolment at the Law School, probably even the Kennedy School, for your name, and when they couldn't find it, they must have thought you were coming in from outside.'

This was very possible. Perhaps the student body did not see the Education School as a hotbed of political activism from whence a chairperson for such a panel would be likely to be drawn.

The conference had been judged by the organisers, despite all the upsets, to have been very successful. When it was over we discussed the attempts made to suppress academic freedom of expression, a value we all thought to be held dear by institutions such as Harvard. We had learned, however, that it was not held equally dear by all members of the student body, and the faculty, too, was susceptible to pressure to silence discussion and debate, even on global matters.

Next day, in the Gutman Library, I was confronted by one of my students who had participated in the demonstration against the Indians the previous day.

'How dare you invite the PLO and not the Jews? Why weren't we allowed to speak on that panel?' I was asked in a very loud voice, which immediately attracted the attention of the security guard who checks students' identification as they come through on the door.

'Me? Do you think I invited the people on the panel? I was asked to do a job at the conference by my hosts here, the Indian people, and I agreed. Who they wished to have on their panel was their own business.'

'So you agree with them. You must, or you wouldn't have gone along with it.'

'Of course I agree. This is their country and they can invite anyone they like. Your people are not indigenous, to this country. You say you're Jewish, so you're a guest here yourself. Why can't you respect that? The Indians don't go to Israel and tell Israelis who they can have as visitors and who they can't.'

'Well, we're an oppressed minority ourselves, we should have had equal time.'

I waved away the security guard, who was hovering in case of trouble. I am not easily put off by a lone raised voice, though I understood that in a library it was not likely to be tolerated for very long. Still, the youth had jumped up and accosted me, giving me an opportunity to at least provide him with food for thought.

'As I understand it, no group of people that participates in this sort of forum can be both an oppressor and also claim to be an oppressed.'

'An oppressor? The Jews are oppressing the Palestinians? Is that what you're saying?'

'No. I'm saying that there are whole sections of this country, America, that are under Jewish occupancy and control. Has the Jewish community here made its peace with the Native American people? When the Jewish people are prepared to hand back to the Indians those lands which they occupy and control, without the consent of the Indian people, maybe then you can talk about who they can and can't invite. But in the meantime, you—just like me—are a guest in the land of the Indian people, and I wish you'd remember that.'

Strangely, when this young man next resumed his place in my class, he did not raise his opinion as a subject for discussion amongst the other students. Out of courtesy to him, neither did I. The event became just another part of the kaleidoscope of experiences that typified the impossibility of my coming home and making any definitive statement about the America I had found.

I had felt from the very beginning a close affinity with the Indian people whom I had met. During my first year, I had felt privileged to be asked to attend a mourning ceremony. It was held annually at Thanksgiving. While non-Indigenous Americans celebrated the arrival of the Pilgrims, their equivalent of Australia's First Fleet, Indians from across the country gathered at Plymouth, the site the first landing, to pray to their gods and wonder in ceremony why so many people had come to take over their lands. During this event, Indians from many North American tribes related their various and different histories, and I learned a great deal. Like many of my generation, I had read Dee Brown's monumental work, *Bury My Heart At Wounded*

K*nee*, and knew something of The Long Walk, the butch-
ery and battles, as well as the distribution of poisoned
blankets. Although not surprised, I was saddened to
realise that, just like the Black community in Australia,
the pain of these events had reverberated down
through the generations. It had never lost its intensity
because the Indians had not been addressed or barely
acknowledged by the descendants, and inheritors, of
those who had perpetrated the crimes and benefited
from their commission.

The following year, I tried to convince some of
the Black American students that they, too, should
support the Indians by travelling to Plymouth at
Thanksgiving. I was gratified with my efforts when some
of them joined up with us on that day. During my third
year, and with the help of some of those Black students who had attended the previous year, we whipped
up so much enthusiasm that a bus was hired to convey
everyone who wished to participate. Now that my studies were almost completed, I worried about whether
there would be anyone left on campus after my departure to try to bridge the gap I saw yawning between
Blacks and Indians. I believed they had so much to
offer each other by way of historical forgiveness and
support.

'What do you think about America?' I was to be
often asked on my return. Depending on the day I was
having I would say 'good' or 'bad' or, mostly, a mix-
ture of both. In the main, however, I'd plead off
answering at all. Instead I would tell the inquirer that
my view of America, without opportunity to travel
across the land, had been limited to just the eastern
corridor. I didn't consider it fair then to make any
assumptions at all. America had offered me an

ROBERTA SYKES

educational opportunity not afforded to me in my own country, and I did not want to be so rude as to come back home and relate positive, or negative, microcosmic events out of context.

13

The remaining few weeks of my last complete semester at Harvard flew by in a flurry of gleeful activity. I wrote to the Australian Council of Churches, telling them of my good fortune and giving an estimate of when I thought I would have my work completed. I decided I would contact colleagues in Australia involved in education, whose opinions I hoped to include in my thesis, when I returned home because, in my absence, people had moved around. Also there were new people working in the area. There were regions around the country where I had never been before that I hoped to explore. I wanted to visit the traditional communities I had heard about that were breaking into new frontiers as far as access to, and in some cases control of, European education were concerned.

On our return to Sydney, I purchased an economical round-Australia ticket with part of my Peter B. Livingston prize. Although prestigious, in cash terms the award was very modest, as I had come to realise when I sat down to work out my budget. It would enable me to travel to the places I wanted to go but it did not stretch to accommodation or on-ground transport. I would need the support of members of the Black community at each destination. In my heart, though, I knew this would be forthcoming. Although most of the people I knew had very little, there was such a generosity of spirit in the Black community that I felt the success of my project was assured.

The sheer length of the air-ticket I was issued proved to be a thrill. Each leg of the journey warranted a separate ticket, and they were all stapled to each other. When I held the ticket up the pages gently unfolded and reached right to the ground. Aunty Glad and Mum, who had come down to Sydney again to meet me on my arrival, laughed to see such a thing.

'We're coming over to your graduation,' Mum told me gaily, very pleased with herself and her own daring. This mother who, for decades, had shunned air travel because, as she'd said, she was so old that she still remembered 'fools jumping off chicken sheds with bits of wood strapped to their arms', had at long last taken the plunge and been to visit Della in New Zealand while I was away. On the strength of this comparatively brief trip, she and Aunty Glad had decided they could now fly halfway across the world. Mum was almost eighty years old.

'Mum, I'm not staying for my graduation. I plan to be back in Australia by Christmas and graduations aren't held until June.'

'Well, we'll just come over to visit you then.' Inwardly, I groaned. Such a visit would be a major interruption during the most intense part of my work, which I hoped to complete in the shortest possible time. Even more importantly Mum had absolutely no comprehension of what an arduous journey this would entail.

'Mum, you'd be in the air almost twenty-four hours. Do you understand what that means? I'd have to meet you both at the airport with an ambulance!'

'But,' she said sulkily, 'Glad and I want to go to New York. We'll go there first—or maybe you can even take us there.'

Opposition to any of her notions had always been the surest way to get this contrary woman fired up and even keener about the idea, so I agreed. 'Okay, we'll see.'

Silently I mused: first Mum says she is going to die if I go, and now she wants to come herself. Hopefully, if I don't object but at the same time, offer no encouragement, her idea will just dwindle away.

In my absence Russel had completed the Bachelor stage of his university course, and I felt terrible. We had missed not only his birthday once more but also his graduation. I was deeply saddened to learn that he hadn't even attended, feeling he had no family available with whom he could celebrate the occasion. This quest of mine was costing us all very dearly. I hoped that the future would enable me to make up for some of the sacrifices we had all had to endure. I was relieved to learn that he intended, the following year, to complete an Honours degree, giving me an opportunity to show him how profoundly proud of him and his achievements I was. Still, I couldn't help but recall the old Black women in Boston who turned up at every Harvard graduation to welcome the bright new future assured by each crop of Black awardees and congratulate each one on their success. I was saddened to think that our Black community had enjoyed no such history of academic success which might have led to the community embracing Russel's achievement. His qualifications would make him the first and only Black Australian psychologist on the entire Eastern seaboard.

I spoke to MumShirl and Brian Syron about the lack of acknowledgment of Russel's success, and they both shared my distress.

'Why didn't he ring and say something?' MumShirl demanded. 'I'd have organised a big mob to go out to the university and see him. Don't even worry about him—it would have been wonderful for the kids to see that one of our own has done it! They need that example.'

'I guess he might have felt it would be too much like bragging, Mum, to ring up and ask people to come to his graduation.'

'Yeah, but it wouldn't have been. He's always been a quiet achiever. So you've got to tell him—he's got to share his success, he's got to let these other Black kids know it's not impossible for them to get in there and do it. There's nothing else around the place going to let them know that.'

In preparation for my data collection trip, I dug into an old trunk where I had stored some of my things while I was away, and hauled out my tape-recorder, and a few summer clothes for the northern climate. Then, equipped with notebooks and pencils, I prepared to set off around the country.

Starting with the Sydney interviews, I rang Margaret Valadian, the first Aboriginal graduate, who was then running an Aboriginal adult education program in Balmain, but was told she was unavailable. Bob Morgan, then Chair of the New South Wales Aboriginal

Education Consultative Group, was delighted to see me. We talked about who should be included in my interview schedule, who had moved where, and I was able to catch up on some of the many changes that had occurred during my absence. Bob agreed to be interviewed and to be a sounding board when I arrived back with my data. He was very happy to be involved in the pursuit of this first Black community doctoral degree. He supplied me with a list of current phone numbers of people around the country and, at the end of our meeting, quite uncharacteristically, gave me a warm and ecstatic hug which said much more than words. 'Use the phones here,' he told me. 'Ring anyone you want. Our first doctorate, eh. Oh, yeah, right on!'

Proceeding anti-clockwise around this vast country, I flew into my home town, Townsville, first. Dr Neville Yeomans, a psychiatrist and friend from days of yore, invited me to use his home, in Belgian Gardens, as a base there. My dear friend Koiki Mabo, whom I had not seen for years, was, amongst his numerous enterprises, operating an innovative Black Community School. He was enthusiastic about his work and opinions being included in my thesis. We had a lot of catching up to do and talked for hours about his family, changes in the Townsville Black community, the state of the ongoing feuds between different family groups and their ideological positions. Then I set up my tape-recorder—only to find that I had stupidly, and in haste, placed it in storage with the batteries inside and acid had leaked out and completely ruined the entire unit.

Well, the loss of my recorder looked like it could turn my whole mission into a major disaster, and I had no funds with which to purchase another. Luckily, Neville produced one for us to use, but I remained worried about how I would cope for the rest of the trip.

Neville felt, and Koiki agreed, that I should contact the Education Department of James Cook University and let them know what I was doing. Although given short notice, I was invited out to a morning tea, and Neville offered to drive me. Both Neville and Koiki thought that the appearance of a local Black woman in the final stages of gaining a degree from Harvard University would help shatter any illusions the white university staff may have had about the inability of Blacks to succeed.

Unfortunately, this was not the case. To begin, I found myself to be the only Black person at this gathering, which, coming so soon after the academic meetings I had attended in Cambridge, heightened my sense of isolation. I felt that, even though they might not have had any Black staff, they could have invited some senior Black students to attend. Then, instead of allowing me to give a presentation to the group as a whole, staff merely wandered around the room and I found myself being required to answer the same questions many times from individuals delicately balancing their cups, saucers and cake plates.

'What exactly are you doing?' I was repeatedly asked.

'Writing my doctoral thesis on Black perspectives on the white education system,' I constantly replied.

'Hmm, very interesting. I'll be very happy to help you,' came so many disconcerting replies. For a start, I wasn't asking for their help, and, since they weren't Black, I was not at all interested in including their perspectives. White people had historically decided, and written about, what they thought was best for Blacks in education and every other area. My thesis was to be a chance for Blacks to have their voices heard, not more of the same.

Still, I continued to be polite. 'And what exactly are *you* doing?' I, from time to time, inquired of those who came forward to question me, careful to use their same words. I wondered if any of them was working on a project similar to my own. My question, however, made them very uneasy, and it became obvious that I had forgotten the unspoken rules. Blacks, I recalled, do not question whites. At Harvard I had become used to a degree of equality which was not available to me in Townsville, not in this setting, and I realised that my new ways were not being appreciated.

I was called aside and asked if I would go outside to allow the university photographer to take some shots of me for inclusion in the campus newspaper. When I returned, Neville Yeomans was very agitated and immediately urged me to leave.

Neville could not contain himself even as we walked across the carpark.

'As soon as you left with the photographer,' he said, 'they looked around the room and saw only white faces, they didn't realise I was with you, and so they dropped their guard. They were saying the most racist things I have heard in many years. They said you don't know what you're doing, and there was a lot of the old "wink-wink, nudge-nudge" to imply how you are getting yourself through Harvard. I felt sick. I had to get out of there. Coming out here was a dreadful mistake.'

I couldn't help it, I just burst out laughing. Change had hit them in the face and all they could do was resort to the same old racist and sexist reactions. Sleeping my way through Harvard? The very idea had me doubled over with hilarity. I had had about thirty teachers, the majority of them female, my thesis supervisor, Professor Courtney Cazden, was a woman. Indeed, most of the faculty and students at the Education School, now that I came to think about it, were women. There were checks and balances all over the school which militated against the likelihood of sexual exploitation or manipulation occurring, and even against the appearance of such an event occurring. Perhaps, I thought, they are saying more about themselves than about me.

I reflected on this episode, especially in light of the lessons I had learned about racism during Chet Pierce's classes. If I did not tell white people what I was doing, then obviously I did not *know* what I was doing. And white people, regardless of what I was doing, or their own level of expertise, felt that they could advise me, that I would be unable to accomplish my exercise if left to my own devices.

I travelled on to Cairns, where I stayed with my good friends Marjorie and Thommo, who had moved north. Mick Miller, a local Black community leader who had taught at the high school for seventeen years, and was then director of the North Queensland Land Council, put all his resources at my disposal. He organised a huge community barbecue in my honour on land that had recently been returned to the Aboriginal community. He was keen to contribute his experience and perspectives towards my thesis, and delighted to explain to people the implications of having one of their own attending Harvard and gaining a doctorate. He would even hail folks from across the street and in passing cars to introduce them to me and took the opportunity to make sure that everyone was aware, and felt themselves to be a part, of my undertaking.

I had known for a long time about Strelley, a community in a remote area in Western Australia which I was keen to visit. However, when I had suggested to people, both Black and white, that I would like to go there, I had been strongly advised against it. The Blacks at Strelley, I was told by those who claimed to know, were 'hostiles', traditional Aborigines who allowed no strangers into their area. Even Port Hedland police were only permitted to come as far as the gate, and had to conduct any business they had with the Elders at this border. Beyond the gate, everything was in the control of the Elders—policing, education, health, welfare, the works. They were unlikely to allow a strange Black from the eastern states to come in and start asking questions.

I shared these thoughts with Marjorie, who 'pooh-poohed' them immediately. Marjorie's people came from around that area, and she had a special place in her heart for that land. 'Yes, Strelley has a hard reputation, and it got that way when old Don McLeod became a spokesperson for the rightful owners. With someone to speak English for them, and to speak true for them, they were able to stop the onslaught of white culture and hang onto their own ways. They are the strongest mob in the west, and other communities from all over go to them for advice and assistance when they're trying to restore traditional law in their areas.'

The more I heard, the more fascinated I became, but would I be allowed to enter, to see for myself what headway they were making in the field of education? Marjorie gave me names and phone numbers, and said she would ring ahead to ensure me of a welcome.

'Well, as a rule, people are supposed to go through

Don McLeod, who lives in Perth, to get permission to
enter. The old men of the tribe trust him. But since
you're arriving from the opposite direction, you go right
on in and talk to Don McLeod later. The Elders will
make you welcome, you'll see. They know one of their
own when they see one,' Marjorie reassured me.

I had other ports of call on my schedule before I
was to reach Western Australia, and took off next for
Alice Springs. Years ago, with Germaine Greer and her
photographer friend, I had been appalled by the racism
in this town, and was looking forward to seeing what
changes had transpired since that time.

The first difference that hit me was virtually upon
my arrival. I took the airport bus into the township
and went straight to the nearest phone box and
opened the phone book. Where, less than a decade
earlier, there had been only one entry under
'Aboriginal'—the Aboriginal Inland Mission, under the
direction of white church people—now there was a
whole page and a half of Aboriginal organisations
listed. My heart sang. My phone call, to an Aboriginal
woman, Freda Thornton, led immediately to a van
being despatched to pick me up. Accommodation? No
worries, she had contacts all over the place, and I was
soon found a bed. The word was sent out to Yipirinya
Community School, and Elders sent back messages of
their availability and willingness to show me their projects and participate as a group in interviews.

'Would I,' asked Freda, 'give the local Aboriginal
radio program an interview myself?'

Next morning I was taken to the radio station, which
consisted merely of a few tiny air-conditioned cubicles
on the edge of a barren, very dry and dusty block.
Two quite young Black women stood outside, drawing

patterns in the dirt with their bare feet and toes. After a short discussion, I was asked to step forward and meet them. They were the language experts who broadcast radio programs for the several language groups in the catchment area.

On air, I was asked, 'When we began broadcasting that we were going to interview you this morning, a listener rang in and said you aren't an Aboriginal. What do you have to say about that?'

'What do *you* have to say about that?' I inquired. 'How did that make you feel?'

'Well, I thought he was saying that Aborigines aren't smart enough to go to Harvard, and...that made me feel very bad.'

'That's what I think people who say things like that really mean, too, and I know it's not true, so I'm not going to even bother answering his question. Is that okay with you?'

The interviewer gave such an enormously relieved sigh and a quietly conspiratorial glance that it was obvious she felt we had put that listener right in his place. The interview continued about more local issues, creating an opportunity for me to learn of the social and educational difficulties still being experienced in the area and what the Black community was trying to do to counteract them.

I was taken on a tour to look at how the outreach program was attempting to cater to the educational needs of those young people who lived in camps scattered throughout the town, without access to proper housing, water or electricity. This was followed by an extremely fruitful and open meeting with Elders on the Yipirinya Community School Council. Then I was on the plane to Darwin.

Peg Havnen, Curriculum Development Specialist and lecturer at Darwin Community College, and Barbara Graham, a graduate of the Aboriginal Task Force in South Australia and, at that time, working with the Department of Community Welfare in Darwin, arranged for me to meet and talk with a host of people about their myriad situations and difficulties. I learned of several Black students who had excelled educationally only to have their—and their family's and community's—hopes dashed by barriers which prevented them from being appropriately employed. 'We can keep our kids in school,' said many of the parents, 'but we can't give them jobs when they come out the other end. Some of these kids do well in school and speak several languages, but they still aren't able to even get a labouring job.'

I had confided in Barbara that my next step was to go to Strelley, which pleased and delighted her. She came to visit me again on the eve of my departure and said she was envious of my freedom to travel to this place which she had heard of and yearned to visit. She slipped a slim bottle of white wine into my bag so that I could have a toast to the future there upon my arrival.

I had been assured that I would be met at Port Hedland airport, which was tiny and located quite a way out of town. On my arrival I waited for someone to collect me. Eventually, the last of the workers, whose hours are based around the arrival and departure of the few aircraft that land there, pulled away leaving just a trail of dust lingering in the twilight. Then I found myself sitting on my case, all alone.

Oh, well, there were bound to be a few hiccups, I thought, quite pleased with myself and all my colleagues to date that things had actually gone so smoothly. In the distance I could see the silhouette of a building, and, gradually, as external lights came on, I realised that it was a motel. I hauled my case over my shoulder and picked my way through the loose rocks, sand and stubby bushes towards it.

My efforts to contact anyone on the numbers I had been given for Strelley went unrewarded. So I booked myself in, had a meal and went off to bed, trying to contemplate what I should do next. I understood Strelley to be at least two or three hours of rough travelling time away, and there was no sign that a hire car was available, although I could not have afforded to rent one, even if there was.

I spent a restless night. I was so close, and yet so far away, from an educational setting and traditional community which was the envy of many, and which seemed to have struck fear into the hearts of people across the country. Had my best laid plans to visit there gone astray?

What a relief then, to learn from the front desk in the morning that I would be picked up in a few hours, though I had no idea by whom. I checked out and waited around outside this lonely outpost, alternately sitting on my case and standing, watching carefully the few passing cars to see if any of them was looking out for me. A big shining eight-cylinder sedan cruised past, turned around, came back, and a white middle-aged man stuck his head out the window.

'Want a lift, luv?' he asked, with a thick European accent, and I knew instantly this was definitely not the person who had been sent to get me.

Another hour passed and the day was beginning to heat up, when a dusty big old four-wheel drive lumbered into the driveway of a little building right next door. An elderly Aboriginal man, dark as midnight, peered out from beneath a battered hat pulled down low over his brow. As I walked towards the vehicle, I could see there were others in the cabin—another man, a woman holding a child on her knee. The second man, also Aboriginal, spoke and room was made for me in the cabin while my bag was hoisted under the cover on the back.

We went into Port Hedland, where there were obviously errands they had come to take care of. The woman and child took off, I thought towards a clinic, mail was collected from the post office, and boxes and bags of supplies loaded in the back. Throughout, no one actually spoke directly to me, and the brief discussions that took place amongst themselves were low-pitched and in their own language which I did not understand. I just sat quietly in the cabin, glad of the company, happy at the thought that eventually we would be moving towards my destination, Strelley.

Once again on the road, and we stopped at a roadhouse, where the old man indicated I should purchase a drink if I wanted. It was the last store we would pass.

Although I am usually very alert when I'm being chauffeured by anyone whose driving skills I am not familiar with, the old man obviously knew every inch of the road and could have safely navigated our way wearing a blindfold. After a comparatively short distance, we turned off the bitumen highway and onto a dirt track. The old man weaved the truck around dips and potholes in the road, boles almost unseen jutting out from the sparse undergrowth, without slowing down and with barely a movement of the steering wheel. The heat, my restlessness the previous night, the speed at which I had been hurtling, combined with

the tranquillity, confidence and self-centredness ema-
nating from the driver, lulled me to sleep, my chin on
my chest.

I awoke with a start to find the truck stopped at a
gate stretched across the roadway. From that point on,
I sat up alert, drinking in my surroundings. We travelled on a few more miles before a scattering of low-set
buildings could be seen in the distance. Then the man
drew the vehicle up beside a long building which consisted of an open breezeway with prefabricated steel
rooms at each end. Near one of these rooms stood a
caravan.

A whole lot of laughing, shy children came out of
nowhere at the sound of our arrival, frolicking around
and eyeing me curiously. One or two white people also
came out, introducing themselves as teachers and
resource people, and explained where I was to sleep.
The traditional Aboriginal people lived beyond this
area. Everyone else had to stay in the mobiles and
cabins that had been built to accommodate them.

It was already late afternoon, and some of the older
children toted my bag to the room where I was to stay.
I was to freshen up and come back to eat at one of
the staff houses.

It was great to be away from the strident noises of
the cities and towns, with the more gentle sounds of
the bush massaging my ears and my heart. Although
June, and therefore mid-winter, the intense heat had
afflicted me with a sense of torpor. Now it was lifting,
and evening came on gently.

I had barely begun exploring the digs I'd been allocated when there was a knock at the door. A tall white
man about my own age introduced himself, Adrian
Sleigh. He was a friend of Marjorie's, he said, a doctor

and also a Harvard graduate, and he flew the Strelley plane.

The Strelley plane? Yes, he told me, this was a unique place, a special community, and they had bought themselves a plane. The government had refused their request for funds for a plane, which they required to cover their large area, especially for medical emergencies, so they had bought it themselves. No one had known how to fly it, and there wasn't money to hire a pilot. So the community had advertised for a doctor, which they could afford, stipulating they wanted a medico who also had a pilot's licence. Adrian had come up from Melbourne.

He waited while I tidied myself and my few belongings, before escorting me to the house where we were to eat. Should I, I asked as I was rummaging through my case and came upon the bottle of wine Barbara had given me, bring the wine to dinner so we could all have a toast?

'If I were you, I'd just put that back in the bottom of the bag and forget about it until you're back in the city. This is a dry reserve, and the Elders would be very unhappy to even know that you've got it with you.' Chastened at my own ignorance, I carefully wrapped and returned it to the bag.

As we walked through the dusk, Adrian explained how the Elders ruled their lands with wills of steel, demanding complete sobriety, travelling long distances to haul back any of their members who fell victim to this vice. Alcohol had caused a lot of problems for some of the traditional groups in the area, and the Strelley mob were determined that these problems would not take hold there.

Over dinner, the teachers and resource people

explained their roles. These teachers didn't actually teach the children, there were young Black adults who did that, and these positions were places of honour. The teaching advisers met with the Aboriginal teachers each morning and worked with them on their teaching plans for the day. Elders dictated what they wanted taught, how it was to be taught, even ensuring that they make their own books, in both traditional language and English. The students learned their culture and their own history as well as being trained in English literacy and numeracy. There were no white people at Strelley who were not directly in the employ of the Aboriginal community, and the respect and adherence to traditional Aboriginal wishes and directives flowed quite naturally through this relationship.

How refreshingly different, I thought as Adrian escorted me back to my digs. What a turnaround from the contempt, powerplays and hypocrisy I had seen elsewhere in Aboriginal education providers. Things *can* be different, and here they *are* different.

Next day I was shown around, and found the long building with the breezeway to be not just the school but the centre of most community endeavours. The community functioned around the training and education of its young people. The caravan housed technical equipment for the production of the school books based on stories generated from the past. I was given a selection of these books from a store room at the end of the building. Some Elders came by during the day and, through interpreters, I was able to further my inquiries.

That night I again met with the white staff to discuss my observations, and the conversation turned to the teaching of English. The Elders, I was told, were very keen to have the young people learn English so that they could deal directly with the white people, particularly the police and government officials, who came to the gate to try to force their will on the local community.

'Is this the sort of English skills you are teaching the young people?' I asked.

'Well, no, not yet. We're teaching them English, and that's what the Elders want us to do.'

'But you and I know that the mere speaking of English is not the same as having the skills to deal with white people. Those interactions are about power. The students would need to learn about stance, attitude, nuance, as well as things that run counter to Aboriginal culture, such as looking people who might be older than yourself in the eye and staring them down.'

'That's true—but how can we tell the Elders that?'

'If you don't, then by your silence you'd be deceiving them, wouldn't you? Letting them think that the language skills you're imparting will enable the next generation to stand up to the negative and culturally destructive forces outside, which are trying to get in and force their will on people?'

'You mean the Department of Aboriginal Affairs?'

'I mean anyone, insurance salesmen, mining companies, government officials—all those people outside who think they know better what should happen to the land, and to the people, than the people who have lived here for thousands of years.'

'God, if you could tell us how to teach that sort of English, the English of the powerful, we'd be glad to try.'

I cherished those teaching advisers for their genuine and sincere desire to work with the community through the very difficult transition that was being forced upon them. The Elders could feel the pressure of the intrusion of a rapacious and insatiable European presence straining just beyond the gate to take over. And they had resisted—were resisting—with all the skills and energy they could muster. They had my deepest admiration, but still I worried for them for the future, their future and my own. Could they, as I hoped, hold out? Only in concert, these Blacks in their remote, far-flung homelands, together with others who worked in Canberra and the capital cities, only if all these people kept their eyes on the prizes of respect and equality, could the two ends of the circle—the past and the future—be drawn together. Only this would ensure the continuity of the relationship between the eternal spirits, the timeless land, and the custodians.

What a deep and moving place, I thought as I picked my way along the path back to my room. Adrian had flown out that afternoon, presumably to make a medical call at one of the out-stations. I was being delivered back to Port Hedland airport to continue my journey next morning. I regretted the brevity of the time I had available to spend here, in this environment so ideal for the contemplation of the larger questions. The night sky, with its thick carpet of stars, seemed endless, blending gently and easily into the landscape of grandeur, trees in silhouette, night birds calling in the distance. I stood outside for a long time, reflecting on the peace and magic I felt there. Yet I was acutely aware that one wrong paper signed in Perth, or in some distant part of the globe, could set in train the machinery to destroy that which had withstood the forces of man and time over all these centuries. Will I, I wondered, next time I come through

this way, hear the shudder and clang of mining equipment booming repetitiously throughout the night,
disembowelling this peaceful world—or will the Elders
hit upon the exact combination of words and power
to prevent the destruction of their place?

Perth glittered in the afternoon sun as the small plane
came in to land. The city seemed to have grown enormously since I had last visited in 1972 for the Lionel
Brockman trial. Geraldine Willesee had moved back
from Sydney to the west, and she had invited me to
stay with her for the few days of my stopover. Gerri
had a car and cheerfully drove me to appointments
with Oriel Green, who worked in Basic Childcare at the
Aboriginal section of the state Education Department,
and other venues, such as the Aboriginal Medical and
Legal services.

When speaking with Oriel, I happened to mention
Strelley. 'Oh, are you thinking of going there? You
won't get in there, you know. They don't like anyone
coming in.'

'I've just come from Strelley. It's not true that they
don't let people in. In fact, Elders came and collected
me from the airport, everyone made me feel very welcome. I think, at least as far as the Black community
is concerned, access is being controlled by rumour.
Have you ever tried to go there?'

'Oh,' replied Oriel, 'I'm going to a childcare meeting
in Port Hedland in a couple of weeks. Maybe I'll—'

'I think it might be a very good idea. I don't think
a big mob should try to go at once, but whatever support you might be able to muster for them in the long
term, I feel sure they'd appreciate it if you turned up
to help.'

I rang to make the courtesy appointment with Don McLeod, as I had promised to do, and Gerri again said she'd be happy to drive me. 'Oh, you can even come in, bird,' I told her affectionately. 'I'm sure you want to hear what he's got to say.' Gerri was an old and dear friend, and we often talked to each other in this loose way.

Gerri filled me in with her considerable knowledge of Don McLeod, whose presence amongst the Blacks had spread fear into the hearts of all those who sought to oppress them.

From everything I had heard, I was therefore not surprised to find a rather short, old, very cocky man waiting for us, though several other things did astonish me. It was a warm and sunny day outside, but he was huddled in sweater, coat and rugs in front of a radiator, which had forced the room temperature up to a near heatwave. He sat in a gloomy room behind a desk, with papers and books heaped around him.

Don had a foul mouth, and we were barely seated before he slyly began to tell me about 'trouble-makers', 'yellow-fellows from the south', 'half-castes and so on', peppered liberally with invectives. He mentioned by name some of these people whom he professed to despise, Gary Foley and others of my acquaintance. 'I've heard of you, too,' he said flatly.

'Well, if you've heard of me, then you know I don't accept this sort of language. If you intend to be rude, and to talk badly about people you don't even know, some of whom happen to be friends of mine, I'm leaving.'

I gave Gerri the nod and we both rose.

'Okay. I won't swear,' he said brusquely just as we reached the door. 'Anything else?'

I turned back towards him. 'There'll be no talk about "yellow-fellows" and "half-castes". I hate those sorts of expressions. Do you think people had a choice about whether they were going to be white or black or yellow, as you call it?'

'Oh, alright,' he said, sulking a little as though I had spoiled his good fun.

After that we spent the next hour in quite reasonable discussion about a range of subjects which affected not only Strelley but state and federal politics. He may not have met everyone he claimed not to like, but he was widely read on most of the important issues.

As we left, Gerri summed him up. 'The old bugger was lonely.' He had drawn out our visit as long as he possibly could, bringing up new topics each time he thought we were getting restless and likely to leave.

'Yeah, but he's obviously been a tough nut in his day. I wouldn't have liked to be a copper trying to cross him, he would have been ferocious.'

Gerri laughed. 'Yes, he was. He out-talked and out-witted all those who came around trying to con the Strelley mob out of anything. But he could also sit for days on end with the Elders until they came to a consensus about which way they wanted to go. That's one of the main reasons why they respect him, I think.'

'Knew when to talk and when to shut up, eh? Well, he didn't practise much of the latter today.'

Gerri, a diabetic, was cramming her mouth with sweets which she kept in the glovebox for just that purpose. 'Let's go and get something to eat, eh. I'm starving. The old bugger didn't even offer us a cup of tea or a biscuit.'

I grimaced. 'With the state of that room, I don't know

if I would have trusted drinking out of his cups,' I replied as Gerri gunned the engine and we drove away.

There were just two more stops, Adelaide and Melbourne, to be made before I finished off my program with some interviews in Sydney. At Barbara Graham's insistence and on her glowing recommendation, I had contacted the Aboriginal Task Force in Adelaide, and been asked to give a presentation to students as I passed through. There I met Mary Ann Bin-Sallik, who was destined to become the third link in my chain of Australian Black Harvard graduates, and the second to achieve her doctorate there.

In Melbourne, I interviewed Wayne Atkinson, Colin Bourke and Hyllus Maris, all of whom were actively involved in innovative educational endeavours. Hyllus also talked about her writing and the screenplay, *Women of the Sun*, co-written with her friend, Sonia Borg, a ground-breaking saga in four episodes.

Arriving back in Sydney, I was exhilarated by the degree of support I had received in what could have been an impossible task. People everywhere had facilitated my passage, arranged accommodation, transport and interviews and made valuable suggestions for inclusion in my thesis, and even brought their own tape-recorders when they'd learned that mine had died.

The only person I had contacted well in advance of my arrival, and again when I had first landed in Sydney, was Margaret Valadian. Despite this, I was unable to interview her. I went to the college she was operating in Balmain and spoke to her colleague, Natasha McNamara. Margaret was willing, I was told, but she just didn't have any time.

I rounded off the project with interviews with Bob Morgan and Errol West, then Deputy Chair of the

National Aboriginal Education Committee, and Kevin Cook, General Secretary of Tranby Cooperative College for Aborigines in Sydney.

On arriving home from Boston, I had contacted the Health Commission to arrange an extension of my study leave. I also explained, with regrets, that I would not have time to do my usual three months' work for them. When I rang again I was told that the Minister for Health, Laurie Brereton, had asked to see me.

I went into the government offices and sat waiting in a little anteroom on the top floor. A couple of slender young men walked past and one of them spoke to me briefly, saying I would not need to wait long. Still I waited. Then one of these young men came to the office door as the other left, and signalled me to enter. It was only then that I realised with a shock that I had forgotten what Laurie Brereton looked like, I had been expecting an older man, more like the rotund executives and ministers I was accustomed to. I felt a bit of a fool as I sat, legs neatly crossed at the ankles, wondering what I was expected to say to this minister whom I had not recognised.

Laurie was relaxed, but apologised that our meeting would be necessarily brief because he had been called back to Parliament to vote on some important issue. Would I, he asked, come out to his house for dinner? His wife, Patricia, would be delighted to see me again, and we could catch up with the changes that had been occurring, in the Department as well as the political arena, in a more convivial atmosphere.

'Sure,' I agreed. Laurie gave me an address in Kensington and stood up to leave.

'Can I bring my son? I don't have a car now, and he could drive me.'

'No worries, he'll be welcome.'

When I told my friend Maureen Morales, who was also Laurie Brereton's sister-in-law, about the dinner invitation, she asked if I would mind if she came along too. As Maureen also didn't own a car, Russel could drive both of us.

Patricia was a bit flustered with children, preparing the meal and tidying the house, when we arrived. She also seemed a bit upset, because someone had recently stolen her Longines watch, and she appeared to miss it.

When Laurie arrived, he took a quick look at Russel and said to me, 'You didn't need to bring a bodyguard.'

'This, Laurie, is my son. His name is Russel. You recall I asked if it would be okay to bring him, he's the only one who has a car.'

He was probably surprised to find himself looking up at Russel, who stood a few inches taller than Laurie and kept himself remarkably fit. He worked with young street people at an inner-city refuge and felt he could ill afford to look as though he was unable to take care of himself if the need arose.

We spent a pleasant evening, talking about wide-ranging issues of government policy, how they impacted on young people, such as those who came through the refuge, the Health Commission, the prisons, while tucking into the great meal that Patricia had miraculously whipped up in next to no time.

As the evening drew to a close, Laurie leaned across the table towards me and said, 'You don't need to worry about your job at the Health Department. We've kept your position open for you.'

'Laurie, I was doing that job before I had two degrees from Harvard. I want to do another job.'

'But—you're already the most senior Black in Aboriginal Health.'

'Exactly. And there are no courses in Aboriginal anything at Harvard.'

He stared at me for a moment before a flash of comprehension came into his eyes.

'Oh, God. I know what you're saying.'

'Yes, well good. I want to do another job when I come back. Okay?'

'Okay.'

We all took our coffee into the lounge room where Laurie produced a cigarette and began to smoke it. The Health Department had recently launched a non-smoking campaign, and I couldn't resist the urge to tease him.

'The Minister for Health smokes?' I said, mock sternly.

'Well, no. Not in public. One a day. That won't kill me, will it? And I'm trying to give that one up, too.'

The next to last item on my agenda was to visit Norma Williams and see how her preparations towards applying to Harvard were going. I found her much happier than when we had last met. She was in the middle of a course on teacher education, she told me, which she would finish the following year. She was very much enjoying the challenge of polishing up her study and essay-writing skills, and felt sure she would be ready and confident to begin tackling the quest for a Harvard Master's degree by the time I returned. She was slowly making arrangements within her family for her children to be cared for in her absence, even though, if her application was accepted, she would not be leaving for just over a year.

One thing was really bothering her, she confided in me. Her marriage to the father of her children, Gary Williams, had long since broken down. Now she wanted to get a divorce so that her Harvard educational certification could appear with her maiden name, Ingram. This, she thought, would also be inspirational to other members of her family and her Wiradjuri clan, as the Ingram name was well known and respected within this circle. She would love to be able to bring credit to it in this way.

I gave her the phone number of my friend Eric Strasser, who had already proved to be extremely helpful to me with legal matters for more than a decade. 'Eric will help you with this,' I told her.

'But I've no money for a divorce. I can't afford a lawyer.'

'Then Eric's just the man you need.'

I was grateful for the small coterie of friends and supporters I had built up over the years. Eric Strasser, in particular, had always prove to be a stalwart. He would probably be pleasantly surprised, I thought, that the task I was leaving him to look after this time was fairly simple, nothing like the major criminal matters I'd had cause to load him up with in years gone by.

'Mum,' said Russel next day as I began packing for my return to Boston, 'I heard people take years to write their thesis. Are you sure you'll be back by Christmas?'

I stopped, sat down, took his hands in mine. He had again agreed to look after his sister until my return in just over three months, and he sounded so worried.

'There's one thing I know for sure, child, and that's how to write. I worried about the coursework, because that was something I'd never done. But I've finished that now, and all I have to do is turn those,' indicating the pile of interview cassettes I had amassed for my research, 'into a few hundred pages. For others, that might be hard work, but for me, it's the easy part. I'll be home by Christmas, and that's a promise.'

He brightened, whether to please me or because he believed me, I had no idea.

So, this is it, I thought as I winged my way back to Boston to complete the final assignment of my doctoral requirements. Now, nothing could stop me.

My abstract had been accepted, my literature review was finished, there was just the data analysis and compilation, and the writing to go. I had a crystal clear idea, based on the interview material I had collected, how the diverse subject matter would need to be linked in order to make sense. I had initially thought about a sequence in which to place the subjects, but rejected that notion in favour of a constellation. This would be the only way to give each area and issue the full attention it required, favouring neither the urban nor the traditional voices over the other.

I spent a couple of weeks letting the constellation spin in my head, before it settled down into a logical form. Scholars normally transcribe their interviews and shuffle through them in paper form. In my case, though, the words of my interviewees were still indelibly implanted in my memory. I would have no trouble accessing them, turning to the tapes only to verify the direct quotes once I had written them down.

Then, for ten days I did nothing but write, rising early in the morning to begin, falling into my bed late each night. When I had all but completed the work,

Dick Katz offered me the use of his computer. I could go to his house each day after his family had left, and put everything into the computer, where it could be changed or altered as required.

The problem, as I confided in him, was that I was unfamiliar with computers. I had never used one except to look up references in the library. 'Oh, that's okay. You just type everything in, and either my wife or I will help you to print it out,' he said.

So for two weeks I worked in Dick's house, but as I went home every night I felt empty and dissatisfied. I was used to working with a typewriter, and at the end of the day seeing a very satisfying pile of completed pages sitting on the desk beside me. After using the computer all day, I seemed to go home with nothing more than the few notebooks I had brought with me in the morning.

Words disappeared from the screen, sometimes whole paragraphs, and I spent what felt like a lot of time on the phone to Dick's wife, with her prompting me with the combination of keys to strike to recover the missing text.

The computer ran an early word-processing program and in American. Dick joked one morning that he had spent most of the previous night running 'Search' to locate all the instructions to 'centre' the work, instead of 'center' the work, which I had inserted. I knew he was just making an effort to help me overcome the computer anxiety I was experiencing, but instead I grew even more alarmed that I'd never be able to cope this way.

Things got worse when I tried to print out my chapters. Spaces I had left in which to insert diagrams came out split over two pages. I became increasingly embarrassed about calling Dick or his wife at work for help.

I noticed a comma missing on a page, and when I inserted it and tried to print it out again, this tiny change had nudged that line into another, causing all subsequent pages to be one line over.

On the day of the first winter snow, as I trudged through the cold to catch my bus back to Fresh Pond, I came to a decision. It might possibly take me weeks to master the computer sufficiently so as to turn out my work in perfect form, where it would only take me ten days if I were to type it up on the old typewriter I had borrowed. I was running out of time and my mind was made up.

Different students, friends of mine, came by in ones and twos and sat reading four or five pages at a time each, for sense and for typographical errors. A page with a serious typo was typed again, but fortunately there were few of them.

I had imbued my thesis examiners with my own sense of urgency and, when I had finished the work, they read it with a speed that I could only have hoped for. The Dean agreed to be on the committee for my orals examination, and we were to gather in his house for this part of the assessment. When we arrived, he had a bottle of champagne sitting up prominently on the table in an ice bucket, and said this was for the celebration as he was sure I would pass. He knew, as my examiners also did by this time, that I was so familiar with my material I could recite it in my sleep—and probably did so.

The technical support system around Harvard is really quite fantastic. One only needs to take a set of papers, a completed thesis, to the copy shop late in the afternoon, and by early next morning as many copies as were ordered are all ready and collated. I imagined an entire troop of workers tending copy machines in the bowels of buildings surrounding Harvard Square, working non-stop around the clock. Miraculously, overnight copies are even cheaper per page than having them done during daylight hours.

Thesis passed, and I next had to find a binder. Leather-bound copies for the school, for the library, and, if requested, for readers, are a formal requirement for completion. Not many of my friends had reached this stage, but they dived into phone books on my behalf, locating binders who were the best, the cheapest, and the closest to my apartment. Before long I was looking at a set of beautifully bound copies.

I had run out of money, but I felt it was imperative that I buy a crimson robe, to which I was now entitled, even if I never got a chance to wear it. I had crossed my fingers, though, that such an opportunity would arise, even though I wouldn't be in Boston to attend my own graduation. I wrote to Mum. Would she please, please lend me the money?

An envelope arrived from her and within it a heartening note, surprisingly lucid. 'It is not every mother who gets the chance to buy their daughter a Harvard doctoral robe,' she wrote. 'The enclosed is not a loan, it's a gift.'

I was then in a whirlwind of packing, preparing to box up my Boston life and come home, home to Australia. My friends arranged a farewell party for me, and came in bearing gifts and congratulations.

'When you said you'd be finished by Christmas, sistah, I thought you was having me on. But damn, girl, you been and done it.'

'Well, you've made us all look like snails. I've been working on my thesis for three years. You're an inspiration, sistah, and now I'm going to be graduating out of here myself come spring.'

'You'll write, won't you? I don't want to lose touch. Having seen you come in and out of this place in record time is just so motivating. Don't think I've ever seen anyone work so hard and so fast in all my life. Girl, you be going *somewhere*, and I want to stay in touch so I know where you're at!'

Kenton had become fascinated by the idea of far-away Australia, and decided to accompany me home to visit for a week. He wanted to see if there was any possibility of emigrating, of continuing our relationship now that my studies had come to an end. I realised I would be embarrassed by my derelict house and our family's living standards, but he assured me that he had come from a poor home too. We drove through a blizzard to depart from JFK Airport, New York, leaving his car with my friend Adrienne Jones, in foreign service at the Australian Consulate.

On the long journey home I had a lot of time to reflect on my life and how far I had come. A Black girl born in a country which had let me know early on that my value would only be measured by my ability to scrub floors and do laundry. Abandoned by my father, whoever he might be, raped, my body thrown into the bush, I had, as a consequence, been left to my own devices to survive and ensure the survival of my two children alone. I had taken what few opportunities the spirits had arranged should be extended to me, and worked hard to do the very best I could with them. The crimson robe and mortar board in my suitcase, I felt, were testimony not just to my academic ability— but to the ability of Black people everywhere, in the face of all manner of hardship, to continue to survive.

The summer sun was shining brightly and my children stood blinking as we came out of Immigration at Sydney Airport. I had been in touch with the Harvard Club of Australia and had learned that they were looking forward to staging a degree presentation ceremony for me, as soon as my testamur arrived.

I felt warm and happy as my daughter hugged me and my son loaded the suitcases into the back of his van. I was home in time for Christmas, and that's all, at that moment, that mattered to us.

Epilogue

Early in the year of 1984, I single-handedly, and to warm applause, integrated the Harvard Club of Australia, as the first Black Australian to become a fully fledged member. Ironically, this occurred at a luncheon at the American National Club where, almost two decades earlier, I had worked as a waitress.

Dr Margaret Guild-Wilson, another Harvard Education School graduate, was the driving force behind the Harvard Club of Australia's sponsorship of a special graduation ceremony where I was presented with my testamur several months later. Held on 24 May, 1984 in the Great Hall of the University of Sydney, the oldest tertiary institution in Australia, this was, I believe, the first Harvard event ever held outside its own campus with its full cooperation and consent. The music for the Harvard anthem was flown over especially for the occasion, the majestic sounds of the organ adding to the ambience and significance of the night.

Dr Guild-Wilson informed me that she had already made representations on my behalf to have Sydney

University Press publish my thesis, *Incentive, Community and Achievement: An Analysis of Black Viewpoints on Issues Relating to Black Australian Education.* I was very gratified by her support.

I stood looking down at the assembly from a small anteroom upstairs where we were robing for the procession. As I did so, I was momentarily overcome by nervousness at the culmination of this train of events which had been set in motion by the visiting Black scientist, Professor Chester Pierce, years before. I felt my debt of gratitude to be enormous. As others helped me to don my crimson robe officially for the first time and adjusted it around my shoulders, I realised that it was symbolic of the weight of responsibilities which I had chosen voluntarily to assume—to create a chain of Black Australian Harvard graduates. This thought was foremost in my mind.

My sister Della had moved back to Australia from New Zealand, and she and her daughter flew in from Adelaide for the ceremony. Another young girl from the Black community whom I took briefly under my wing, Mandy Hamilton, also attended. Naomi, Mandy, and Della's daughter Carlena, played a major part at the ceremonial finale, racing up to the stage and presenting me with enormous bouquets. My son, Russel, was also present, beaming his good wishes to me throughout.

I was disappointed that my youngest sister, Leonie, chose not to attend. We had grown increasingly estranged, though it would be difficult to put a date on when this process had begun. I had, much earlier, exacerbated the rift perhaps with a sharply worded reply to a letter she had written while she was in hospital recovering from cosmetic surgery—in pursuit of earthly and transient beauty by having 'tummy tucks'. I thought it hypocritical of her, as a Jehovah's Witness, to place herself in a position where she might have required a blood transfusion if complications arose, and then court death by her refusal of this medical procedure. Re-married and still deeply involved with this religion, she wrote to me now saying that she was 'not allowed' to come to my graduation.

Mum, by this time obviously well along the road towards senile dementia, had to be cajoled and bribed to attend. She said she was unable to come to Sydney because it was too cold. I had to promise that she could wear my kangaroo skin coat before she agreed. She was seated in the front row, where she spent a few minutes making small talk with the woman beside her before being introduced. For the next few weeks we all heard, repetitiously as the demented are inclined to do, how surprised Mum had been to learn that 'the nice lady' who sat beside her and talked with her was none other than Lady Black, the wife of the Chancellor, Sir Hermann Black, who officiated at the ceremony.

Many Harvard doctoral and other graduates flew in from around the country, and, in their crimson robes, provided the spectacle and pageantry required of such formal proceedings. Dr Nugget Coombs, though not a Harvard graduate, had written to me supportively throughout my studies, and made a point, each time I was home in Australia, of taking me to lunch to brief me on changes in the political situation in the country. As Nugget had been adviser to seven Prime Ministers over the years, I considered these briefings added to my understanding of Australia's history and contemporary situation enormously, and I insisted he be invited to give an Occasional Address.

My dear friend Sandra Bardas, as a surprise for me, made arrangements through the university's technical department to have the event filmed on video. And she and husband David flew up from Melbourne to attend.

How pleased I was to look around and see how many friends were in the audience, amongst them Fred Hollows, Lloyd McDermott (the first Aboriginal law graduate), Glenda Humes, and oh, too many to list here. I was grateful to be able to share the occasion with them.

Not everything was idyllic. I had put out a general invitation to members of the local Black community, only to learn later that many had feared the formality and felt unable to turn up. An Aboriginal Health Conference was being held elsewhere in the grounds of Sydney University and I had asked Naomi Mayers to tell the participants that they would be very welcome to walk over at the end of their day's meeting to attend. I even phoned the conference organisers again on the morning of the event to remind them to make such an announcement. No announcement was ever made.

Marjorie Baldwin, who had flown down from Cairns to be present at my graduation, was walking back through the university grounds when she came upon an Aboriginal woman whom she knew, sitting on the lawn. The woman, a participant at the Health Conference, was upset to learn from Marjorie that she had missed a very special and joyful moment in history. She said that she would have attended because she was just sitting around bored, wishing she had something to do. I was very sad when I heard this, and astounded anew at the extent of envy and jealousy which existed in some quarters of the Black community. I wondered whether they were mindful of the negative effects this was having on the people they claimed to be helping.

I felt very proud when, during the presentation, John Doherty, then-president of the Harvard Club of Australia, informed the audience that not only was I the first Black Australian to have gained a doctorate from any university in the world, but also only the fourteenth Australian to have earned a doctorate from Harvard.

My heart thumped when Sir Hermann Black, speaking of the Peter B. Livingston Award I had won, the many talks I had given on Australian race relations at universities in the American east, and the exhibitions that I, at times assisted by Peter McKenzie, had organised, said, 'I feel a special humility in the presence of Doctor Sykes since, as a post-graduate student myself at Harvard, long ago in the years 1936–37, I cannot match the academic achievement of this distinguished woman during her stay there.' I wondered would I too be permitted to aspire to anything like the lofty heights achieved by Sir Hermann in Australia, or would racism continue to be a barrier to my achievement?

Both speakers applauded the contribution of the ordinary Australians who had, through their financial, practical and emotional contributions enabled me to be conferred with this degree, and I was deeply gratified to hear them being so recognised.

The Institute for Aboriginal Studies in Canberra, though, sent a carload of Aboriginal representatives. These young people carefully positioned themselves to ensure that I met them each individually so that they could shake my hand, introduce themselves and congratulate me. The evening had been such a high moment, and they were flushed, as I was, with the sheer spirit of it all.

Any official Australian Government involvement or endorsement was conspicuous by its absence. However, Bronson Dede, the Nigerian Ambassador, came up from Canberra to attend. Following the official part of the evening, Bronson hosted a dinner in his suite at the Regent Hotel, to which he asked me to invite any of my friends. Regrettably, by the time he was able to reach me with this offer, a large number of my friends had departed or made other plans. Our small party included the Aboriginal artist Phemie Bostock, who presented me with a sculpture she had made to commemorate my success, and Geraldine Willesee, who had helped shuttle members of my family to the ceremony, and my sister Della.

I arrived at the Regent Hotel a little late as I'd had to take my mother and the children home. So I called at the front desk to check Bronson Dede's room number. The clerk glanced at his computer and gave me the number. As I walked away, he called, 'Dr Sykes, Dr Sykes', and it was a moment before, with a thrill, I realised he was speaking to me.

I turned to hear—'Dr Sykes, the Ambassador is expecting you.'

Was I, I wondered, walking towards the elevator on clouds, just dreaming?

Yes, dreaming, it occurred to me then. Snake dreaming.